BLACK MOSAIC

D1548149

Black Mosaic

The Politics of Black Pan-Ethnic Diversity

Candis Watts Smith

NEW YORK UNIVERSITY PRESS
New York and London

NEW YORK UNIVERSITY PRESS
New York and London
www.nyupress.org

© 2014 by New York University
All rights reserved

References to Internet websites (URLs) were accurate at the time of writing.
Neither the author nor New York University Press is responsible for URLs
that may have expired or changed since the manuscript was prepared.

LIBRARY OF CONGRESS CATALOGING-IN-PUBLICATION DATA
Smith, Candis Watts.
Black mosaic : the politics of Black pan-ethnic diversity / Candis Watts Smith.
pages cm
Includes bibliographical references and index.
ISBN 978-1-4798-2354-3 (cloth : acid-free paper)
ISBN 978-1-4798-0531-0 (paper : acid-free paper)
1. African Americans—Race identity. 2. African Americans—Relations with Africans.
3. African Americans—Relations with Caribbean Americans. 4. African Americans—
Relations with Hispanic Americans. 5. Blacks—United States—Politics and government.
6. Immigrants—Political activity—United States. 7. Pan-Africanism—Political aspects—
United States. 8. Cultural pluralism—United States. 9. United States—Population. 10.
United States—Race relations. I. Title.
E185.625.S63 2014
305.800973—dc23
2014018127

New York University Press books are printed on acid-free paper,
and their binding materials are chosen for strength and durability.
We strive to use environmentally responsible suppliers and materials
to the greatest extent possible in publishing our books.

Manufactured in the United States of America

10 9 8 7 6 5 4 3 2 1

Also available as an ebook

GARY PUBLIC LIBRARY

For André

GARY PUBLIC LIBRARY

CONTENTS

ACKNOWLEDGMENTS

I think about the butterfly effect quite a bit. It is the idea that a minute change in one point in time could lead to an incredibly different outcome much later. As far as this project goes, I would say that the first flap of the butterfly's wings was my acceptance and participation in the Mellon Mays Undergraduate Fellowship program, which was at the time and still is gracefully run by Debbie Wahl. I started this project when I was a Mellon fellow in college. Then in an accidental conversation with Kerry Haynie, I learned about the Ralph Bunche Summer Institute, headed by Paula McClain and Scott DeMarchi. I was considering graduate school before I went to RBSI, but that program helped me to solidify my decision. And now here we are. Apparently, there are just over 9,300 political science faculty in American colleges and universities; of those, 461 are Black political scientists, and among those, 161 of them are Black women. I am a statistical outlier. The thing about these types of programs is that they are trying to put themselves out of business; they try to make people like me the norm rather than the exception. I hope, in some way, this book serves as a small testament to the good programs such as MMUF do and RSBI can do when given the opportunity.

With that said, let me acknowledge those people who helped me write this little testament. Kerry Haynie, Paula McClain, Eduardo Bonilla-Silva, and John Aldrich were my advisers and guided me through the initial writing process. Both Kerry and Paula have been and continue to be wonderful mentors, and I am certain that I will always feel deeply indebted to them.

Jim Rogers and Ken Meier invited me to come for a year to Texas A&M, where I worked on transitioning my research into a book manuscript. Actually, I invited myself, but thankfully, Jim and Ken welcomed me and provided the resources I needed. During my year at TAMU, a number of people helped me to step back and see the project from a new perspective: Jureé Capers, Kim Yi Dionne, Francisco Pedraza, Misha Taylor-Robinson, Breanca Thomas, and Joe Ura. Thank all of you for making my time in College Station fruitful and, dare I say, fun. I also received helpful feedback and encouragement from a number of fantastic individuals: Portia Cropper, Chryl Laird, Taeku Lee, Natalie Masuoka, Shayla Nunnally, Efrén Pérez, Gabe Sanchez, Karthik Ramakrishnan, and Neil Roberts. When I got to Williams College, Lori DuBois and Sharron Macklin helped me with some of the very technical aspects of the manuscript. I appreciate them for sharing their time with me. Thanks to Ilene Kalish, Caelyn Cobb, and their editorial team at New York University Press. I especially want to thank Andrew Katz for his meticulous copyediting. Thanks to the reviewers who remained anonymous for their excellent and helpful critiques on various versions of the manuscript. Also, I must thank my respondents. I wish I could name them.

It turns out that all of my closest friends are brilliant and also very gracious. Thank you, Kim Bickham, Rose Buckelew, Sarah Mayorga-Gallo, and Danielle Spurlock for reading this book in manuscript and providing feedback. Thank you for your kind words and for using lots of exclamation marks along with those words. Finally, I would like to thank my family—Anthony and Sheila Watts, my parents; and Terrell Smith, my husband—for all of their love and support, and André, who took just enough naps and gave more than enough smiles for me to put the finishing touches on this project.

Introduction

Many people have some of their first interactions with groups of people they have never met before during their first year in college, and these interactions often lead people to think more deeply about their own identity. Mary Waters, in *Ethnic Options*, discusses this phenomenon for white college students who, for their entire life, may have identified as Irish or Italian and then go to college and realize that there are actually people from Ireland and Italy who would use the same ethnic labels; this experience leads these people to reassess their identity in the face of "authentic" ethnic white international or immigrant students.[1] This was true for me as well as for a number of other people in my incoming class. A Trinidadian friend of mine, for example, told me that I was the first Black friend she had that was actually from the United States—that is to say, someone who had a long African American lineage. She lived in Miami and mentioned that all the Black people she knew were from one island in the Caribbean or another. And I met two Afro-Latina women who were best friends. One of them had a Black father and a Mexican mother. The other had a Black mother and a Puerto Rican father. They were connected at the hip and identified as Black (both pledged a historically Black sorority), but when they fought (in Spanish), they would make remarks about the other's Mexican or Puerto Rican roots. I realized that my ideas concerning who was Black were actually very limited and constrained.

My undergraduate institution, like other elite schools in the U.S., had a large proportion of Black students who were first- and second-generation immigrants; the exact numbers are undocumented by the institution, but with a group of friends and a yearbook, we approximated that 30 percent or so of the Black students in our incoming class were immigrants or had at least one parent who was an immigrant.

Black immigrants compose 8 percent of the Black population nationally.[2] While almost all the Black students belonged to the Black Student Alliance, many of them also belonged to clubs particular to their ethnic group. Black students were proud of where they came from, but at times you could feel a tension between the various Black ethnic groups. I can recall quite clearly a time when a woman asked me, "Where are you from?" I replied, "My family lives in North Carolina"—a response that I used because my family was an Army family. She, in turn, asked, "No, where are you *from* from?" So I said, "Well, my parents are from Chicago, and my grandparents are from Mississippi." And then she said, "So you're telling me that you've managed to accomplish all that you have, and you have no immigrants in your family?" I didn't know exactly what she meant then, but her comment piqued my interest. Was she giving me a backhanded compliment, or was she simply insulting African Americans?

Throughout my college career, it became clear to me that while there was a sense of unity among Blacks on campus due to our shared racial identity, there was also potential for tension to crop up due to ethnic differences depending on the context. At Duke, people like me whose families are nth-generation African American were labeled "regular Black," then there were Nigerians, Trinidadians, Dominicans, Haitians, Ethiopians, Ghanaians, "halfsies" (people who had one parent who was African American and the other who was not), and so forth. We united because we were a minority on a predominantly white campus, and we did not want to disagree with one another in front of people outside our racial group; we did not want to "air our dirty laundry." Black students knew there were differences among us due to socioeconomic status, ideology, and sexuality but also due to ethnicity. Sometimes we reacted to these differences with appreciation, while at other times we reacted with cynicism: "I'm not Black. I'm Nigerian. You all have funny names like LaQuisha," or "You only checked the Black box so could get into this school; you're not *really* Black."

With an increased attention in the news and the academy to ethnic diversity among Blacks, especially in elite institutions of higher education,[3] I began to recognize that Duke was a microcosm of the country, as it concerned ethnic diversity among Blacks. The migration of Black immigrants from Africa, the Caribbean, and Latin America has served to increase the ethnic diversity of those who are ascribed a Black identity in the United States. As more first- and second-generation Black students began to develop student groups around their ethnic identity—Duke Africa, Duke Ethiopian Student Association, Students of the Caribbean Association—I thought this must also be going on across the country and in larger ways. I wanted to know what this diversity would mean for Black politics. Sometimes Blacks of various ethnicities worked together and embraced an identity that was inclusive of ethnic diversity. At other times, the groups differentiated themselves, and conflict ensued. Black politics has been intriguing because of the homogeneity in political attitudes and behaviors that derives from a shared history and collective memory, but what happens to Black identity and, consequently, Black politics as Black immigrants are incorporated into American society?

Black Mosaic is an examination of the ways in which the boundaries of Black identity and the contours of Black politics are (re)shaped by the increasing ethnic diversity among Black people in the United States. Ultimately, the answer to the larger question concerning the nature of the boundaries of Black identity and Black politics will rest on answers to a set of secondary questions raised in this book: Considering the fact that ethnicity continues to be a salient identity within a racialized context, how do African Americans and Black immigrants conceptualize who is Black? Do Black immigrants embrace or reject a Black racial identity that is inclusive of Blacks native to the U.S.? Similarly, do African Americans embrace an identity that is inclusive of Black immigrants? Do Black immigrants share a sense of group consciousness similar to what has long been documented for African Americans? To what extent are the political and policy attitudes of Black immigrants and African Americans similar or different? Finally, what are the prospects for intraracial coalitions of African American and Black immigrants across the country?

My experiences as well as those who have shared their time with me in interviews for this book push me to go beyond the question of whether Black immigrants' and African Americans' political attitudes and behaviors are similar or different. Instead, I am compelled to examine the more complex and necessary concerns—to what extent and under what conditions are these groups likely to develop a pan-ethnic identity and to work in coalition and under what conditions are we are likely to see interethnic distancing and intraracial conflict? The intent here is to develop a theory that helps us to explain what we see empirically and to predict when and under what circumstances the boundaries of Black identity and politics are likely to be more rigid and when they are likely to be more permeable.

We know from the study of Latino and Asian American politics that differentiations due to ethnicity, country of origin, generational status, and levels of acculturation complicate what we know about these panethnic groups. This level of diversity exists among Blacks in the U.S., but little attention has been paid to the effects of this diversity on Black politics. Due to the rapid changes in the American population, generally, and the Black population, more specifically, it will become increasingly important to establish whether what we know about Blacks in the United States is actually relevant to those immigrants who are ascribed a Black identity but may or may not identify as Black. If that knowledge is (or is not) relevant, then we need to know why and under what circumstances this might be the case.

Dynamic Boundaries of Black Identity and Black Politics

In recognizing that *Black* is not only a racial category but also a panethnic identity, we must also realize that a more nuanced analysis and explanation of the group's identity and political attitudes and behavior are required. That is to say, taking into consideration the ethnic diversity of Blacks brings with it a myriad of complexities that have to, at least, be acknowledged. There are two major groups of scholars whose shoulders I stand on in the development of a theory that helps us to more thoroughly explain what we see empirically and what we should expect for Black politics as ethnic diversity increases.

The first body of literature is that which is concerned with the political attitudes and behaviors of African Americans. One of the primary reasons African American politics has been of interest to political scientists is due to the homogeneity of political attitudes and behaviors among African Americans in the United States. African Americans tend to have a sense of linked fate, and Michael Dawson explains that because African Americans have been treated as group members rather than individuals, they use the well-being of their racial group as a proxy for the well-being of the individual when making political decisions; he calls this rule of thumb the "black utility heuristic."[4] Consequently, African Americans have overwhelmingly supported the political party and political policies that they feel best represent the interests of Blacks in America. For example, for the past five decades, at least 60 percent of African Americans have supported the Democratic Party despite the increased number of Blacks in the middle class.[5] We typically expect Americans who make more money to support the Republican Party, but this is not the case for African Americans; racial group consciousness is key to understanding this paradox.

Dawson further argues that we should continue to see Blacks behaving similarly because of the constraints of America's racialized social system. But there is intraracial diversity in political attitudes and behaviors.[6] There has always existed diversity among Blacks in the United States, but the differences within the group are becoming ever more blatant. Cathy Cohen explains: "the dominant myth of a monolithic black community is tearing not only at the seams but throughout its entire fabric."[7] There are at least four significant sources of diversity among Blacks that influence Black politics, some of which have received more attention than others. Scholars have focused on the diversity that exists among Blacks due to ideological differences,[8] an increasing class bifurcation between middle- and working-class Blacks,[9] and gender.[10] But the fourth, political diversity as a result of ethnic diversity, has received less attention.[11] This source of diversity and its effects on Black politics are the focus of this book.

The second body of literature that is of importance to this study focuses on Black immigrants. One emerging consensus in the literature is that (first-generation) Black immigrants' ethnic or distinct cultural identity is often more salient and central than is their racial identity. A consistent finding in these studies is that Black immigrants often make an effort to differentiate themselves from African Americans or even to place themselves in a superior position in America's ethno-racial hierarchy.[12]

Scholars of American politics and Black politics have primarily focused on the centripetal forces of unity among Blacks in the United States. Scholars of Black immigrants have primarily focused on the notion of distancing between African Americans and Black immigrants. But empirical reality, what we see in the real world, shows that the situation is more complicated than that. There exists diversity among Blacks and diversity in their political attitudes and behaviors. Further, there are times when Black immigrants and African Americans are in conflict with each other, but there are also times when they embrace an identity that is inclusive of ethnic diversity and build political coalitions.[13] We need a new theory for Black political behavior that helps explain the very contextual nature of Black identity, Black intraracial relations, and Black politics.

I develop a theory of *diasporic consciousness* to help explain what we see empirically and what we should expect for Black politics as ethnic diversity increases. My central thesis is that while African Americans and Black immigrants may at times see differences marked by ethnic boundaries, they will generally see each other as members of the same group and as partners in a struggle against racial inequality. As a result of contemporary racism and racial inequality, first- and second-generation Black immigrants are likely to believe that their potential status as first-class citizens is imperiled just as a many African Americans do, and consequently, their racial identities are likely to be mobilized just as African Americans' racial identity is politically mobilized. I recognize that there has been significant change in the racial landscape in the United States, but I would argue that many of the factors that led African Americans to develop a sense of group consciousness historically still exist today. And we should, in turn, see that Black immigrants' identities are similarly shaped by those structural constraints.

But there is more complexity for which we must account. A theory of diasporic consciousness is motivated to account for both similarities and differences, for conflict and coalition, for distancing and mutual embracing, and asserts that even though America's racialized social system continues to have a homogenizing effect, Black immigrants are likely to bring along with them different ideas about what race means (both its definition and its implications), different interpretations of political issues, different ideas about the role of government, and different ideas about how to improve the status of a broader, pan-ethnic group. Speaking more generally, differences between groups typically bring conflict and tension, and ethnic diversity is likely to do the same at times.

Put simply, we can think of diasporic consciousness as *the (mental) tightrope that people of African descent who live in the United States walk as they try to balance their superordinate racial identity (and the political interests associated with it) with their subgroup or ethnic identity and its closely associated political interests.* The diversity that exists among Blacks across the country calls for a nuanced theory that helps us to understand when we should expect similar outcomes of the identity-to-politics link among native- and foreign-born Blacks and when we should see differences. Diasporic consciousness is an effort to satisfy that need.

Since I label this new conceptual framework *diasporic* consciousness, I imagine some readers are wondering how the theory I present departs from Pan-Africanism. Proponents of Pan-Africanism claim that "there is an underlying unity in the New World black experience," while focusing on "important uniformities in the black experience—that indeed, the trend is toward complete uniformity."[14] Critical race scholars and diaspora scholars show that people of African descent across the globe are in similar straits, and they challenge scholars to gain an understanding of how processes of inequalities are connected from one country or region to the next.[15] Moreover, Pan-Africanism largely focuses on the dispersal from a common Black homeland, the making of memory around that homeland, the recognition of marginalization in the new location, a commitment to the restoration of the homeland, and a desire to return and continue a relationship with the homeland.[16] The concept presented here—diasporic consciousness—centers on the idea that within the borders of the United States, native- and foreign-born Blacks must navigate the U.S.'s racial hierarchy. At times, strategies to navigate this hierarchy will lead to unity among various Black ethnic groups, while at other moments, strategies to navigate this society will lead these groups to be at odds with each other.

Diasporic consciousness, in contrast to Pan-Africanism, focuses on the idea that various groups of Blacks must balance two things: (1) their shared pan-ethnic identity and the (political) interests that are associated with this superordinate group and (2) their disparate, subethnic identity and the sometimes differing interests associated with that identity; Pan-Africanism focuses largely on the former aspect. Again, by not thinking of Black identity as simply a homogeneous racial group but instead thinking of "Blackness" in the U.S. as a pan-ethnic identity, we recognize the need for flexibility in a theory of contemporary Black politics. The theory of diasporic consciousness, in short, allows for a more accurate depiction of Black identity and more satisfying explanations of Black political behavior.

Why Focus on Ethnic Diversity Now?

The implications of ethnic diversity on Black politics are the focus of this book for three primary reasons. The first reason has to do with the sheer number of Black immigrants who are coming to the U.S. This change in demographics compels us to think about the influence that these newcomers and their interactions with native-born Blacks will have on Black identity and Black politics as we know them. National immigration policies such as the Immigration Act of 1924 and the Hart-Cellar Act are often cited by scholars of identity and politics as factors that have served to dramatically change the racial and ethnic makeup of the United States' population, especially due to the rigid exclusion of or substantial increase in the number of Latino and Asians immigrants.[17] But the ethnic makeup of the Black population in the United States has also been influenced by these national immigration policies. For example, prior to Immigration Act of 1924, which favored the admission of northern European immigrants, there were no limits on West Indian immigration. In 1924, approximately 12,000 Black immigrants came to the United States, but in 1925, only 791 Black immigrants entered the United States.[18] Ira Berlin notes, "by 1965, the United States was no longer a nation of immigrants," as the foreign-born proportion of the American population fell to rates lower than before then 1830s, about 5 percent of the population.[19]

Looking retrospectively, the 1965 Hart-Cellar Act has changed the racial makeup of immigrant waves to the United States ever since. Just as the 1965 act increased the diversity of the American population in general due to a mass influx of immigrants from Latin American and Asia, the act also increased the ethnic diversity among Black people in the United States who come from the Caribbean and Africa. In 1965,

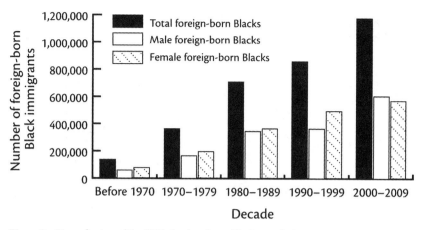

Figure I.1. Year of entry of the U.S.'s foreign-born Black population

there were only 125,000 foreign-born Blacks in this country. This number increased to 816,000 in 1980, and a total of 2.8 million foreign-born Blacks resided in the U.S. in 2005.[20] Figure I.1 provides U.S. Census Bureau data on foreign-born Black immigration to the country over the past five decades.

Although Black immigrants only compose about 8 percent of the Black population nationally, there are several states across the country where Black immigrants make up a significant portion of the Black population (see figure I.2). New York is a historical destination for many groups of Black immigrants, and consequently, foreign-born Blacks account for about 28.4 percent of the Black population in that state. Foreign-born Blacks also compose 28.4 percent of the Black population in Massachusetts, a less studied destination. Additionally, Black immigrants make up a significant portion of Blacks in several other states: Minnesota (25.5 percent), Florida (19.3 percent), Connecticut (17.2 percent), Washington (17.2 percent), and New Jersey (14.4 percent). There are also large populations of Black immigrants in less traditional destinations: Arizona, Colorado, Nevada, Maryland, and Delaware.[21] Furthermore, foreign-born Blacks contributed 20 percent of the growth of the Black population in the United States between 2000 and 2006.[22] Black immigrants are likely to have an increasing influence on Black politics, especially in these places where their voices, which may be quite different from African Americans', are likely to be more

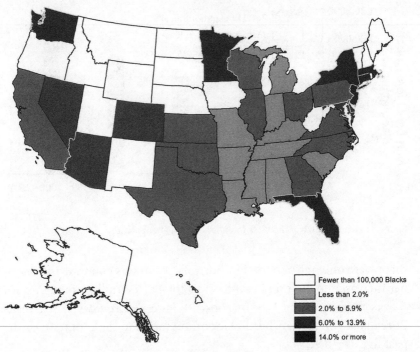

Figure I.2. Foreign-born black population, 2004. *Note*: Percentage of the state's Black-alone population that is foreign-born. Data are based on a sample limited to the household population and exclude those who are institutionalized or living in college dormitories or other group quarters. *Source*: U.S. Census Bureau, 2004 American Community Survey, Detailed Tables, B06004B.

resounding. The demographic shifts in the American population, in general, and in the Black population, more specifically, call for the need to think more critically about the interactions between African Americans and Black immigrants, because while they are grouped in the same racial category, it is unclear how well or whether they will get along.

Connected to shifting demographics, this book focuses on the increasing ethnic diversity of Blacks in the United States because increased interactions between native- and foreign-born Blacks are likely to influence change in the meaning of "Blackness" and Black identity in the United States. Increased diversity among Blacks in the United States along with the dismantling of formal racial segregation in the post–Civil Rights era has sparked a debate among Black people in the

United States around notions of Black identity and Black politics.[23] Black immigrants, on the one hand, bring with them alternative frameworks of racial identity, thereby expanding the ways that people who are categorized as Black understand their racial and ethnic identities. Many of these immigrants do not necessarily see themselves as Black (or white) or at least do not feel that their racial identity will influence their life chances, as African Americans historically have.[24]

The Civil Rights era also loosened the rigid Black-white dichotomy. Historically, Black immigrants' racial identity was more psychologically and politically salient to first- and second-generation Black immigrants—in comparison to contemporary immigrants—because formal laws and informal customs of segregation were based on racial identity rather than ethnic identity.[25] In some ways, Black ethnic identity was irrelevant in public spaces prior to the 1960s, but over the past five decades, both Black and non-Black Americans have increasingly paid attention to ethnic diversity among Black people in the United States. White employers, for example, are reported to prefer foreign-born Blacks to native-born African Americans.[26] Further, 37 percent of Blacks suggest that African Americans and Black immigrants are not actually members of the same racial group, with this feeling being the most salient among younger Blacks, between the ages of eighteen and twenty-nine.[27]

The notion that white ethnic immigrants became white—or were eventually included within the boundaries of whiteness and called white—is well documented.[28] But the boundaries of Blackness in the United States have also contracted and expanded. Previously, the debates around Black identity concerned whether those with mixed-raced ancestry should be included within the group, but the informal "one-drop" rule, which was later codified into law, made this a moot point. All those members of society with one Black ancestor were ascribed an all encompassing Black identity that failed to account for any differences among group members. But the increasing ethnic diversity among Blacks in the United States at this moment in American history has served to respark and reshape this debate around racial labeling and racial belonging.

Due to the influx of Afro-Latino, Afro-Caribbean, and African immigrants into the United States, the definitions of "African American" and "Black" are being challenged both by native-born Black people and by foreign-born people of African descent and their children. Berlin reports that many African immigrants feel that they should make claim to the term "African American," challenging native-born Blacks because many of them have not been to Africa, nor can they trace one of their ancestors to a specific African country.[29] Likewise, many Haitian immigrants tend to distance themselves from African Americans in their effort to avoid "being Black twice"—or, in other words, being at the bottom of the racial hierarchy in two countries.[30] Afro-Caribbeans often see themselves as Black but argue that "Black" and "African American" should not be seen as synonymous.[31] Meanwhile, many Black elites have tried to make the boundaries of Blackness more rigid in efforts to protect civil rights gains for African Americans. Lani Guinier, for instance, reportedly suggested that Black immigrants represent a threat to African American educational interests, stating, "I don't think, in the name of affirmative action, we should be admitting people because they look like us, but then they don't identify with us."[32] The debate over who is and who is not Black as well as who should be able to adopt (or reject) various racial labels is by no means new, but it certainly has become more intense.

The final, and perhaps most important, reason that ethnic diversity is the focus of this book is because it is my intuition that immigrants— Black or otherwise—can be likened to a canary in a coal mine. Assessing the well-being of immigrants of color can help us to gauge the toxicity of the racial environment in society. America is a nation of immigrants. Immigrants come to the United States with a particular set of goals and ideas about American society. Many Black immigrants, like many other types of immigrants, come to the U.S. with the ideas that meritocracy reigns supreme among the tenets of the American creed and that their hard work will be rewarded without regard to their race. Following the progression of immigrants' identities, attitudes, behaviors, and outcomes will ultimately help us to distinguish the historical influences that led Blacks to be placed at the bottom of America's ethnoracial hierarchy from the contemporary influences. African Americans have a long history and deep understanding of America's racial structure and what that means for citizenship; their political attitudes and behaviors are largely shaped by a four-century-long legacy and relationship with American social, political, and economic institutions.[33] Further, many of their economic outcomes are due to intergenerational transfers of debt, or lack of wealth.[34] In contrast, immigrant-replenished communities and the experiences of immigrants in the U.S. provide an excellent anchoring point to assess the role and effects of contemporary levels of racism.

Scholarship on African Americans and Black immigrants tends to analyze these groups separately. This approach might best be characterized as what Claire Jean Kim calls the "different trajectories approach," which "examines racialization . . . as an open-ended, variable process that has played out differently for each subordinated group."[35] We know that African Americans and Black immigrants are not mutually exclusive groups since they live in a society that groups them together at the bottom of its ethnoracial hierarchy. By comparing immigrants' outcomes and experiences with those of native-born minorities, we gain a better idea of how far we have actually come in reducing the levels of racial toxicity in American society.

Methodological Approach

To address the questions I raise in this book about the changing contours of Black identity and Black politics, I pursue a multimethodological design, which includes survey analysis and analysis of semistructured, face-to-face interviews, to test a theory of diasporic consciousness. The survey analysis employs data from the National Survey of American Life (NSAL), 2001–3. The NSAL was developed by the University of Michigan Research Center and supported by the National Institute for Mental Health. The survey was conducted between 2001 and 2003, and respondents include over three thousand African Americans and sixteen hundred Black Immigrants of Caribbean, Latin American, and African descent. The survey is concerned with cross-cultural differences among African Americans, Afro-Caribbeans, and white Americans across the United States.

I also incorporate semistructured, face-to-face interviews. Interviews are an excellent way to understand how people make meaning around issues that affect them. This analysis draws on thirty face-to-face, in-depth interviews conducted between March and July of 2010. I interviewed a total of thirty college-age African Americans and first- and second-generation Black immigrants. The respondents include seventeen African Americans and thirteen Black immigrants. Among the Black immigrants, three of them are first-generation Black immigrants, three of them were born in another country but moved to the U.S. as a child (1.5 generation), and the remaining seven of them are second generation—that is, at least one of their parents is an immigrant, but they were born and raised in the United States.[36] The Black immigrants include students from the Caribbean, Latin America, and Africa. Three of the African American respondents are biracial. Twenty of them are or were students at a small private university in the South (henceforth, Private Southern University, or PSU), and the remainder of them attended colleges across the country. Their families come from various socioeconomic statuses; further, some of them live in economically and racially homogeneous neighborhoods, while others were raised and live in very diverse neighborhoods (appendix B includes a table of the respondents' attributes).

The interviews were conducted in North Carolina, but only one of the respondents called North Carolina home. In 2000, foreign-born Blacks constituted 30 percent of Blacks in New York City, 28 percent of those in Boston, and about 25 percent in Montgomery County, Maryland. Seven of the respondents here live in or near these cities. The other respondents live in various places around the United States, representing all of the major regions of the United States. These data have the added value of furthering our understanding of Black immigrants outside New York, where the majority of studies on this population have been conducted.

Respondents were recruited through snowball sampling procedure. The initial participants answered an advertisement emailed to cultural groups and summer programs. The semistructured interview schedule consisted of questions concerning themes of identity and personal experiences, as well as political attitudes and behaviors. The interviews lasted between forty-five minutes and two hours. The taped recordings of the interviews were transcribed verbatim, and most of the respondents selected their own pseudonyms.

The qualitative data analysis involved a multistep processes. First, a coding scheme was developed inductively. Then, I organized data into analytical categories. Once the interviews were coded, a series of patterns became clear. I analyzed these patterns across ethnic groups and across generational status.

I chose college students as interview subjects for three reasons. First, this group of individuals comes into contact with various types of Black people; they have had experiences with communities that are ethnically and racially homogeneous as well as ones that are diverse. Second, there is quite a bit of talk on college campuses about the ethnic diversity of Black people in the United States,[37] so it is likely that they have thought seriously about what it means to be Black, who they feel constitute members of "the Black community," and what the implications are for aggregating African Americans and Black immigrants into one racial group. Third, it is typically assumed that first- and second-generation Black immigrants, who are projected to move upwardly on economic and social ladders, are resistant to identifying with Blackness—as an identity and its associated politics.[38] This well-educated group of people provides a stringent test for the proposed theory.

Overview of the Book

Black immigrants have always taken part in Black politics, but they, for the most part, have been invisible. Chapter 1 examines the historical legacy of foreign-born and native Black relations. At times, African Americans and Black immigrants worked together, while at other times, the groups were in direct conflict. Similarly, we have seen Black immigrant politicians distancing themselves from African Americans to gain votes from whites and Blacks immigrants, while at other times we see them identifying with African Americans. The ways in which African Americans and Black immigrants interact today is, in part, an outcome of what occurred in the past; chapter 1 brings this history to light. Further, this chapter touches on contemporary examples of political conflict and coalition between Black immigrants and African Americans. This chapter sets the backdrop for the reader to understand the various paths that Black *intraracial* politics might take, which a theory of diasporic consciousness seeks to understand and predict.

Chapter 2 more thoroughly examines the concept of diasporic consciousness, which is the central theoretical framework I use throughout this book. The basic argument is that because Black people in the United States do not compose a monolithic racial group but instead make up a diverse pan-ethnic group, we should expect similarities and unity as well as differences and discord. That is to say, we should expect a resemblance to exist between African Americans' and Black immigrants' identity and political attitudes and behaviors due to the constraints of America's racialized social system, but we should also expect distinctions to arise due to ethnic diversity. The U.S. places Blacks—despite ethnicity—at the bottom of an ethnoracial hierarchy, leading foreign- and native-born Blacks to embrace a pan-ethnic identity; but with ethnic diversity comes different interpretation of problems, different perceptions about the role of government, and different notions about how to improve the status of the group. A theory of diasporic consciousness both appreciates the factors that lead to unity among Blacks and problematizes the notion that unity will always be the best characterization of Black politics as diversity increases. Ultimately, diasporic consciousness captures the complex notion that African Americans and Black immigrants find themselves trying to balance the (political) concerns of their shared, overarching racial identity with the sometimes competing concerns closely associated with their more exclusive ethnic-group membership and identity.

Chapters 3 through 6 analyze each step or transition in the path that links identities to politics: group membership, group identity, group consciousness, and finally, political attitudes and behaviors. Chapter 3 is concerned with the link between group membership and group identity. First, this chapter examines how racial labels and group boundaries are understood and constructed among people of African descent. Here, I use data from the National Survey of American Life and in-depth interviews. Black immigrants' and African Americans' responses illuminate how Black people discuss issues around racial group membership. These respondents help us to better understand how African Americans and Black immigrants define who is Black as well as the extent to which Blacks of various ethnicities embrace or reject an identity that is inclusive of ethnic diversity. Ultimately, the respondents' answers elucidate how group membership (whereby individuals are involuntarily assigned to a racial category) transitions into group identity (or the development of an attachment to people in your racial category). Chapter 4 expounds on the findings of the previous chapter by exploring the determinants of racial identity with data from the NSAL. This chapter investigates various dimensions of Black racial identity, and the quantitative analysis allows us to compare the determinants of racial identity of African Americans with those of Black immigrants.

Chapter 5 moves us to group consciousness. Racial group consciousness is a critical step in the identity-to-politics link for African Americans, but it is unknown whether a sense of group consciousness influences the political attitudes and behaviors of Black immigrants, much less what the determinants of group consciousness among Black immigrants are. Here, I explore the extent to which African Americans' and Black immigrants' identities are politicized. Interview respondents explain the connection between their racial identity and their political attitudes and behaviors, and then the remainder of the chapter analyzes the determinants of racial group consciousness among native- and foreign-born Blacks as well as the political consequences of group consciousness. I employ the NSAL to develop a series of analyses that shed light on the role of group consciousness on political attitudes and levels and types of political participation among African Americans and Black immigrants.

Chapter 6 is concerned with the last portion of the identity-to-politics link: political outcomes. This chapter is primarily concerned with the prospects for intraracial political coalitions. In an effort to answer questions around issues of coalition and competition, the chapter explores the issues of importance to African Americans and Black immigrants and asks whether there is one cohesive Black agenda or whether there are distinct Black agendas as a result of ethnic diversity. Informants' responses as to whether African Americans and Black immigrants should form coalitions to progress the racial group illustrate a spectrum of possibilities for the future of Black politics. Finally, in the concluding chapter, I discuss the major findings of the book and also the implications that the results have for what we know about and how we understand American politics in general and Black politics more specifically.

A Note on Nomenclature

I use the term "Black" to describe all people who are categorized as racially Black despite their ethnicity. I use the terms "African American" and "native-born Black" interchangeably to describe Black people whose ancestors have been in the U.S. for several generations. Finally, I use "foreign-born Black " and "Black immigrant" to describe people who are categorized as Black in the U.S. but are first-, 1.5-, or second-generation immigrants to the U.S.; this group includes Afro-Caribbeans, Afro-Latinos, and Black Africans.

1

Black on Black History

In 1939, Ira De Augustine Reid took note of the fact that "between 1899 and 1937 approximately 150,000 Negro aliens were legally admitted to the United States" and in turn asked, "How does a group theoretically regarded as biologically unassimilable in the United States' melting pot accommodate?"[1] Historically, Black immigrants melted into a larger Black racial category.[2] Contemporarily, some scholars argue that the significance of race is declining in today's society, thereby allowing Black immigrants to make claim to distinct ethnic identities rather than being required to adopt an undifferentiated Black racial identity.[3] The fact of the matter is, however, race still influences individuals' life chances and the well-being of racial groups as a whole, and furthermore, "choices" of identity remain constrained, especially as we move down the racial hierarchy. Reid's question, then, is still quite pertinent.

This chapter lays the groundwork for a theory of diasporic consciousness. First, this chapter includes brief descriptions of the racial landscapes of the regions from which many Black immigrants come. Black immigrants do not come to the U.S. as blank slates, but rather they have been socialized in a racial context quite different from that of the United States.[4] Racial socialization—or the process by which people learn the meaning of their race and racial status in a particular society—shapes the way we understand our identity as well as how race might affect social status, culture, and group history.[5] In this chapter, I compare and contrast how race is constructed in the U.S., Latin America and the Caribbean, and Africa in an effort to better predict how diasporic consciousness is shaped among Blacks. Identities are heavily influenced by the construction of race in people's country of origin; hence, when Blacks of different ethnic origins interact within the boundaries of the United States, it will be helpful to understand how race is conceptualized in different societies.

But again, centering on Reid's question, what happens when Blacks from across the globe collide and interact within American society? Scholars have primarily focused on the aspect of African American and Black immigrant relations that may be characterized as hostile, antagonistic, and competitive, but history shows that the relationships between native- and foreign-born Blacks are very complex and contextual, as they are dependent on a number of factors—domestic and international. There are times when African Americans and Black immigrants are in accord and focus on the problems that they face because of their shared racial identity. And there are times when native and immigrant Blacks are at odds with each other. This chapter takes a brief look at the historical interactions of African Americans and Black immigrants. These relationships are not new, so homing in on what happened in the past will surely help to provide a foundation on which to more accurately predict when African Americans and Black immigrants will be racially united or ethnically divided.

Race and Place

Definitions of race as a concept as well as the boundaries of racial categories change over time and from place to place.[6] "Racial identity, as an organizing mechanism, is situationally emergent. It is shaped by cumulative social experience and is enacted in reaction to context-specific social interaction."[7] Thus, race is a social construct. The best way to understand what "socially constructed" means is to look comparatively at how race is structured and understood in different societies. Similarly, the most optimal way to understand what immigrants bring to the United States is to have a grasp of how race is shaped in their countries and regions of origin.

Race in the United States

The introduction of race to the U.S. began with slavery as well as the expropriation of Indian lands by white colonists.[8] Blacks and American

Indians were racialized in order to legitimize the enslavement of Africans and the expulsion and genocide of American Indians at a time when whites needed to justify America's looming contradiction and dilemma. The American creed is predicated on egalitarianism, but discrimination and inequality is deeply embedded in the foundation of America's political, economic, and social spheres.[9]

Black and white racial identities have been developed in tandem in the U.S and in other parts of the world, too; historically, whiteness was identified by the absence of Blackness in the United States. Those who had at least one ancestor of African descent were identified as Black. Eighteenth- and nineteenth-century scientists "determined" that Blacks were inherently and genetically (although that language did not exist at the time) inferior to whites, and they suggested that any mixing between "pure" white blood and "tainted" Black blood would contaminant and dilute the purity of whiteness; consequently, the boundaries of white identity became very exclusive.

This idea of hypodescent, or the "one-drop" rule, developed by "scientific" communities was incorporated into the workings of American political institutions, including the courts, state legislatures, U.S. Congress, and other bureaucratic institutions. These institutions created and maintained laws based on racial pseudoscience for most of America's history. Even through the twentieth century, the notions around the contamination of "black blood" and "miscegenation" contributed to shaping the boundaries of white and Black racial groups, despite the fact that race as a biological reality was denounced at least three-quarters of a century ago.

In the United States, "Blackness" and being racialized as Black is a ubiquitous phenomenon. While some Americans and new immigrants to the United States have challenged the notion of the "one drop," or the idea that one Black ancestor requires one to identify as Black, this notion of hypodescent still affects those with identifiable African attributes.[10] Black racial identity in the United States has historically been "a particularly and peculiarly totalizing identity that has been applied to anyone of African descent, even when it fails to capture the social heritage of individuals whose cultures and identities were not formed in the particularly American context of slavery, discrimination, and segregation."[11]

Race in Latin America and the Caribbean

Many people argue that because race in Latin America and the Caribbean is not constructed as it is in the United States, race does not *really* exist, or if it does, it is not an important determinant of an individual's life chances.[12] Scholars, in particular, who subscribe to such a notion argue that a strict "Black-white" dichotomy as well as practices such as Jim Crow laws and antimiscegenation laws have made the United States a particularly vicious place for nonwhite people; they would suggest that since none of these laws existed in Latin American and in many Caribbean societies, racism does not exist. In Latin American countries, more specifically, some suggest that Spanish and Portuguese colonialists were much more apt to mix racially, so slavery in Latin America was not nearly as brutal as it was in the United States. Researchers and lay people in this camp tend to go on to assert that while there might be some discrimination in Latin American societies today, it is "benign" and largely based on color and/or class.[13] In the Caribbean and in Latin America, people are categorized by their skin color, thereby creating a spectrum from light to dark, denoting various degrees of racial mixture.[14] Race in these regions is not simply a matter of physical features, but ancestry, social class, education, wealth, and occupation also serve to determine one's racial identity.[15] While race relations in Latin America and the Caribbean, for the most part, have never been based on strict racial categories, racial discrimination and hierarchy did and do exist.[16]

Nancy Foner explains that in the West Indies, income, occupation, living standards, and personal associates are important in determining a person's life chances, in addition to skin color. Most people in the Caribbean are Black, and Blacks tend to fill the most prestigious, lucrative, and professional positions in Caribbean societies; but whiteness is still associated with wealth, privilege, and power.[17] Foner asserts that while people are aware of shade differences, "blackness is not in itself . . . a barrier to upward social mobility or to social acceptance at the top."[18] Milton Vickerman explains that in addition to the fact that Blacks are the supermajority of the population in the Caribbean, Caribbean political leaders and representatives tend to propagate the notion that their societies are diverse places where members of various races peacefully coexist.[19]

In many Latin American countries, a similar ideology is also promulgated through notions of *mestizaje* and racial democracy. *Mestizaje* is the idea that a prevalence of mixed ancestry in a society means that its citizens are racially homogeneous; the logic of *mestizaje* leads to the erroneous conclusion that racial differences cannot be made because everyone is racially mixed. Historically, many Latin American countries had large Black populations as well as high rates of miscegenation. In turn, many of the elites were negatively implicated by dominant American and European science at the time. Elites, who identified as white, too could have Black relatives and children or even be Black themselves if they had adopted the U.S.'s "one-drop" rule. Instead, elites reshaped their history and interpreted science to their benefit. They argued that racial mixing would *improve* the racial stock of their countries through "whitening." Racially mixed people would be whiter than their Black parent.[20] Over time, this legacy has evolved into *mestizaje* and racial democracy ideologies.

The basic tenets of these "colorblind" racial ideologies are (1) race does not exist, only color; (2) physical appearance and not origin (or race) determines a person's color; (3) there is no discrimination because there have not been laws that allow portions of the population to be second-class citizens; (4) educated mixed-race people and lighter-skinned blacks will be economically, culturally, socially, and politically assimilated into the white establishment—this is called the "mulatto escape hatch," and (5) the continued existence of the social hierarchy by color is simply a leftover from slavery rather than current-day discriminatory behaviors and ideology.[21]

People in Latin America and the Caribbean may suggest that they have a "shade" problem rather than a race problem, but the distinction between race and color cannot be so easily made.[22] The primary reason is because race and racism undergird notions of color and prejudice. The denial of Black ancestry is one of the most blatant manifestations of Latin American racism.[23] Further, it should be noted, "skin color stratification requires both racism and colorism."[24] The notions of "whitening" and *mestizaje* were and are predicated on the perceived necessity to eliminate any signs of African "origin." That is to say, the real target of color discrimination is, in fact, race.[25]

This "shade" problem also has material consequences. Those who are at the lighter end of the spectrum are provided more benefits; meanwhile, those who are on the darker end are provided more disadvantages from society. There are many nonwhites who occupy higher economic and social strata in Latin America and the Caribbean, but for the most part, an overwhelming proportion of poor and politically powerless people are darker skinned and/or nonwhite.[26] Such a system can be characterized as a pigmentocracy—or a social hierarchy based on skin color.[27] It looks very similar to America's racialized social system.[28] Whether one views race in Latin America and the Caribbean through the lens of *mestizaje* or through the lens of pigmentocracy, it is important to keep these ideas in mind when we consider how Black immigrants from these regions understand and develop their own racial identity while in the United States.

Race in Africa

Research concerning identity, difference, and hierarchy in Africa predominantly centers around notions of ethnicity, and ethno-political, tribal, or national identities,[29] but there is a small body of literature that discusses race as an important identity in African societies. Scholars who explore racial issues in Africa primarily focus on the development of racial identities due to the white colonization of several African countries.[30] A major theme in this body of literature centers on the notion that European colonists fused notions of race and nation. More specifically, when white colonists in countries such as South Africa, Zimbabwe, Sudan, and Tanzania seized African territories to create "formal" states, they also dictated who would be citizens within that space.[31] Just as we saw in the United States, the boundaries of citizenship in many African countries were exclusive, allowing only those who were ascribed a white identity entry into the polity and the privileges of citizenship. As such, a race-conscious colonial hierarchy served as a major force in racializing Africans as well as Indians and other Asians in various African countries.

James R. Brennan paints a more complex picture of racialization processes prior to European colonization; he asserts that while European concepts of race and civilization were brought over and broadly disseminated through schools, the press, and colonial propaganda, "it would be a mistake to overlook earlier discourses that elaborate ideas of race."[32] Brennan, whose work focuses on East African countries, shows that there existed racial hierarchies in these countries, whereby an Arab identity was viewed as dominant and mainstream, and it was this identity that was most associated with high status.[33] Brennan explains that the Kiswahili term *ustaarabu* means "to become Arab," and in order to assimilate into precolonial Swahili society, one had to distance oneself from slave origins, to claim deep roots in Islam, and to become "culturally" Arab.[34]

While race, as we understand it in the U.S. context, is not easily translated into the contexts of various African countries, one can see important similarities. First, we see that even in countries where ethnic or tribal identities are emphasized, there still is possibility for hierarchy among ethnic groups. Rwanda provides an excellent example. Philip Gourevitch shows that even though there were few differences in phenotype and other physical features between most Hutu and Tutsi Rwandans, issues of power and hierarchy were at the foundation of the 1994 conflict in Rwanda.[35] What is more, while there may not have been physical differences, both of these tribes had stereotypes associated with them; the association of stereotypes with value-neutral group labels is a racialization process. Further, we see that in many African countries, European colonization processes lumped together various African ethnic groups, blurring distinctions between them, and then excluded these groups from enjoying equal rights. The racialization processes and the racial hierarchy that we see today in postcolonial African countries very much mirror the United States' racial history.

Black Meets Black: Intraracial Interactions between Native- and Foreign-Born Blacks

In 1850, there were 4,067 foreign-born Blacks in the United States. Two decades later in 1870, this number reached 9,494, of which 28 percent were from Canada, 21 percent were from Africa, 16 percent were from the West Indies and other Atlantic islands, and the remainder were from Portugal, Spain, and Mexico. Today, approximately three million Black immigrants live in the United States. Black intraracial interactions are not born out of a vacuum but instead are built on historical relationships.

Black immigrants have historically played a role in Black politics, but societal conditions under which pre-1965 immigrants were incorporated constrained the latitude that Black immigrants had in making public claim to an ethnic identity.[36] Because Black immigrants were subsumed into an all-encompassing Black category, Roy Simon Bryce-Laporte has described Black immigrants as doubly invisible, in both the study and the practice of Black politics:

> On the one hand, *as blacks*, their demands and protests as a constituent group have been responded to with the same disregard shown by the larger society and its leaders toward efforts of native American blacks to reshape the society to meet their particular needs and cultural orientation. On the other hand, while black foreigners (and their progenies) have held a disproportionately high number of leadership and successful positions and have exercised significant influence in black life in this country, their cultural impact as *foreigners* has generally been ignored or has merely been given lip service in the larger spheres of American life. On the national level, they suffer double invisibility, in fact—as *blacks* and as *black foreigners*.[37]

Bryce-Laporte's observations are still valid today. For example, Colin Powell, Eric Holder, and Barack Obama are all prominent Black politicians who are of foreign-born Black stock.[38] They are generally known for being the first "Black" person to be in their positions, but it is likely that relatively few people know that they are second-generation Black immigrants. In general, little is known about the political attitudes or behaviors of Black immigrants because they have generally been subsumed within the larger Black category, but historians provide incredible insight into Black intraracial relations.

The presence of Black immigrants in the United States is by no means new, so we may be able to gain a sense of the circumstances under which a pan-ethnic identity can be developed as well as to sketch out an illustration of diasporic consciousness by analyzing historical Black intraracial interactions. Historically, foreign-born Blacks moved to such places as Florida and New York, as well as to Washington, D.C., to some extent. Through an examination of "Black on Black" relations within the borders of the United States and within the context of an American racialized social system, we see that these relations are complex. The quality of these relationships wax and wane depending on changes in American society as well as due to political shocks across the globe.

Afro-Cubans and African Americans

African American and Afro-Cuban relations in Florida show that native- and foreign-born Black relations can be (and have been) heavily influenced not only by American domestic policies but also by international and transnational politics. Florida's "Black Codes" defined anyone with at least one great-grandparent of African descent (one-eighth) as Black, thereby categorizing Afro-Cubans (and practically all Cubans, for that matter) as Black.[39] Nancy Mirabal explains, "as Cubans living and working in an immigrant community, they [Afro-Cubans] occupied a fluid, in-between position where they were neither white nor necessarily 'black.'"[40] But, immediately after the Supreme Court decided that "separate but equal" was constitutional in *Plessy v. Ferguson* (1896), Florida's legislators implemented a series of Jim Crow laws, further entrenching the state's existing practices of legal segregation.[41] These laws essentially revoked the rights of anyone ascribed a Black identity. These changes had severe implications for Cuban intraethnic relations as well as Black intraracial relations.[42]

When Cubans first came to Tampa and Miami, Florida, in the late nineteenth century, "they were locked together in a revolutionary nation-building project."[43] This project, led by José Martí, emphasized Cuban independence from Spain, anti–American imperialism, and racial solidarity. In addition to the fact that there was a language barrier between African Americans and Afro-Cubans, Afro-Cubans did not share the same political concerns with African Americans. What is more, Afro-Cubans had access to jobs in cigar factories and social networks that were open to all Cubans, despite race, therefore providing an incentive to distance themselves from African Americans.[44] Further-more, Afro-Cubans in Florida did not belong to any of the same clubs, lodges, or organizations as African Americans, although some Afro-Cubans did belong to the Republican Party.[45]

Interestingly, occurring at about the same time, Jim Crow was offi-cially launched by the Supreme Court's *Plessy v. Ferguson* decision (1896), José Martí died (in 1895), and the Spanish were defeated in Cuba (1898). These shocks provided incentives for white Cubans to dissoci-ate from Afro-Cubans just as Afro-Cubans had distanced themselves from African Americans. One of the most well-known manifestations of the racial wedge that developed between white and Afro-Cubans arises in the story of La Union Martí-Maceo. In Tampa in 1899, a group of Cuban men formed a recreational club, El Club Nacional Cubano (founded on October 10), that was open to Cubans across the color and racial spectrum. However, soon after its development, the Afro-Cuban men were summarily banned from the club.

José Rivero Muñiz, a Cuban who lived in Tampa during the time of the split, explained, "It was necessary to overcome difficulties that were based more on custom than on law. . . . But in this part of the United States it was necessary to face the reality of the facts. . . . They began to look for a solution, in spite of the fact that there was opposition among those who believed in equality for all. The idea was to organize two different organizations."[46] But, as Susan D. Greenbaum points out, the "custom" of the time was that if "white Cubans continued to share social space with their black compatriots, the result would have been to define all Cubans as 'niggers.'"[47] Nancy Raquel Mirabal similarly explains, "the decision of white male Cuban members to eject the Afro-Cuban male members of the October 10 Club reinscribed the Afro-Cuban members, and by extension the Afro-Cuban immigrant community in Ybor City, as 'black.'"[48] White Cubans made an effort to distance themselves from Afro-Cubans in the United States in order to avoid being placed at the bottom of the society's racial hierarchy.

Afro-Cubans were also well aware of the "custom" of the time, and they too sought to distance themselves from African Americans.[49] The former members of the October 10 Club formed their own Afro-Cuban club, La Union Martí-Maceo, but they did not allow African Americans to join their club in an attempt to maintain their "in-between" status in a binary racial social system. But this could only go on for so long. Jim Crow laws forced Afro-Cubans to interact with African Americans. Residential segregation required Afro-Cubans to live in historically Black areas, such as the Scrub; they had to share schools, hospitals, movie theaters, and the like.[50]

The laws of Jim Crow compelled Afro-Cubans and African Americans to interact, but not all these interactions were necessarily negative. In fact, it is likely that through the experience of persistent racism Afro-Cubans and African Americans were able to develop amicable social relations and, over time, work toward political coalitions. For example, Cuban baseball teams were automatically declared "Black" teams because they were racially integrated. Afro-Cubans and African Americans were thoroughly intertwined in baseball due to the racial politics of the United States. Lisa Brock and Bijan Bayne, in their study of Black intraracial relations in baseball, suggest, "objective conditions and common interests, not paternalism and resentment, shaped the ensuing history of black American and Cuban interactions through baseball."[51]

African American and Afro-Cuban relations also improved over time, especially because Afro-Cubans began to embrace a racial consciousness, recognizing that while their ethnic identity provided benefits at times, their place in America's ethnoracial hierarchy was largely based on the color of their skin. Additionally, as the boundaries between Black and white Cubans crystallized, the ethnic wedge between Blacks dissipated. In 1908, a member of the Martí-Maceo club proposed that the members set up a school for "hombres de color de ambas nacionalidades," or men of color of both nationalities, but this idea was rejected by the other members; however, seven years later, the Afro-Cuban male members of the club voted to permit all eligible Blacks into their club.[52] Mirabal explains that twenty-six of the members voted for other Black males' admission, four voted against, and thirty-two abstained; the vote, then, simultaneously showed that the Afro-Cuban men were ambivalent about extending their hand to African Americans and that there was a clear increase in solidarity between members of these groups.[53]

The bond became even tighter in the aftermath of World War II. After World War II, the Servicemen's Readjustment Act of 1944—better known as the GI Bill—provided incredible benefits to individuals who served in the U.S. military, but these benefits were doled out along racial lines, especially in the South.[54] Consequently, white veterans, including white Cubans, were able to attain benefits that allowed them to move into new suburbs and that brought them accelerated advances in education and employment; Afro-Cubans, however, did not have access to the same advantages. In turn, disparities between groups intensified on the basis of race and color rather than ethnicity.[55] Just as African Americans, especially GIs, espoused the Double V campaign for civil rights in the United States, they were joined by Afro-Cuban GIs who faced the same challenges due to their ascribed racial identity. By the 1940s, young Afro-Cubans and African Americans in Florida began to work together on local issues of voting rights and desegregation.

Haitians and African Americans

The story of Haitian and African American relations is not as picturesque as that of Afro-Cubans and African Americans in the early twentieth century. But the relationship does show that there is variety in intraracial interactions that needs to be mapped. Haiti was, historically, a symbol of pride for African Americans, but this view has changed particularly due to the facts that Haiti has been led by brutal dictators and is currently the poorest country in the Western Hemisphere. Haitians, on the other hand, are not particularly proud of African Americans either, since they are at the bottom of America's racial hierarchy. African American and Haitian-immigrant relations can best be characterized as tense. Neither group wants to associate with the other, but they also are not prepared to participate in American-style racism either.

During the 1950s and 1960s, many Black immigrants bypassed the South because of its oppressive racial politics, but the civil rights victories of the 1960s and 1970s made Florida more attractive to Haitians and other Black immigrants from the Caribbean.[56] In addition to coming to the U.S. for voluntary reasons, many Haitians came to the U.S. as political refugees. Marvin Dunn explains that when Haitian refugees began to come to Miami in the mid-1960s, "generally, local blacks were not inclined to help the Haitians assimilate into the larger population. . . . In fact, Haitians met outright hostility from some resident blacks."[57] Nonetheless, a small coalition of Blacks and Black churches—Liberty City's Friendship Missionary Baptist Church and the Black Baptist Alliance—did help to provide food, shelter, and clothing for newcomers.[58]

Haitians continued to come to Miami as refugees during the 1970s, and by the 1980s, the numbers grew large enough that members of South Florida's political elite complained to the federal government. In turn, the Immigration and Naturalization Service (INS) began to control the flow of Haitian immigrants with harsher tactics. Alex Stepick explains, "the campaign included the imprisonment of new arrivals, the denial of work permits to those who were allowed out of jail, [and] the wholesale rejection of Haitian claims for political asylum."[59] The curtailment of the Haitian refugees' rights coincided with the welcoming of Cubans in the late 1970s and 1980s as well as Nicaraguans in 1989. The intersection of events, whereby Black refugees were turned away and others were not, prompted Black leaders to speak out against what they saw as a racial inequity. By the late 1970s, the National Council of Churches as well as the Congressional Black Caucus, led by Shirley Chisolm[60] and Walter Fauntroy, pressed the federal government about the disregarded rights of Haitian refugees, a policy they characterized as racist.[61]

In 1992, during an increased flow of Haitian immigrants, George H. W. Bush issued an executive order requiring the return of intercepted Haitian refugees to Haiti, thereby denying them the opportunity to request asylum from the United States. Again, the Congressional Black Caucus, which had nearly doubled in size after the 1992 election, was a critical force in reshaping the U.S.'s policy toward Haitian refugees; the new policy, announced by President Bill Clinton, reversed the policy of returning Haitians and instead allowed the INS to conduct asylum hearings for those Haitian refugees who were intercepted at sea. The National Association for the Advancement of Colored People (NAACP) was also active in shedding light on the U.S.'s racist patterns in immigrant and refugee policies.[62]

In essence, African Americans supported Haitian refugees because they had a shared sense of racial group consciousness, but these shared feelings did not characterize day-to-day interactions between group members. On one hand, many African Americans resented the immigration laws that negatively affected Black immigrants. While the U.S. treated Cuban refugees favorably because they were considered to be politically motivated, it denied entrance to Haitian refugees who were making the same claims. African Americans viewed the U.S.'s policies toward Haitians as racist.

Yet, in spite of this shared racial consciousness, African Americans were (and are) wary of Black immigrants and of immigrants in general. Since native-born Blacks constitute a disproportionate number of Florida's poor and many of the Haitian immigrants who come to Miami are poor, intergroup tensions arise from "competition for limited resources, particularly with respect to public facilities such as health clinics, schools, public housing, emergency relief support, and general welfare services."[63] Similarly, Haitians in Florida are, at best, ambivalent about African Americans, or, in the words of Stepick, "for their part, Haitians accept black American support in their trials against racism, but Haitians do not wish to be identified with what they view as the most downtrodden group in the United States."[64]

Here, we see that African American and Haitian relations are contextual, and our characterization of the relationship between these two groups depends on whether we are looking at their relationship from the point of view of political elites or from the perspective of the masses. African American elites—including political representatives and community leaders—tend to feel a strong sense of group consciousness and have led the way to producing amicable relationships with Haitians in the U.S. through the policymaking process. But the on-the-ground relationship between average African Americans and Haitians is less positive. Since this text focuses on everyday individuals, throughout much of the remainder of this book we will get a better understanding of the perspective of members of the masses on cross-ethnic relations.

Afro-Caribbeans and African Americans

The most famous interactions between African Americans and Afro-Caribbeans are often represented by a relationship between two prominent Black political figures: W. E. B. Du Bois and Marcus Garvey. Du Bois and Garvey led major pan-African movements aiming to improve the welfare of Blacks across the globe. Even though Du Bois believed that Garvey's methods lacked "plain sense," he did admit to sharing Garvey's "main aspirations."[65] Similarly, Garvey, like Du Bois, recognized that racial inequality was not just an American problem or a colonial issue but that the color line belted the globe, and both men "would brook no compromise of the principles of absolute racial equality and eventual rule of Africa *by* Africans."[66] The men's visions of how to advance the rights of Blacks were quite different, however.

It is typical that the ethnicity of Black leaders in the first quarter of the twentieth century is unknown or, at least, underplayed, but much of the rhetoric that Du Bois and Garvey spewed toward each other in their respective newspapers often included insults about each other's heritage in their explanations of why their opponent's movement was flawed and would ultimately do harm to Blacks. This was especially true as Garvey's Universal Negro Improvement Association (UNIA) and Black Star Line became increasingly formidable organizations in the eyes of the Black masses. Garvey often made reference to Du Bois's mixed-race heritage, suggesting that you could not trust Du Bois's integrationist strategies to improve the plight of Blacks because Du Bois, and the Black elite—many of which were light skinned and mixed race—would be the primary beneficiaries, leaving poor and dark-skinned Blacks behind.[67]

Similarly, Du Bois would make every effort not to insinuate that it was because Garvey was West Indian that he was unstable and unable to be a serious leader, but Garvey's "being a West Indian subject of the British Empire had become a convenient substitute for reasoned criticism."[68] Du Bois was, at times, complicit in the anti–West Indian counterattack as Garvey's organization gained momentum. When W. A. Domingo pushed Du Bois and asked him about his xenophobic turn, Du Bois explained that his problem was with Garvey and not his heritage.[69] However, David Lewis explains that "the issue may not have been one of West Indian origins, but it certainly came down increasingly to knocking West Indians who were Garveyites."[70]

The relationship between Du Bois and Garvey does represent some of the interactions between African Americans and West Indians, but Du Bois and Garvey's relationship can primarily be characterized as antagonistic. The relationships between African Americans and West Indians were and are more complex than that. For one, there were West Indians who worked for and with Du Bois and against Garvey. Similarly, many angry and poor African Americans worked with Garvey, turning their backs on Du Bois. Second, the relationship between these groups' members has changed significantly over time, waxing and waning from positive and mutually inclusive to negative and exclusive depending on major events, such as transformations in U.S. immigration policy, fluctuations in the size of either group's population, and changes in the racial policy mood of the American electorate.

From the point of view of African Americans, the introduction of West Indians into New York between the 1910s and the 1930s was both a gift and a curse. First, the new immigrants were much more educated than were those African Americans who already lived in New York. Since these newcomers were ascribed a Black identity by white Americans, they were unable to pursue their white-collar work in the ways that they imagined they could, because of racial proscriptions; however, Black immigrants were able to monopolize specialties in Black neighborhoods. This, of course, was problematic in the eyes of African Americans because Black immigrants increased competition for jobs, Black business, and eventually, political influence.[71]

Nonetheless, since these newcomers tended to be highly educated, many African Americans, including Du Bois, felt that immigrant Blacks were more readily able to show white America what Blacks were able to do if they had access to quality education.[72] Alvin Tillery and Michell Chresfield, in a content analysis of prominent Black newspapers published between 1900 and 1940, found that although Black immigrants were often framed as "prone to criminality and other forms of social deviance," African Americans also viewed first-wave Afro-Caribbean immigrants as "model minorities" due to the fact that Afro-Caribbean immigrants, on average, possessed high socioeconomic status (on some indicators) and high levels of educational attainment.[73]

An added consideration for African Americans was the notion that West Indians did not understand the racial landscape of the United States; again, this was both a gift and a curse for African Americans. West Indians, like African Americans, were appalled by the racism in the United States. Some West Indians, however, chose to distance themselves from African Americans and relied on their option to return to their country of origin in order to cope with racial degradation. This strategy often irritated African Americans who felt that if West Indians were going to live in the United States, they should become citizens so that they—native- and foreign-born Blacks alike—could exercise the power of the ballot and work to improve the well-being of all Blacks living the United States.[74]

Harold Cruse, in *The Crisis of the Negro Intellectual*, was particularly critical of Black immigrants from the West Indies and Africa for employing this tactic. Cruse lambasted Black immigrants who delved into African American communities to take part in the arts, "yet on American Negro experiences on the social, political, economic and civil rights fronts, he often refuses to commit himself."[75] Much of Cruse's ire about Black immigrants derived from his observation that African and West Indian immigrants criticized African Americans for their position in American society, but from his point of view, these immigrants failed to recognize a contradiction: the conditions of immigrants' homelands were so dire that they immigrated to the U.S., but even in a land "without American Negro Black Power," the U.S., immigrants were still able to fare better economically. Furthermore, Cruse noted that Black immigrants often encouraged African Americans to rise up as minorities against whites but felt that this was disingenuous because, according to him, Afro-Caribbeans were unwilling to do the same in places where they were the majority.[76]

There were some Black immigrants who did get involved in politics, but they did not necessarily join African Americans. For one thing, they did not have any attachment to either major party, and many West Indians joined the Democratic Party—which actually helped African Americans later when the Democratic Party began to vie for the Black vote—or other political parties, such as the Socialist Party.[77] And, as John Walter explains about Black immigrants, "confronted with even deeper racism than they had left at home and uncertain of the easy rewards rumored to be found in America, a significant percentage found release of their frustrations in radical quasi-political and political behavior."[78] Prominent Black political figures such as Hubert H. Harrison, W. A. Domingo, Otto Huiswood, Cyril V. Briggs, Richard B. Moore, William Bridges, and William Ferris were all of West Indian descent. Harrison, for example, in his efforts to get African Americans to disassociate from the Republican Party and join the Socialist Party felt the wrath of Booker T. Washington, who arranged to get Harrison fired from his job as a post office clerk because he spoke poorly of Washington and his political affiliation and ideology.[79] Cyril Briggs came in direct conflict with Du Bois. Du Bois recognized a pattern of Blacks gaining rights after participating in American war efforts and, in turn, argued that Blacks should "close ranks" and join white Americans in the war effort.[80] Briggs as well as Garvey argued otherwise; more specifically, Briggs suggested that "the Negro had no interest in fighting a white man's war and that the Negro's foremost duty was to fight in the war at home against lynching."[81]

Black immigrants, in general, were perceived as and stereotyped as being dangerous radicals by the U.S. government, which sent in investigators to observe the radical Black political movement that came out of the Harlem Renaissance.[82] Ira Reid suggested that the introduction of West Indians and their radical politics may actually have served to accelerate African Americans' calls for equality. Reid argued, "The presence of a foreign Negro population has broadened the social vision of the native Negro group. It has helped to speed up the forces of aggressiveness and self-assertion in the direction the prejudice would suppress them."[83] But there were many African Americans who felt otherwise and predicted that radical movements would actually serve to threaten Black citizenship.[84]

Taking a step back, however, one can see that the "differences between African American and West Indian politicians were matters of style, not of substance"; in fact, during the early part of the twentieth century, West Indian politicians were not "West Indian" politicians per se but instead were Black political leaders who happened to be of West Indian origin.[85] That is to say, there were not any identifiable West Indian issues, and prominent West Indian politicians often did not think of their political personas as being West Indian, due to the constraints of the color line. In fact, W. A. Domingo, who was saddened by the *Messenger*'s insinuation that West Indian countries were more likely to produce "jackasses" than the United States was, wrote a letter to the *Messenger* suggesting that he thought of himself as a Black person who happened to be of West Indian descent; he thought that it was unfair to suggest that because he was of West Indian origin, he should be thought of as different from or inherently inferior to African Americans, especially since he was fighting toward racial equality just as many African Americans were.[86]

By the end of the 1920s and during the 1930s, there were more alliances between African American and West Indian political leaders. Marcus Garvey, who was in many ways a divisive character, had been arrested and deported; his UNIA organization dissolved. And the Johnson-Reed Act of 1924 curtailed the number of immigrants to the United States. In 1924, 12,000 Black immigrants came to the United States, but in 1925, only 791 West Indians were admitted.[87] Between 1924 and 1965, the proportion of foreign-born people in the United States had declined dramatically due to immigration restrictions.[88] All these changes managed to foster intraracial harmony. This might be best marked by the fact that many leaders of the Civil Rights Movement were of foreign-born stock; activists such as Kwame Ture (also known as Stokely Carmichael), Harry Belafonte, and Sidney Poitier as well as political leaders such as Shirley Chisholm were either foreign-born or born to immigrant parents. But during the time they fought for civil rights and Black representation, their identities, as first- or second-generation immigrants, were not necessarily central to the task at hand.

Philip Kasinitz describes a sinuous relationship between African Americans and Black immigrants in New York, placing ethnic entrepreneurs at the center of gravity.[89] He points out that in the 1920s and 1930s, race determined place of residence, jobs, school placement, and day-to-day treatment, thereby lumping West Indians and African Americans together. Kasinitz claims, however, "changes in the role of race in American culture since the late 1960s have made West Indian political distinctiveness possible," such that "race is not the monolithic force it was when the first cohort of West Indian migrants came to political consciousness."[90] Both Kasinitz and Foner suggest that due to a loosening of the role of race, both Caribbean and white politicians began to court West Indians as West Indians rather than as members of a larger Black community and further created "ethnic constituencies," all of which served to make salient ethnic identities rather than racial identities.[91] What is more, the Immigration Act of 1965 served to increase the number of Black immigrants across the country, especially in New York. West Indians began to notice that there was a large enough constituency of coethnics to gain representation separate from African Americans.[92] Previously, a dramatic decrease in the immigrant population served to encourage Black immigrants to work with African

Americans (in New York as well as in Florida). But as the West Indian population grew, Black immigrants recognized that they did not need to build race-based coalitions with African Americans in order to make their political desires a reality.

But yet another shift in African American and West Indian relations in New York occurred by the late 1980s. At the end of the 1980s, there was an increase in intraracial Black electoral unity because the racial climate of New York City was deteriorating. In 1986, Michael Griffith, a young Trinidadian, was chased onto a highway by a group of white youths and was killed by car. Soon after that, a group of New York City police officers killed a Jamaican street vendor. Racial tensions ran high especially between working-class and middle-class Caribbean residents and the police, as police harassed young Blacks.[93] In the late 1970s and much of 1980s, candidates recognized the potential to split the Black vote along ethnic lines, but in 1989, West Indians and African Americans formed a voting bloc, which helped to elect New York City's first Black mayor, David Dinkins.

This increase in racial tension at this time also brought about other types of coalition between African Americans and Black immigrants in the 1990s. Claire Jean Kim's *Bitter Fruit* is primarily about a drawn-out conflict between Blacks and Korean merchants in New York, but the Red Apple Boycott began when a Haitian woman, Ghiselaine Felissaint, was allegedly beaten by a Korean store owner in a Caribbean and Haitian neighborhood.[94] Kim documents the sixteen-month coalition of Haitian, Afro-Caribbean, and African American activists who recognized that Felissaint's treatment derived from the anti-Black attitude that Korean merchants directed at Black people in general—not just Haitians. African Americans, Haitians, and West Indians were aware that they all had been similarly racialized as Black despite their ethnic, cultural, and linguistic differences and acted together to demand better treatment.

Reuel Rogers provides evidence for the other extreme.[95] He suggests that race will not be a site for coalition building among nonwhite minority groups. In his study on Afro-Caribbean political elites in New York, he finds that relations between African American and Afro-Caribbean leaders tend to weaken when confronted with issues of descriptive representation. That is, Afro-Caribbeans are interested in being represented by one of their ethnic cohort just as African Americans have also sought to be represented by someone who shares common experiences with them. Furthermore, Rogers suggests that while many Afro-Caribbeans feel connected to African Americans and have a sense of linked fate, we should not expect them to mobilize around their racial identity in the same way that African Americans have, especially around issues of racial inequality.[96]

New Intraracial Interactions in the American South: Afro-Mexicans and Somalis

African Americans have interacted with Haitians, Afro-Caribbeans, and Afro-Cubans for at least a century now, but there are new groups that derive from the African diaspora that have only recently arrived in the United States. Not only are they recent immigrants, but they are also locating in a region that has not seen much change in its racial makeup since the Civil War: the South. The South has seen drastic population shifts over the past two decades; this shift largely stems from the new immigration patterns of Hispanics to the area. Cities such as Charlotte, Greensboro, Winston-Salem, Raleigh, and Durham in North Carolina have seen significant increases in the Hispanic population; Nashville and Memphis as well as Greenville, South Carolina, and Atlanta, Georgia, have also seen their traditionally binary or white/Black population become more diverse.[97] Afro-Mexican immigrants in Winston-Salem, North Carolina, and Somali refugees in Tennessee provide contemporary case studies of African American and Black immigrant relations. Even though these two immigrant groups are fairly new to these cities, there are striking similarities in the ways in which African Americans initially perceived and received these groups. There are also important similarities concerning the ways in which white racial animus in these two southern cities has shaped how African Americans have come view these groups as well as how Afro-Mexicans and Somalis view themselves.

The extent to which Hispanics and African Americans are "getting along" in various southern cities has recently caught the attention of scholars,[98] but if we zoom in a little closer, we find that the Hispanics who are coming to the U.S. are racially diverse; this is especially true in North Carolina. Afro-Mexicans make up approximately 1 percent of Mexico's population, but it is estimated that that they make up 80 percent of the Hispanic population in Winston-Salem.[99] Scholars have typically assessed that Hispanics and African Americans are and will continue to be at odds with each other, largely because Hispanic migrants tend to have negative stereotypes about African Americans and because African Americans feel that Hispanic immigrants compete for jobs and resources, such as affordable housing.[100]

Bobby Vaughn and Ben Vinson assert, "Generally speaking, however, the differences in everyday life experiences, buttressed by cultural and historical differences, have thus far prevented a socially viable solidarity between Afro-Mexicans and African Americans" in Winston-Salem.[101] Even though African Americans and Afro-Mexicans are members of the African diaspora, they have not viewed themselves as members of the same racial or ethnic group. It has been noted that Afro-Mexicans tend to be unaware of their racial history. Instead, there is a story that has been passed down in the Costa Chica, where most of the Afro-Mexican population that resides in Winston-Salem originate, suggesting that they are the descendants of individuals who were supposed to be slaves but escaped in the wake of a shipwreck or that they are descendants of Aztec warriors who have been darkened by the sun.[102] What is more, Afro-Mexicans are often mistaken for African Americans by American whites and are not seen as "legitimate" Mexicans or Latinos by other Mexicans. These experiences lead many Afro-Mexicans to feel animosity toward African Americans.[103] African Americans, on the other hand, tend to racialize Afro-Mexicans as Hispanic or Mexican rather than as Black.[104] All of these factors serve to hinder the development of a positive relationship or potential for coalition between these groups.

Despite these observations, there are signs that a shared sense of identity may develop between African Americans and Afro-Mexicans. Jennifer A. Jones points out that Winston-Salem is city that has a "long history of separation and quiet distrust. . . . With few exceptions, one becomes part of the black community or the white community, irrespective of class and potential for upward mobility."[105] In turn, Afro-Mexicans have largely been racialized by whites as "other" and potentially as "Black." According to Jones, recent shifts in policies concerning immigrants (e.g., 287(g) is a policy that has been used to target Latinos and deport those who are undocumented; undocumented immigrants have also been deprived of the ability to get driver licenses) have led Afro-Mexican immigrants to think less about the "American Dream" and more about American racism.[106] Afro-Mexican immigrants are now likely to incorporate experiences of racial discrimination and hostility in their consideration of their identities, just as we have seen African Americans do historically.

While African Americans received Afro-Mexicans coldly because of the perception of economic competition, African Americans, particularly through churches, have begun to reach out to Afro-Mexicans, as they have become more empathetic with the ways in which immigrants have been treated in the state. "Blacks reach out to the Latino community as well as other blacks by explaining the immigrant struggle through the experiences of blacks."[107] This is not to say that Afro-Mexicans and African Americans have simultaneously developed a shared sense of Black identity, but there is something to be said about the effects of the racialization process. The case presented here looks a lot like several of the aforementioned cases: at times, social interactions are characterized as hostile, especially in the beginning, but at other times, the intraracial interactions are supportive; the latter stage generally comes about in the face of racial discrimination.

As mentioned, the case of African Americans' relationship with Somalis in Tennessee is also quite similar to the one between African Americans and Afro-Mexicans in North Carolina. Beginning in 2004, Somali refugees were placed in Shelbyville, Tennessee; between four hundred and one thousand are estimated to have settled in the small town of about seventeen thousand due to a taxpayer-funded refugee aid resettlement program.[108] There is not much academic scholarship about this town, but the documentary *Welcome to Shelbyville* does an excellent job of laying out some of the dynamics between the newcomers, Latinos, African Americans, and whites in the town.[109] The film documents the attitudes and behaviors of politicians, citizens, and members of the media between November 2008 and May 2009.

Shelbyville is a town whose economy spiraled downward due to the exit of several manufacturing plants. Tyson Foods was one of the few plants left, and many of the remaining jobs went to Somali refugees. Consequently, citizens of Shelbyville—both Black and white—felt that the refugees represented an economic threat to them. In addition to the fact that longtime Shelbyville residents felt that Somalis were "stealing their jobs," they also had negative stereotypes about the refugees. County Mayor Eugene Ray, an African American man, went on record stating, "In the last ten years, it was Black and White, mostly here. But as we move along, we started getting Hispanics. And the one good thing about Hispanics, they are nice, you know. Easy to talk to, easy to deal with. Then about two years or three years after that, now you've got Somalians. Somalians are not nice and easy to talk to." Throughout the documentary, Somali refugees (including children) were characterized by Shelbyville residents as aggressive and primitive. Additionally, due to national media presentations of "homegrown terrorists" who traveled to Somalia to receive terrorist training, Shelbyville residents, largely represented by an African American woman named Miss Beverly, were particularly suspicious of the newcomers. Finally, most of the refugees were also Muslim, which added insult to injury from the perspective of most Christian Shelbyville residents. The combination of all these issues caused American-born Shelbyville residents to distance themselves from the refugees.

But there was an impetus for African Americans to change their attitudes toward the Somali refugees. Brian Mosely, a white journalist for the *Shelbyville Times*, wrote a series of articles that reinforced negative stereotypes about the refugees. Responding to the hostility inspired by these articles, an African American woman who spoke at a "Community Unity" event stated,

> I have been on the other end of the totem pole like the Somalis, that we were all put in the same category. We are not all in the same category. They thought all Black people were dirty. We were not dirty. You're not all these things that people want to put you in one pot. That all white folks hate Black folks. That's not true, so we need to educate ourselves again, I say. We need to educate and communicate, and see what these people's standards are. And then we'll have to change and find out you're just as good as I am. We have to change our attitudes, and we also have to change our actions. You've got to walk the walk, and talk the talk.

The speaker in this short speech provides a number of insights. First, she notes that even though the refugees are African, they are not necessarily the same as African American Shelbyville residents; nonetheless, she notes, the stereotypes people had about African Americans are now being placed on Somali refugees, which in her view is wrong. Additionally, in her speech, which was applauded by the African American attendees, she notes that it is not enough to change the way people think about these newcomers but that people also should behave differently—more fairly—toward them, especially considering that African Americans were in the same position that the Somalis are in now. Similarly, at the end of the documentary—six months after the Unity event—Miss Beverly, who was initially skeptical of the refugees, says, "I could be that Somalian woman. I could have been her, but God chose for me to be over here. It's just . . . No. I could have been one of them." Her level of empathy had also increased for this group of Black immigrants as she recognized both their struggles in their country of origin and their struggles in the United States.

Again, it is unclear how the relationship between African Americans and Black immigrants will fare in these two cities, or cities like them, but what is clear is the pattern of an initial cold reception followed by a recognition that Black immigrants and African Americans are racialized similarly and face similar challenges in the face of racism. These shared experiences are not only largely responsible for shaping how Black immigrants come to see themselves, but also these experiences often manage to bring native- and foreign-born Blacks to one accord politically.

* * *

In summary, history reflects multiple possibilities for Black intraracial relations. This chapter shows that there is quite a bit of overlap in the ways in which Black immigrants and African Americans experience race in the U.S., but it also shows that there is room for potential political conflict. African American and Black immigrant relations are not only dictated by shared racial group consciousness or lack thereof but also are heavily influenced by forces external to these communities:

U.S. immigration policy, fluctuations in racial tension, changes in demographics, political entrepreneurs, and the extent to which Blacks enjoy or are denied civil rights and freedoms on the basis of their racial group membership.

Coalition and cohesion tend to occur when there is an incentive for African Americans and Black immigrants to work together. We saw this between African Americans and West Indians in New York as well as between Afro-Cubans and African Americans in Florida. Ginetta Candelario also points out that during the 1960s and 1970s in New York, African Americans were not particularly empowered, and consequently, Black immigrants tended to distance themselves from African Americans. This disempowerment sought to reinforce "the prevailing Dominican association of blackness with low socioeconomic standing."[110] Meanwhile, in Washington, D.C., during the same two decades, Dominican immigrants found it beneficial to work with and identify with African Americans because African Americans were politically and economically empowered. Black people experienced social mobility in D.C. due to the political activities of African Americans, and the potential for economic and social success served as an incentive for Black immigrants to assimilate into a Black racial identity.[111]

Pan-ethnic identities also appear to become more salient when Black immigrants gain a sense of racial consciousness and recognize that they are disenfranchised and discriminated against primarily because of their race. On the other hand, distancing and "disidentification" tend to occur when ethnic entrepreneurs present incentives based on ethnic identification rather than an overarching racial or pan-ethnic identity,[112] when Black immigrants feel that there is not a need to mobilize against racial disparities,[113] or when African Americans feel that their political gains through the Civil Rights era are threatened by expanding the boundaries of Blackness.[114] The historical research on native- and foreign-born Black relations, however, is generally descriptive rather than theoretical, lacking a general explanation of why at times race is a unifier and at other times ethnicity is a divider among Blacks in the United States. A theory of diasporic consciousness, which is outlined in the next chapter, aims to fill this gap.

2

Diasporic Consciousness

Theorizing Black Pan-Ethnic Identity and Intraracial Politics

Sociological literature focusing on Black immigrants tends to imply that African American and Black immigrant relations will be primarily characterized as antagonistic, with elements of hostility, distancing, and competition. These predictions are primarily based on studies that show that first-generation Black immigrants tend to have negative stereotypes about African Americans and, in turn, seek to distance themselves and their children from native-born Blacks.[1]

Classical Black politics literature, on the other hand, primarily helps us to understand racial unity among Blacks in the United States. This literature suggests that as long as Black people feel that their fate is linked to the members of their racial group and believe that their life chances are highly influenced by their race, they will think about their racial group when making political decisions; that is to say, we should expect unity from Blacks as long as race is a defining element in their lives.[2] Michael Dawson notes, "The relative homogeneity of black public opinion has generally been considered one of the few certainties of modern American politics."[3] Literature spanning decades provides a great deal of empirical evidence for this "relative homogeneity" of Black political attitudes and behaviors as well, so much that homogeneity and unity are now the conventional wisdom.[4]

Yvette M. Alex-Assensoh, nonetheless, brings to our attention her observation that "the so-called lack of diversity in Black Politics is *also* due to the singular research on native-born African Americans, who represent only one segment of the increasingly diverse black population."[5] Furthermore, while I agree that the existing sociology literature provides an abundant amount of evidence suggesting that Black immigrants tend to distance themselves from African Americans, historical accounts paint a more complex portrait of African American and Black immigrant relations.[6] There have been and are times when African Americans and Black immigrants embrace a mutually inclusive identity and mobilize this shared identity toward common political goals, as illustrated in the previous chapter.

Just as unity has become the conventional wisdom in the Black politics literature, distancing and competition have taken center stage in the sociological literature on immigrants of African descent. These two bodies of work stand seemingly in contradiction to each other. Consequently, we need a new theory of Black politics that better explains when and under which circumstances Blacks build intraracial coalitions and develop a pan-ethnic identity as well as when and under what circumstances interethnic conflict and intraracial distancing prevail. In order to gain a better understanding of Black politics in the face of increasing ethnic diversity, we need a more complex and nuanced theoretical model. This theory not only must highlight the historical factors that initially shaped Black politics as we know it today but must also account for the contemporary influences of America's racialized social structure. It needs to incorporate the notion that Black identity is contextual and fluid; that is to say, the extent to which Blacks feel that their race is salient and central to their self-image is situational.[7] This fluidity influences Black political behavior and attitudes as well as the potential for intraracial conflict and coalition. I propose a theory of diasporic consciousness as an important addition to the scholarship on Black intraracial relations. As previously mentioned, we should conceptualize diasporic consciousness as the (mental) tightrope that people of African descent who live in the United States walk as they try to balance their superordinate racial identity (and the political interests associated with it) with their subgroup or ethnic identity and its closely associated political interests.

This chapter, ultimately, seeks to fully delineate this theory. I begin this chapter by engaging with the concept of the identity-to-politics link, which helps us to understand how an individual's racial identity can be mobilized toward political action; but even this link needs to be contextualized due to the complexities that arise in linking individuals' pan-ethnic identity to pan-ethnic political action. This chapter lays a foundation to do so with discussions concerning the processes of racial-ization and the factors that affect inter- and intraracial politics. Finally, I describe, in detail, the theory of diasporic consciousness as well as outline a new, more complex set of expectations for Black politics that arise with the help of a theory that paints a more accurate depiction of Black identity, political behavior, and political attitudes.

Identity-to-Politics Link

Rawi Abdelal and his colleagues point out that "the wide variety of con-ceptualizations and definitions of identity have led some to conclude that identity is so elusive, slippery, and amorphous that it will never prove to be a useful variable for the social sciences."[8] Nonetheless, it is well known that the structural constraints that African Americans (and many other minority groups) face due to their racial categoriza-tion affects their decision-making calculus in the political realm. Sim-ply being involuntarily placed in a racial category, however, does not necessarily mean group members will act or think in a particular way. Instead, there are a number of steps that link "demographic classifi-cation to a collective political choice."[9] We can consider four of those steps here: group membership, identification, group consciousness, and political behavior.[10] This link is depicted in figure 2.1.

The first step, classification or group membership, is "defined as 'objectively' belonging to a particular social group."[11] People in the United States are, for the most part, assigned a racial category; they are involuntarily ascribed a racial identity.[12] Institutions, such as state legislatures, courts (including the Supreme Court), and the U.S. Cen-sus have all played a role in developing racial group categories as well

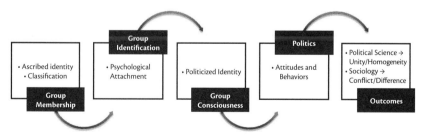

Figure 2.1. Identity-to-politics link

as instructing society on which members belong to which categories.[13] People of African descent, including those with "one drop" of Black blood, or a single ancestor of African descent, have traditionally been ascribed a Black racial identity in the United States. While there have been changes over time in the ways in which people have been racially classified, the U.S. Census contemporarily describes a Black or African American person as "a person having origins in any of the black racial groups of Africa." It further instructs, "Terms such as 'Haitian' or 'Negro' can be used in addition to 'Black or African American.'" Individuals from North Africa, however, are classified as "white." Categorization may seem innocuous, and even a bit haphazard, but racial categories are constituted in racial hierarchies; how one is classified can have major consequences on one's life chances.[14]

The second step is group identification, which is quite different from group membership. Group membership leads one to have an ascribed group category, but identification is a psychological attachment to one's group.[15] Group identification is often a consequence of group membership, but the first step does not always lead to the next. Zoltan Hajnal and Taeku Lee point out that there are times when "the set of individuals who might conceivably identify with a given category does not correspond perfectly or sometimes reliably with the subset of individuals who actually identify with that category."[16] This may be the case for Black immigrants, who are assigned to the Black racial category but may or may not identify as Black.

The third step is group consciousness. Although psychological attachment is a necessary condition toward political action in the name of one's racial group, it is not sufficient on its own to promote political behavior. It is only when this identity is politicized—when one's sense of group consciousness is raised—that we see a change in behavior, or a completion of the identity-to-politics link.[17] Group consciousness is "in-group identification *politicized* by a set of ideological beliefs about one's group's social standing as well as a view that collective action is the best means by which the group can improve its status and realize its interests."[18]

The final step is political action. Those who have a strong sense of group consciousness tend to participate at higher rates, to have an increased interest in politics, and to feel a sense of group pride and political efficacy in comparison to those with a weaker sense of group consciousness.[19] Group consciousness tends to lead group members to act collectively toward improving the status of the group.

The African American Link

The scholarship on African Americans' political and racial solidarity swelled in the 1960s and the 1970s in reaction to the Civil Rights and Black Power Movements as well as a "New Black Politics that fused protest and electoral forms and had a strong base in organizations."[20] African American political behavior caught the attention of scholars because "New Black Politics were putting blacks in office and mobilizing blacks to register to vote in numbers unimaginable since the days of Reconstruction."[21] After the 1965 Voting Rights Acts, Blacks were able to participate in electoral politics in ways and at rates that they had not been able to since the 1880s, and they moved from the Republican Party to the Democratic Party.[22]

This resurgence of Black political participation was marked by group solidarity, and it became clear that African Americans' racial identity and sense of group consciousness played a role in the ways in which they participated in American politics. Scholarship that focused on racial solidarity and racial group consciousness reveals that African Americans' racial identity can be mobilized into political action. For example, Sidney Verba and Norman Nie found that African Americans who viewed the world through a racial lens were more likely to be participatory than were those who did not believe that race was at the center of many issues.[23] They suggested that a sense of racial group consciousness was a political resource for African Americans. Richard Shingles expounded on Verba and Nie's notion of black consciousness, showing that this consciousness has such a dramatic effect on African Americans' political behavior because it "contributes to the combination of a sense of political efficacy and political mistrust which in turn induces political involvement."[24] Black consciousness appears to be the link between identity and political action for African Americans.

While the scholarship on the role of racial identity and group consciousness began to surge in the 1970s, the idea that Black racial identity is linked to Black political behavior is deeply rooted in history.

The most well-known example of how racial identity influences political behavior for African Americans is partisanship. For the past five decades, African Americans have supported the Democratic Party, but this was not always the case. Prior to the 1950s, African Americans were supporters of the Republican Party. This partisan switch was made because prior to the New Deal, the Republican Party—the party of Lincoln—endorsed laws that were beneficial to African Americans. When it became clear that the Republican Party was no longer a good fit for the group, African Americans chose to support the Democratic Party. A shift in national partisan politics resulted in a steady movement of African Americans from a party that no longer advocated for them to a partisan organization that would do so.[25]

Michael C. Dawson in his seminal text, *Behind the Mule*, argues that it is a combination of African Americans' history and current status in the United States that connects their racial identity to their political behavior. History shows that when African Americans are able to participate politically, they tend to support the political parties and candidates that best represent their racial group rather than their individual social or economic interests. Dawson argues that such is the case because African Americans have been treated as group members rather than as individuals, despite their class status or attained level of prestige. Further, since African Americans' life chances are significantly influenced by their racial group membership, they tend to behave politically as a group. Dawson characterizes this feeling as a sense of linked fate, a sense that the well-being of the group will have very much to do with the well-being of the individual.

While there is some dissent about the extent to which group consciousness is a helpful explanation of African American political behavior,[26] many political scientists value the use of group consciousness as an explanation for the overall homogeneity in political behavior among African Americans as well as for the participation rates among this group.[27] The evidence showing that racial identity and consciousness are excellent predictors of African American political behavior is quite strong. Katherine Tate finds that racial identity serves as a unifying factor among African Africans, transcending variations in socioeconomic status, ideology, and region.[28] Dennis Chong and Reuel Rogers build on Tate's work and find that in statistical models, racial identity alone accounts for some of the effect in African American political participation, but they also find that group consciousness is a critical factor that underlies the propensity of African Americans to participate in politics. Chong and Rogers find that racial identification and consciousness, indeed, have positive effects on voter turnout as well as other campaign activities, including petitioning government officials and participating in boycotts and protests.[29]

Black Immigrants: Identity to Politics

Mary Waters suggests that the successes of the Civil Rights Movement and civil rights legislation have allowed immigrants of color, including Black immigrants, to have a broader array of identity choices.[30] That is, they may choose to identify racially as Black or even as African American, but they may also embrace various ethnic identities such as West Indian, Nigerian, or Cuban, for instance. But Reuel Rogers reminds us that ethnicity, on the one hand, is generally a matter of cultural nostalgia, while race, in contrast, has real political, social, and economic implications, even for Black immigrants.[31] Black immigrants must negotiate their racial and ethnic identities while living in the United States, but very little is known about how these identities influence their political behavior.

One emerging consensus in the literature concerns the observation that first-generation Black immigrants' ethnic or distinct cultural identity is often more salient and central for them than is their racial identity.[32] Most scholars have focused on Afro-Caribbeans' tendency to make their ethnic identity known. A consistent finding in these studies is that Black immigrants often make an effort to differentiate themselves from African Americans. Scholars offer three general explanations for this finding. One explanation is that Black immigrants use their ethnic identity to distance themselves from African Americans as a consequence of negative stereotypes they know and perhaps hold about African Americans. This tends to be especially true among first-generation Black immigrants.[33] The second explanation is that ethnic identity might be primed or strengthened as a psychological coping mechanism in response to the racial discrimination that Black immigrants experience in the United States.[34] The third explanation is that

making ethnic identity salient may be a political strategy to gain benefits that are restricted to one's ethnic group rather than to a larger racial
or pan-ethnic group.[35]

The research on the children of first-generation Black immigrants
provides more nuanced theories about the development of racial identity. Waters, for example, in her seminal text on Black immigrants,
Black Identities, proposes three identity trajectories or paths for second-
generation West Indians: identifying as African American, identifying
as ethnic or hyphenated Americans, or maintaining their parents' ethnic identification. These "choices" are influenced by class and by gender,
so that poorer respondents and male respondents are supposedly more
likely to identify as African American, while well-to-do and female
respondents are more likely to identify with their ethnicity.[36] Alejandro
Portes and his colleagues have also developed theoretical models suggesting that second-generation immigrants have more complex identity
choices than do their first-generation counterparts, but these choices
are dictated by the "direction" of assimilation paths.[37] More specifically,
these scholars maintain that second-generation Black immigrants may
take a "straight-line" path into the white middle-class majority; may
face "downward assimilation" into an undifferentiated Black, inner-city
"underclass"; or may experience a combination of upward mobility and
heightened ethnic awareness.

According to these theories, these paths have consequences for the
identities of second-generation immigrants of color. These theories predict that those who experience "downward" assimilation will identify
racially, as African American or Black, while those who take "upward"
assimilation paths will identify with an ethnic identity. Some scholars
point out, however, that second-generation Black immigrants are likely
to feel connected to and identify with members from their parents'
country of origin (or ethnic identity) as well as with African Americans (racial identity), revealing that these identities are not mutually exclusive.[38]

Scholars specifically concerned with identity development among
immigrants remind us that acculturation processes are "not a matter
of one's individual strategy where one has the free choice to unproblematically integrate the values of the host culture and one's own immigrant group," but instead immigrants to the United States are always

negotiating their identities in the face of structural inequalities as a result of their nationality, race, gender, and class.[39] While we must consider structure—such as those institutions that "make" racial hierarchy and racialize individuals—we must also take seriously the notion of individual agency when analyzing how people develop identities.

Racializing Immigrants

Immigrants come to the United States with their own ideas about their identity but often very quickly recognize the notion that their racial identity within the U.S. context may be a benefit or a hindrance to their success. Michael Omi and Howard Winant's theory of racial formation via racial projects explains that racial categories as well as the way we racialize individuals and groups is an ongoing sociohistorical process, meaning that both macro-level, social structural processes and everyday, micro-level processes influence the development and maintenance of racialized social systems.[40]

The notions that (1) racial boundaries expand and contract, sometimes becoming more inclusive while at other times being more exclusive, and (2) racial boundaries are influenced from the top down as well as the bottom up contribute to my theory of diasporic consciousness. African Americans and Black immigrants are, at times, differentiated and/or differentiate themselves from each other, while also being grouped together and/or embracing an identity inclusive of ethnic diversity. We see several instances of each on a day-to-day basis. For example, the U.S. Census categorizes native- and foreign-born Blacks within the same racial group. Relatedly, police officers may see all low-income, Black men as potential criminals despite their distinct ethnic backgrounds, as the case of Amadou Diallo illustrates.[41] Similarly, employers may seek Black immigrants, whom they stereotype as "model minorities," rather than African Americans, and Black immigrants may embrace this stereotype and, in turn, distance themselves from African Americans in an effort to gain some economic benefit.[42] And at the same time, Black immigrants may bond with African Americans in a struggle against ongoing anti-Black discrimination; that is to say, despite the potential pitfalls of identifying as or being associated with African Americans, Black immigrants may develop a sense of linked fate or racial group consciousness. Racialization processes occur on several levels of analysis.

Looking historically at the ways in which white and nonwhite immigrants to the United States have been racialized will help us better understand and more accurately predict the mechanisms that may lead first- and second-generation Black immigrants and African Americans who are categorized similarly by mainstream society to decide whether to embrace or reject an overarching or pan-ethnic identity—the first transition in the identity-to-politics link.

To Be(come) or Not to Be(come) White

Whiteness and ethnic studies scholars, through the exposition of the way European immigrants over several generations assimilated into a white American mainstream, illuminate the fact that immigrants to this country arrive with an ethnic or country-based identity. Over time, however, society—via formal and informal institutions—incorporates them into America's racial hierarchy.[43] For example, upon arrival to the United States in the nineteenth century, many European immigrants, including the Irish, Italians, Poles, and Jews, were not identified as white; some of these immigrants, in fact, were identified as, grouped with, and treated the same as African Americans.[44] In many ways, they were racialized as Black. Irish immigrants were subject to racial epithets such as "white negroes" and "smoked Irish."[45] Southern Italian immigrants were identified as "swarthy" and "kinky-haired." Southern legislators, at the time, predicted that Italian immigrants would be an "unassimilable race" and fought to keep Italian children out of "white" schools. Research shows that some Italian immigrants were hanged for crimes not committed, similarly to African Americans.[46]

These immigrants were situated outside the privileged domain of whiteness, but they were, over time, able to work their way into whiteness.[47] In addition to developing political prowess and affecting positive change for their ethnic group through the power of the ballot, one of the major ways that European immigrants assimilated into a white mainstream was by distancing themselves from African Americans.[48] While these immigrants were not originally considered as white, the doors of whiteness were opened to them relatively quickly. For example, white immigrants including Polish, Slovak, and Czech immigrants were able to settle in the South, and within forty years, native whites were "fully reconciled to their presence."[49] Stephen Steinberg suggests that although white immigrants' entry point into the United States was at the bottom of America's racial, social, economic, and political hierarchies, it was not the same bottom that African Americans occupied.[50] White immigrants were in some ways told, "You will become like us whether you want to or not," while the implied message to African Americans was, "No matter how much like us you are, you will remain apart."[51] The histories of how various groups of European immigrants became white are telling of how racial boundaries can be permeable and selectively inclusive or exclusive. These boundaries are also constantly evolving as a result of top-down institutional changes, such as immigration policies, as well as due to the agency and actions of individuals and marginalized groups.

It is also well known that not all immigrants are welcomed into whiteness.[52] The Mississippi Chinese provide an excellent example of the way one Asian group was racialized as an "in-between" racial group. The Mississippi Chinese, like their white ethnic predecessors, found themselves grouped with African Americans. Through distancing themselves from African Americans as well as making concerted efforts to be accepted into white American society, this group was able to remove themselves from an all-encompassing Black identity, but at the same time they were not accepted into the white mainstream.[53] Claire Jean Kim's theory of racial triangulation provides a helpful explanation of the way Asian immigrants, in particular, are racially valorized in comparison to African Americans but are not yet privileged into a white identity because they are civically ostracized.[54]

Some scholars might argue that some Latinos have gained their way into whiteness, citing, for example, the brief period of time when Mexicans were categorized as white in the U.S. Census or the fact that many "white" Cubans have assimilated into a white identity. While it has been shown that Hispanic whites as well as other white ethnic immigrants are able to integrate themselves into dominant white society,[55] Benjamin Bailey suggests that the mere designation of people as "Latino" or "Hispanic" in addition to "white" reflects and reproduces their exclusion from white racial categorization and identity.[56] Whether the boundaries of whiteness are still flexible and permeable remains an unanswered empirical question,[57] but the doors of whiteness seem to be closed for contemporary immigrants of color.

It is generally taken as a given that immigrants of African descent will be racialized as "Black" because racialization processes are taken for granted.[58] Unlike whites, and to some extent Asians and Latinos, people with darker phenotypes and certain facial features are generally categorized as Black, because "the power of race as a socially defining status in the U.S. makes . . . internal differences rather unimportant in interracial setting[s] in comparison to the fundamental black/white color boundary."[59] But it should be duly noted that Black immigrants do have ethnic identities and must also navigate a racialized social system. They, like other immigrant groups, may attempt to distance themselves from or may embrace the Black racial identity that American society ascribes to them.

Forging Pan-Ethnic Identities among Racial Minorities

Identities, including pan-ethnicities, are in some ways a result of both structure and individual agency. Further, the boundaries of identities are negotiated among current group insiders as well between insiders and outsiders. This study takes seriously the idea that Blackness as a category has the potential to be stretched and conceived of as a pan-ethnic identity. The scholarship on the development of pan-ethnic identities among and the racialization of Asian Americans and Latinos serves as a building block for a theory of diasporic consciousness. First, the pan-ethnic identity literature acknowledges that we must be careful in moving directly from ascribing pan-ethnic labels to individuals to assuming that those who share the same label also share experiences, attitudes, and beliefs.[60] Second, the notion of pan-ethnicity is useful to this study because it communicates the notion that pan-ethnic groups are "characterized by the simultaneous coexistence of externally perceived homogeneity and internally lived heterogeneity."[61] That is, the concept of pan-ethnicity includes both the notion that groups are lumped together and racialized by outsiders and, at the same time, that in-group members are aware of and negotiate internal, ethnic boundaries. Third, pan-ethnicity, as a process, focuses on the ways in which ethnic and racial identities change.[62] The concept of pan-ethnicity is also important because it suggests that ethnic identity is not merely a matter of descent but may also be a political identity that can be chosen or rejected by individuals. Pan-ethnic identities are layered—they are one of many possible identities held simultaneously with others; they are fluid and contextual. Diasporic consciousness is built on these ideas.

As mentioned, European immigrants are now understood to have linearly adapted and to have been adopted into whiteness, but the identity paths for immigrants of color have been quite different. Whereas accounts of identity shifts for nineteenth- and early twentieth-century European immigrants suggest that these immigrants shed ethnic markers of language and traditions as they climbed economic and political ladders and intermarried across ethnic lines, the extent to which today's immigrants of color will be "collectively channeled into enduring racially marked subordinate statuses" remains an open question.[63]

Some of the extant research on processes of pan-ethnic boundary formation has focused on the social and historical processes that led to the creation of pan-ethnic boundaries, highlighting the role of formal institutions. One major example of this is the role of state-developed racial categories, best illustrated by the U.S. Census Bureau's role in reifying group labels and group boundaries.[64] Arthur Kim and Michael White emphasize that formal institutions' racial categorizations contribute to essentializing groups and promote the perception of natural demarcations, which in turn become legitimized within institutions and among individuals.[65] Political policies and mainstream institutions, including the media, influence group boundaries by "increasing the symbolic and material value of racial and ethnic identities."[66]

Other scholars maintain that the nature of pan-ethnic identities is best described as instrumental, suggesting that these identities only arise when an incentive or threat is presented. Indeed, pan-ethnic subgroups might have an incentive to forge coalitions and mobilize politically if group members are designated as a "single administrative unit" and resources are allocated to those groups. Pan-ethnic identity may also become salient when subgroup members' rights are externally threatened (e.g., by a change in state policies). Felix M. Padilla, for example, reports that in 1980s Chicago, Mexicans and Puerto Ricans organized in a struggle against language discrimination.[67] The sense of group identity of Latinos of various ethnic groups also increased in the face of Proposition 187.[68] Joane Nagel shows that federal Indian policies that threatened Native Americans created an atmosphere that increased pan-ethnic consciousness, mobilization, and pride among Native Americans.[69]

Similarly, Yan Espiritu shows that after a Chinese man was beaten to death with a baseball bat because two white men believed that he was Japanese, Asian Americans' sense of pan-ethnic identity was raised, as they recognized that the internal subgroup boundaries were unrecognized by a larger American society.[70] We also see this sense of group threat as a means of raising a sense of pan-ethnic identity in the case of the Red Apple Boycott in New York City. After a Korean store owner mistreated a Haitian customer, Haitians, West Indians, and African Americans recognized that the customer was mistreated because of her race rather than her ethnicity. In turn, Black immigrants and African Americans mutually recognized their shared racial identity and mobilized politically.[71]

Structural conditions also serve as mechanisms that influence the development of pan-ethnic identities. Dina Okamoto emphasizes the role of market segregation; she finds that when ethnic groups are concentrated together in the same low-paying occupations, often due to discrimination, they are likely to develop a pan-ethnic identity that can be politically mobilized.[72] This mechanism of occupational segmentation has the potential to facilitate the development of a shared identity among Blacks. First- and second-generation Black immigrants, especially men, tend to be concentrated in the public and not-for-profit sectors and are similarly funneled into the same low-paying, second-tier jobs as African Americans are.[73]

Residential segregation is yet another structural condition that serves to raise a sense of shared identity among subethnic groups. Milagro Ricourt and Ruby Danta find that in Queens the constant interaction among various members of multiple Latin American national groups has led to the development of an overarching identity.[74] Louis DeSipio also suggests that increased contact among subgroups facilitates pan-ethnic identity development.[75] Additionally, in an effort to weigh the relative effect of cultural similarities against structural conditions, David Lopez and Yan Espiritu find that structural processes of racialization have a greater influence in developing pan-ethnic identities.[76] More specifically, they find that geographic overlap and residential concentration are likely to encourage pan-ethnic identities. Research on residential patterns of Black immigrants shows that despite attaining higher average socioeconomic status than African Americans do, Black immigrants have difficulty avoiding discrimination and segregation in the housing market. Black immigrants are generally denied access to predominantly white residential areas and are instead confined to areas of large Black concentrations.[77]

In addition to understanding the ways in which out-group members and external forces, such as state or federal governments, influence the development of pan-ethnic identities, it is also important to understand how in-group members play a role in developing, maintaining, or restructuring a superordinate identity. Okamoto suggests that "mobilizing structures" play a role in pan-ethnic identity development as well. These structures, which are often led by group members themselves, aim to mobilize a constituency toward a political goal and make people aware that political and economic desires are shared cross-ethnically.[78] Ricourt and Danta make a similar argument, suggesting that when leaders espouse a pan-ethnic identity or when organizations, such as churches and neighborhood centers, attempt to attract and serve members of various national groups, pan-ethnic identities are likely to be forged among audience members.[79] Participation in these pan-ethnically aimed mobilizing structures also serves to bolster a psychological attachment to a pan-ethnic identity.[80]

The power of structural conditions, such as spatial and market segregation, and everyday exposure to racism and discrimination do not always lead to ethnic groups uniting under their imposed racial label, however.[81] Pei-te Lien, M. Margaret Conway, and Janelle Wong point out several potential hindrances in the development of pan-ethnic identification and cooperation among racial group members: (1) "divide and conquer" strategies by white labor management; (2) "ethnic disidentification" by some group members to avoid "being misidentified as belonging to other politically or social ostracized" subgroups; (3) political and military conflicts between subgroup members' homelands; and (4) "further diversification of the polyethnic population along class, ethnic origin, race, ideology, religion, and other lines of cleavage" due to ongoing immigration.[82] All these potential hindrances can be found when analyzing the relationships between African Americans and Black immigrants. Scholars find that employers in New York prefer to employ Black immigrants rather than African Americans.[83] Many find that Black immigrants see themselves as superior to African Americans and often distance themselves from native-born Blacks.[84] Ongoing conflicts in Africa, for example, might also influence the ways in which Blacks from that continent feel about uniting under a pan-ethnic identity.

Overall, the potential for the development of an overarching racial or pan-ethnic identity among Black immigrants and African Americans in the United States exists—as do hindrances against it. But again, understanding and appreciating these mechanisms will help us develop better explanations and predictors for a very complex set of attitudes and behaviors in Black politics, as a theory of diasporic consciousness seeks to do.

Inter- and Intraracial Minority Politics

The U.S. Census Bureau projects that by 2042 minority group members will make up a majority of the total U.S. population. These changing demographics make it necessary for social scientists to think more carefully about the ways in which minority groups will behave toward one another.[85] One might expect racial minorities to form political coalitions because they have suffered from social, political, and economic inequalities by the same racialized social system—though in different ways. Looking retrospectively, however, we see that while there have, at times, been temporary coalitions, competition among minority groups across the country has also been quite common.

The notion that minorities would, could, or should work together is based in the idea that they have shared interests; they share many of the same problems, setbacks, and goals. There are, however, other factors that should be accounted for when predicting under what circumstances interminority coalitions might or might not form. Stokely Carmichael and Charles Hamilton argued that four conditions must be met for a successful coalition: (1) parties have to recognize their own self-interests; (2) each party must feel that it will benefit from working with the other groups; (3) each party must have its own base of power and must have control over its own decision-making processes; and (4) each party must be cognizant that a coalition is formed with a specific goal in mind.[86] It seems that minorities have enough common ground to incentivize inter- and intraminority group coalitions, but often there are differences between racial groups and within pan-ethnic groups such that they do not share similar interests. In fact, at times these interests are competing—or at least members perceive their interests as competing. Bilingual education, housing, jobs, and other social resources are often viewed as zero-sum issues between minority groups.[87]

Nevertheless, there have been times when multiracial coalitions have been fruitful. On the local level, the elections of New York's first African American mayor, David Dinkins, and of Los Angeles mayors Tom Bradley and Antonio Villaraigosa all depended on multiracial coalitions.[88] On a national level, the election of President Barack Obama was made possible due to the high turnout of Black voters as well as Latinos, Asians, and young white voters.[89]

But we must also go beyond calculated interests and ideology to understand why minority groups may at times mutually recognize one another as allies while at other times they may attempt to distance themselves from one another. By thinking critically about and accounting for the system in which minority groups encounter one another, scholars of systemic or structural racism help us consider from a broader viewpoint the circumstances under which minority groups interact.[90] Theories of structural racism suggest that racism and racial power "operates not only by reproducing racial categories and meanings per se but by reproducing them in the form of a distinct racial order."[91] No one individual is responsible for such a phenomenon, but individuals do play a part. Minority groups encounter one another within a larger structure marked by white racial dominance and racial power, and they must negotiate this structure, which may lead them to perpetuate and maintain the hierarchy of a racialized social system.

An excellent example of this negotiation is illustrated by the tension that exists between some Black immigrants and African Americans. More specifically, much of the animosity that exists between the groups' members has a lot to do with the adaptation and perpetuation of negative stereotypes by Black immigrants about African Americans. Mary Waters's Afro-Caribbean respondents, for example, tended to espouse some of the most denigrating stereotypes about African Americans.[92] Other scholars show that Black immigrants tend to believe that African Americans are lazy and are likely to be discourteous, to use drugs, and to be criminals, and many Black immigrants blame African Americans for the racial group's lack of success relative to other racial groups.[93] Because of these existing racial stereotypes, Black immigrants have an incentive to distance themselves from African Americans as well as to rely on "white racial frames" to explain African Americans' position in society's racial hierarchy.[94] Paula McClain and her colleagues also find that Latinos hold negative stereotypes about African Americans, thereby threatening coalitions that have worked in the past.[95] Similarly, the stereotype of Asians as a "model minority" tends to lead other minority groups to feel that Asians are not likely to be discriminated against and therefore do not recognize that, indeed, minority groups are pitted against one another to maintain white hegemony.[96] All these examples show how minority groups interact within a specific racial context and at times (unintentionally) perpetuate white racial power in their effort to improve or maintain their status within the larger racial hierarchy.

Group interests, political elites, decision-making strategies, and the perception of a zero-sum game all come into play when predicting or explaining interminority relations. These groups, however, do not come into contact in a vacuum. The context in which they interact must be accounted for when considering the possibilities and pitfalls of political interactions among minority groups. This is especially important when considering the ways in which Black immigrants and African Americans interact because, while they have different historical experiences with racism in the U.S., they also have to negotiate the same racial structure from the same position in America's racial hierarchy.

A Spectrum of Possibilities

As ethnic diversity increases, there is a spectrum of possibilities that exists for Black politics; on one end, you have pan-ethnic unity, and on the other, you have interethnic/intraracial competition. Let us first consider the factors that may push Black intraracial relations toward interethnic distancing and competition. First, there are African Americans—elites and members of the masses—who believe that they need not only to protect the gains made from the Civil Rights Movement but also to maintain narrow membership of those who can benefit from these gains.[97] As such, one might expect that African Americans will distance themselves from Black immigrants; or perhaps African Americans will attempt to gain Black immigrants' support but marginalize their policy priorities. Cathy Cohen calls this process secondary marginalization.[98] Moreover, Shayla Nunnally recently found that while a majority of African Americans do acknowledge Black linked fate, they tend to have more tenuous linkages with West Indians and Africans in the United States, thereby illustrating that maintaining a unified Black politics will be a challenge in the face of increasing ethnic diversity.[99]

Second, there are Black immigrants who aim to distance themselves from African Americans by communicating ethnic differentiation between the two groups. Studies have found that Afro-Caribbeans hold some of the worst stereotypes about African Americans. For example, both Foner's and Waters's West Indian respondents tended to see themselves as more ambitious, harder working, and greater achievers than their "lazy" and "welfare-dependent" African American counterparts.[100] Additionally, Afro-Latinos often do not embrace their African heritage.[101] Reportedly, African immigrants often feel superior to African Americans.[102] There is plenty of potential for Black immigrants to avoid being identified as Black, thereby preventing the development of Black pan-ethnic coalitions.

Third, there is a larger racially stratified social system, maintained by racially coded language (among many other things) to valorize immigrant groups over African Americans as well as the use of pathological and behavioral theories as primary explanations for African Americans' position in the U.S.'s social system.[103] This ideology is alluring to immigrants, and there is incentive to adopt it in a country where Black people are at the bottom of the racial hierarchy. Research has shown that immigrant groups have sometimes attempted to avoid adopting a Black racial identity in order to be more easily incorporated into mainstream society.[104] Groups come into contact with one another within a specific (racial) context, which may provide an incentive for Black immigrants to distance themselves from Black identity and American politics.

Nevertheless, there are also a number of factors that may pull native- and foreign-born Black relations toward the other side of the spectrum. First, while there is a multiplicity of Black identities and Black experiences, there are also multiple points of overlapping experiences with race and racism in the U.S. and abroad. While immigrants of African descent from the Caribbean, Latin America, and Africa have not shared the same experiences of American slavery and racial discrimination, the color line does belt the globe. Immigrants of African descent have had similar racialized experiences prior to coming to the U.S. due to the legacies of slavery, colonialism, apartheid, U.S. military invasion, and inclusionary discrimination that derives from state-enforced ideologies such as "racial democracy."[105]

Second, racial identity is fluid and is contextual. Everyday microaggressors and major racialized experiences will have an influence not only on the way people see themselves but also on the way they see others. First-generation Black immigrants, for example, tend to become more sympathetic with the racial anxieties of African Americans as they spend more time in the U.S., and their own identities are reshaped in turn.[106] Second-generation immigrants do not share the same racial history with Blacks whose ancestry in America extends for several generations, but America's current racial environment tends to make salient their racial identities.[107] And finally, African Americans are likely to recognize the fact that ethnic diversity exists among Black people in the United States and the notion that shared experiences, particularly with racism and discrimination, constitute a major determinant of how to understand their own racial identities and others'.[108]

Constructing Diasporic Consciousness

We know that diversity exists among Blacks across ideology,[109] gender,[110] and class.[111] Despite these categorical differences, African Americans still tend to embrace a unified identity largely because this diversity has been "muted by the persistence of racial discrimination, a collective memory of racial oppression and other factors."[112] At the same time, it is virtually unknown whether Black immigrants will fall in line with African Americans on the identity-to-politics path.[113] Rather than taking the comparison of the identity-to-politics link of Black immigrants and African Americans as an empirical question, either social scientists have generally implied that the relationship between identity and politics is the same for both groups, or they study the groups in isolation and not much comparative analysis gets developed anyway.

Diasporic consciousness, however, takes this inter- and intragroup comparison seriously. These groups are not mutually exclusive, but they certainly are not the same. A theory of diasporic consciousness allows us to conceive of "Blackness" in contemporary Black politics as a pan-ethnic racial identity and allows us to grasp the fact that there is an array of possibilities for Black politics as African Americans and Black immigrants interact. Again, diasporic consciousness is the duality that people of African descent who live in the United States hold as they consider their racial identity and the political issues associated with it along with their ethnic identity and the political matters closely associated with that subgroup identity.

With this proposed theory, we can expect African Americans and Black immigrants both to see differences marked by ethnic boundaries and also to recognize each other as pan-ethnic compatriots in a struggle against racial injustice and inequality. As a result of contemporary racism and racial inequality, first- and second-generation Black immigrants are likely to believe that their potential status as first-class citizens is imperiled just as many African Americans do. Their racial identities, consequently, are likely to be mobilized just as African Americans' racial identity is politically mobilized. A theory of diasporic consciousness accounts for the fact that while Black immigrants and African Americans have not shared the exact same legacy of racial torment, ongoing racism and racial discrimination will be major factors in shaping their racial identities, enhancing racial group consciousness, and influencing both groups' political attitudes. However, we still see and should expect to see differences arise among African Americans and Black immigrants, and these differences must be accounted for as well.

From this perspective, we should expect neither total distancing nor permanent unity among group members. Instead, we should anticipate, on the one hand, similarities to exist between African Americans and Black immigrants due to the constraints of a racialized social system, but on the other hand, we should also expect differences that arise from ethnic diversity. The U.S. places Blacks—regardless of ethnicity—at the bottom of an ethnoracial hierarchy, leading native- and foreign-born Blacks to embrace a pan-ethnic identity. But with that diversity comes variation and, at times, tension and conflict. Variation in ethnicity among Blacks is likely to bring along with it different ideas about what race means (both its definition and its implications), different interpretations of political issues, different ideas about the role of government, and different ideas about how to improve the status of a broader, pan-ethnic group. A theory of diasporic consciousness both appreciates the factors that produce unity among ethnically diverse Black communities and problematizes the notion that unity will always characterize Black politics, particularly as diversity increases.

In recognizing that "Black" is a diverse pan-ethnic group, rather than a homogeneous racial group, we realize how the notion of an identity-to-politics link becomes more complicated; there exists the possibility that there are *multiple* Black identity-to-politics links; the next section provides a more detailed analysis of the ways in which the identity-to-politics link should be reconceptualized in the face of the increasing ethnic diversity among Blacks in the United States.

New Expectations for Black Politics

In taking account of racialization processes, pan-ethnic identity, and theories of political coalitions and conflict, we can map diasporic consciousness onto a Black identity-to-politics link in a way that allows us to more accurately depict Black identity. It will also allow us to articulate more precise predictions about what we should expect for Black politics as ethnic diversity increases. Instead of expecting "unity" as the classical political science literature predicts or "difference" as predicted by sociological accounts, we instead should consider the possibilities for "unity" and "difference" at virtually every step of the identity-to-politics link; consider figure 2.2.

First, concerning racial group identity, we realize that group membership does not always lead to group identity, especially among members of society who are ascribed a stigmatized, lower status in the ethnoracial hierarchy of the United States. Black immigrants may distance themselves from African Americans, and likewise, African Americans

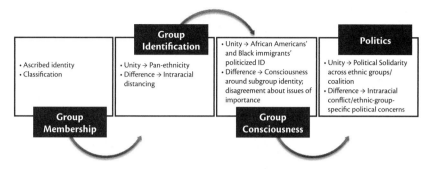

Figure 2.2. New expectations for Black politics

may aim to narrow the boundaries of Blackness. There is also the potential for a pan-ethnic identity, which is itself contextual and situational. We should expect that as native- and foreign-born Blacks experience racism and racial discrimination, they will adopt an identity that is inclusive of ethnic diversity. However, in recognizing the fact that Black immigrants value their ethnic identity just as much as their racial identity, we should see that there are more fluctuations in the ways in which Black immigrants relate to their identities; at times, their racial identity will be salient, while in other contexts, their ethnic identity will be prioritized. The fact that Black immigrants' identities are more contextual may at times make African Americans suspicious of Black immigrants, which, of course, could have negative consequences for intraracial coalitions.

Concerning group consciousness, we should expect those factors that led African Americans to develop a sense of group consciousness also to influence Black immigrants. We might also, however, expect additional factors, such as generational status and level of acculturation, to influence levels of group consciousness among Black immigrants. These factors have not traditionally been incorporated to explain African American political behavior, but I argue that they will become increasingly important to consider as diversity mushrooms.[114]

Additionally, we should expect different outcomes in the effects of group consciousness on Black immigrants and African Americans. Black immigrants may be mobilized to participate in politics, but we should anticipate that the ways in which group consciousness influences their behaviors will differ from the ways it influences African Americans'. African Americans have a long history in the U.S. and are likely to be more cognizant of the ways in which various policies, even those that seemingly have nothing to do with their racial group membership, will affect Blacks more drastically than other racial groups. Newcomers, on the other hand, should mobilize around policies that are directly related to their racial group membership. Further, due to Black immigrants' own experiences with government, they may be less likely to make demands on the state as a means to improve the status of their group. Overall, we are likely to see that political issues will be viewed quite differently among African Americans in comparison to Black immigrants.

Finally, diasporic consciousness predicts that intraracial coalitions will, at best, be semipermanent. Black immigrants' and African Americans' views about what political issues are important are likely to be similar, but it is also likely that there will be some differences concerning the prioritization of issues. In turn, native- and foreign-born Blacks are likely to develop coalitions around issues that affect them because of their racial group, but there is likely to be conflict around those issues that influence groups differently due to their ethnicity; immigration is likely to be a key point of contestation that will challenge political unity among people of African descent in the United States. The subsequent chapters will more closely examine each step and transition of the politics-to-identity link of African Americans and Black immigrants, and furthermore, each chapter includes a series of tests of the hypotheses developed here.

3

From Group Membership to Group Identification

Who is considered Black, the definitions of "Black" and "African Ameri-can," and the criteria for group membership are all shifting as the ethnic diversity in the United States increases. The boundaries of Black iden-tity have traditionally been shaped by historical and ongoing processes of racialization—or macro and micro processes that ascribe Blacks a stigmatized, lower status in the ethnoracial hierarchy of the United States.[1] Furthermore, it is typically assumed that immigrants of African descent will be subsumed into an all-encompassing and homogenized Black identity in a society where internal intraracial (or ethnic) differ-ences are, for the most part, less important than interracial differences.[2]

But intraracial differences do matter, and further, some scholars argue that the combination of gains brought by the Civil Rights Move-ment and the large influx of immigrants of color has served to increase the space to make claim to less traditional racial and ethnic identi-ties.[3] Historically, we have seen this idea manifested in the fact that at times African Americans and Black immigrants are differentiated (or differentiate themselves) from each other while at other times they are grouped together (or through their own agency embrace an identity that is inclusive of ethnic diversity).

This chapter examines African Americans' and first- and second-generation Black immigrants' identity choices in three steps. The first step is to examine African Americans' and Black immigrants' termino-logical preferences. What do various groups of Black people like to be called—what racial and ethnic labels to they prefer—and why? Here, I employ data from the National Survey of American Life (NSAL). Instead of asking respondents a closed-ended question about their racial label preferences, the NSAL allows respondents to report any racial or ethnic label of their preference. This slight but important change in question wording not only allows us to explore the large array of racial labels that Black people prefer, but the data illuminate some important determinants that undergird these preferences.

The second step is to examine the ways in which people conceptualize these racial and ethnic labels. Racial labels are "rooted in historical eras and the prevailing self-definition and self-images of groups. But they also arise out of definitions conferred by the broader society."[4] For this step, I analyze face-to-face interview data. I queried respondents about how they define "Black" and "African American," whether they thought these terms were synonymous or different, to whom they believed these terms applied, and whether they (consistently) used these terms to describe themselves and why (or why not). My respondents' conversations around these issues also reveal that quite a bit of thinking and problematizing goes into seemingly ordinary categories such as "Black" or "African American."

The third and final step is to examine the transition from embracing an ascribed racial or ethnic group label to feeling a sense of attachment with other individuals who have also been placed in that category. In the last substantive section of this chapter, I try to gain a sense of who my respondents perceive as members of their racial group. Who do they believe belongs in "the Black community"? What criteria do they use to assess who could and should identify as Black?

William Cross's theory of *nigrescence*, or "the process of becoming Black," comes to mind here, particularly because "nigrescence is a *resocializing* experience."[5] Cross suggests that there are five stages a Black person experiences as his or her racial identity evolves: pre-encounter, encounter, immersion-emersion, internalization, and internationalization-commitment.[6] People in the pre-encounter stage recognize that they are Black (as a "physical fact") but feel that race plays an insignificant role in their everyday lives. These people see race primarily as a stigma, and they may even have anti-Black attitudes. Cross predicts that the second stage, encounter, may come about after a person is exposed to positive, cultural-historical information about his or her racial group or due to "startling racial episode," such as a racist encounter with the police, at work, or at college; these types of events are likely to "shatter the relevance of the person's current identity and worldview."[7] Thereafter, a person may move to the next stage, immersion-emersion; this is an in-between stage, in which a person has not yet changed but becomes committed to change, begins to develop a dichotomized worldview, and becomes passionately consumed with Blackness. Internalization is a leveling-off phase; it is where we are likely to see a "balancing and synthesizing [of] Blackness with other demands of personhood, such as one's sexuality, occupational identity, spiritual or religious identity and various role identities."[8] It is during this stage that people become aware that racism is a part of the American experience, recognize that they may be a target of racism, and become more likely to blame a larger racialized social system for the outcomes of racism rather than demonize whites or blame themselves. The final stage, internalization-commitment, is marked by a sustained interest in Black affairs.

In many ways, the analysis in this chapter illuminates how some of these stages play out for Blacks in the United States, but this chapter also serves to expand Cross's theory, as it provides a glimpse as to whether this theory is applicable to foreign-born Blacks and their children, as well as to African Americans of the millennial generation. Furthermore, by examining the processes that native- and foreign-born Blacks engage in as they construct their identities, this chapter ultimately helps us to develop a better understanding of how group membership evolves into group identity—the first transition in the identity-to-politics link. By taking seriously the ideas that group identities are in many ways a result of both structure and individual agency and that the boundaries of identities are negotiated among current group insiders as well between insiders and outsiders, we recognize that there are other possible identities Black immigrants might take on. Black immigrants may or may not choose to identify with or psychologically attach to an identity which they were involuntarily ascribed. They, as other immigrants historically have done, may attempt to distance themselves from African Americans in order to gain access into the American mainstream, or in contrast, they may embrace a Black racial identity. Just as well, African Americans may embrace an identity that is inclusive of ethnic diversity, or they may reject those Blacks whom they view as having different cultures and historical experiences.

Through analyses of in-depth interviews with African Americans and first- and second-generation Black immigrants as well as the data

from the NSAL, the chapter shows the complexity of Black identity and identity choices even within the constraints of the American
racial structure. Overall, the results elucidate the tension that is best
conceptualized and predicted by a theory of diasporic consciousness.
Here we will see that Black immigrants and African Americans alike
embrace the notion that "Black" is a pan-ethnic group and pan-ethnic
identity. Members of both groups have developed and embrace an identity that is inclusive of ethnic diversity among Blacks. However, they
also predict and perceive that attempts to flatten this identity—to force
homogenization rather than to recognize its diversity—will lead to tension among the various ethnic groups. That is to say, even though African Americans and Black immigrants conceive of Blackness as being
diverse, they also recognize the potential problems that diversity brings
to the groups' members.

Step 1: What Do Black People Like to Be Called Anyway?

Americans of African descent have changed their preference for group
labels over time; they have gone from preferring and employing "colored" to "Negro" to "Black" to "African American."[9] Whether these
terms are capitalized is another entirely different and complex issue.[10]
One of the most important factors that determine what a group is to
be called is based on the preferences of the majority or the dominant
members of society. Racial classification systems and racial labels have
largely been shaped by American institutions such as the U.S. Census
Bureau, and state and congressional legislators have also influenced the
contours of racial group boundaries.[11]

But minority group members also have a degree of agency in select-
ing a racial label through embracing a term and collectively working to
change the connotation of the term, from pejorative to positive; these
preferences tend to evolve for each generational cohort.[12] For example,
Marcus Garvey preferred the term "negro" over "black" because he felt
that the former connoted more dignity and respect.[13] Malcolm X preferred "black."[14] Jesse Jackson prefers "African American," and through
his position as a civil rights leader, he persuaded other Americans of
African descent to adopt the label. In 1988, Jackson argued that the term
"African American" puts Blacks in the United States "in our proper

historical context" and asserted, "Every ethnic group in this country has a reference to some land base, some historical cultural base. African Americans have hit that level of cultural maturity."[15]

In addition to the racialized policies developed by American political institutions as well as group members' evolving preferences, immigration is also a factor that can influence racial boundaries. Everyone within a racialized social system, such as the U.S., is ascribed a racial identity, but as Jose Itzigsohn and his colleagues explain, "Immigrants are not helpless vis-à-vis external labeling; they can, within certain limits, manipulate the available choices to their advantage. Furthermore, in making racial identification choices, immigrants also shape the work of the classificatory system, changing and expanding its categories."[16] However, the conditions under which immigrant groups are incorporated determine their range of latitude in making claim to nontraditional racial or ethnic labels.[17] Black immigrants have the least degree of latitude in their identity "choices," as they are typically racialized as Black and placed at the bottom of America's ethnoracial hierarchy.

Several scholars have proclaimed that people of African descent prefer to be called "Black" over "African American." Meanwhile, others have suggested that most Blacks in the United States tend to identify with one of two racial labels and have no qualms embracing either of the two—"African American" or "Black"—but these conclusions can be characterized as simplistic, at best.[18] The extant research does not capture the ongoing debate over these racial labels due to three major limits in this area of research. The first limit derives from survey question construction. Polls and surveys have generally asked Blacks closed-ended questions about their identity; for example, Carol Sigelman and her colleagues ask respondents, "Do you prefer the term 'black' or 'African American' to describe your racial identity?"[19] The way this question is worded assumes that there are not other terms that people of African descent might prefer. We see something different empirically. For instance, in 2010, the U.S. Census Bureau included the term "Negro," after dropping it in 2000, because older African Americans prefer that term to either of the more popular terms used among Blacks.

Second, this research assumes or implies that all the individuals of African descent who are captured in survey and polling data are Americans who have been socialized to accept and employ one of these two terms. However, approximately three million individuals living in the United States are immigrants of African descent, and 20 percent of the growth in the Black population, which otherwise has been stagnant, is attributed to immigrant replenishment.[20] In turn, the extant literature has been limited in its ability to ascertain whether Black respondents are African Americans or first- or second-generation Black immigrants. The third limit of the extant research, particularly the qualitative research on racial labels, becomes manifest when researchers do take the time the ascertain whether respondents are native- or foreign-born but then analyze Black immigrants in isolation, never really comparing their understandings of racial identity with African Americans'.

There are reasons to expect the range of labels preferred by people of African descent in the United States to be larger than previously expected and described. The first reason centers on the notion that the space to make claim to nontraditional identities is growing. Consider, for example, that the U.S. Census, largely in response to the "Mark One or More" movement, has broadened the "legitimate" ways individuals can identify in the decennial data collection.[21] More specific to the particulars here, Black immigrants have historically merged and melded into a large, undifferentiated "Black" racial category.[22] But if race is becoming a less significant factor in determining individuals' life chances, as some scholars suggest, immigrants of color currently should have more latitude in making claim to distinct ethnic categories instead of embracing an all-encompassing Black racial identity than they did several decades ago.[23] As the option—and perhaps the incentives—to embrace a broader range of identities is presented to Black immigrants, we may find that they do so in order to distance themselves from African Americans or simply to lay claim to an ethnic identity that is more salient to their self-image.

Nonetheless, there are theoretical reasons to expect otherwise. Some scholars see racial "identity as a psychological connection to a group that engenders dignity in the face of social rejection and enables identifiers to function successfully in a society that is dominated by whites."[24] Although racial discrimination has declined in American society, it has not completely disappeared. Black immigrants are just as, if not more, likely to experience discrimination as African Americans.[25] As such, we might expect Black immigrants, even those who are highly educated, to embrace similar identities as African Americans rather than identifying with a country-specific or ethnic identity since it is likely that experiences with discrimination will be due to their racial identity rather than their ethnic identity. Scholars show that first-generation immigrants who have experienced racial discrimination and second-generation immigrants, those who have been socialized in the United States, are likely to embrace both a racial identity—as "Black" or "African American"—as well as an ethnic identity.[26]

Analytic Strategy and Data

To address the issue of what people of African descent prefer to be called, I draw on data from the NSAL. The survey respondents include over three thousand African Americans and sixteen hundred Black immigrants of Caribbean, Latin American, and African descent. Using this data, I first report the preferences of racial and ethnic labels of people of African descent by ethnic group. Then I explore the predictors that drive these preferences. Since these preferences are categorical, I employ multinomial logistic regression to ascertain why Afro-Caribbeans, Haitians, Africans, and African Americans prefer one racial label over another.

Variable Measurement

Traditionally, surveys and polls generally ask Blacks, "Do you prefer the term 'black' or 'African American' to describe your racial identity?" However, the NSAL asked its respondents, "People use different words to refer to people whose original ancestors came from Africa. What word best describes what you like to be called?" Respondents were able to answer this open-ended question with the label they prefer rather than being constrained to select one of two labels. Over seventeen labels were used. For the purposes of this study, I have created four groups: (1) Black or Black American; (2) African American or Afro-American; (3) Specified Country; (4) Other, which includes terms such as "Negro," "Colored," and "Hispanic."

To discern the source of preference for one of these terms, I employ some of the additional information about the respondents collected in the NSAL. First, I include ethnicity. I coded ethnicity on the basis of the respondents' place of birth or their parents' place of birth. "African Americans" are those who were born in the U.S. and both of whose parents were born in the United States. "Haitians" are those who were born in Haiti or had at least one parent born in Haiti. "Africans" are those individuals who were born in an African country or had at least one parent born in Africa. Finally, "Caribbeans" are those who were born in the West Indies or had at least one parent born in the West Indies.[27]

Additionally, because one's selection of a racial or ethnic label is likely to be influenced by the extent to which an individual feels close to other group members, I account for how closely identified the respondent feels with other Blacks. Black immigrants and African Americans interact within a system that locates people with a darker phenotype at the bottom of the racial hierarchy. Research on Black immigrant identity development shows that Black immigrants who have negative attitudes about African Americans tend to disassociate from their racial identity and from other Blacks.[28] Meanwhile, those immigrants who recognize that their racial identity will influence their life chances tend to embrace an identity that is inclusive of various groups of Blacks.[29] In many ways, these observations reflect Cross's model of nigrescence, as Black immigrants are likely to go from a pre-encounter stage to, at least, the internalization stage as they interact with race and racism in the American context. To account for how close respondents feel to other Blacks, I employ respondents' answer to the question, "How close do you feel in your ideas and feelings about things to Black people in this country?" Respondents can report if they feel "not close at all," "not too close," "fairly close," or "very close."

I also account for generational status. Respondents who were not born in the U.S. are identified as "first generation"; respondents who were born in the United States but had a least one parent who was not born in the U.S. are identified as "second generation."

In addition to ethnicity, closeness to other Blacks, and generational status, I also include factors that have been shown to influence one's choice of racial label. Research shows that respondents' age, level of education, and place of residence influences racial identity.[30] Lee Sigelman and his coauthors found that "younger residents of large cities outside the South [express] more enthusiasm for the label

'African-American.'"[31] Consequently, I account for age, level of education, and region. "Region" accounts for whether the individual lives in the South (where African Americans have historically resided), in the Northeast (where Black immigrants have tended to live), or elsewhere. I also include a measure that accounts for whether the respondent has generally spent time around mostly whites or Blacks; "proximity" measures whether people have lived, gone to school, or worked around "almost all Whites" to "almost all Blacks." Research on Black immigrants shows that gender as well as experiences with discrimination also influence racial identity development.[32] I control for gender, and I also include a variable that measures Blacks' perceived exposure to racial discrimination.

Results

Figure 3.1 shows the distribution of preferences by ethnic group. Among the 3,374 African American respondents, about 56 percent prefer "Black," while 34 percent prefer "African American." Approximately, 43 percent of Caribbean immigrants prefer to be called "Black,"

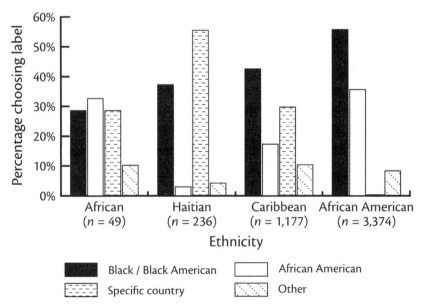

Figure 3.1. Choice of racial/ethnic label by ethnicity

followed by 30 percent who prefer to be identified with their country of origin, and 17 percent prefer "African American." Haitians primarily prefer to be identified presumably as "Haitian" (55.5 percent prefer to be identified by a label based on a specific country), and 37 percent prefer "Black" or "Black American." Finally, of the forty-nine African respondents who were included in the sample, 32 percent prefer "African American," while 28 percent like to be called "Black." Another 28 percent of Africans prefer a country-specific label.

While it is clear that "African American" and "Black" are the top contenders among those who have longer lineages rooted in the United States, Black immigrants have a very different set of preferences. "African American" is the least preferred term among Haitians and other Afro-Caribbean respondents. And African immigrants seem to be contesting the use of "African American," as this is the most preferred label among this group. "Black" also seems to be a popular term among native- and foreign-born Blacks alike. Perhaps, the results here suggest that "Black" might best be understood as a term that is inclusive of ethnic diversity or as a pan-ethnic label rather than just a racial label.

Table 3.1 shows the results of a multinomial regression analysis of preferences for one term or another; the table provides the coefficients and the standard deviations along with the relative risk ratio of preferring the specified term to "African American."[33] African Americans, first-generation immigrants, and men are the comparison groups in their respective categories. The first column in table 3.1 shows that closeness and ethnicity are important predictors of racial/ethnic label preferences among people of African descent. Those who feel close to other Blacks in their thoughts and ideas are more likely to prefer "Black" over "African American." Afro-Caribbeans and Haitians are less likely to prefer "African American" as a term to describe themselves in comparison to African Americans. African respondents showed no significant difference in preference between "Black" and "African American" in comparison to African Americans.

Meanwhile, second-generation respondents are much more likely to embrace "Black" than "African American." Scholars such as Mary Waters and Alejandro Portes and his colleagues suggest that second-generation immigrants who identify as "Black" are those who have "downwardly assimilated" into an undifferentiated Black, inner-city

Table 3.1. Multinomial Logistic Regression Results—Preferences of Racial Labels

	Black vs. African American			Country specific vs. African American			Other vs. African American		
	Coef.	SE	RRR	Coef.	SE	RRR	Coef.	SE	RRR
Closeness	.218**	(.077)	1.2	−.188	(.150)	.83	−.257	(.118)	.77
Ethnicity									
Caribbean	−1.69***	(.280)	.18	5.12***	(.559)	167.6	.271	(.329)	1.3
Haitian	−2.92**	(1.03)	.05	5.47***	(.614)	237.5	.664	(.536)	1.9
African	1.28	(1.13)	3.6	6.94***	(1.22)	1042.2	1.95	(1.43)	7.1
Generation									
Second generation	1.35***	(.312)	3.9	−1.31***	(.338)	.27	−.231	(.434)	.79
Demographics									
Gender (male = 1)	.061	(.110)	1.1	−.239	(.253)	.786	.184	(.190)	1.2
Age	−.011**	(.004)	.99	−.008	(.008)	.992	.013*	(.006)	1.0
Education	.182***	(.052)	1.2	−.011	(.115)	.98	−.018	(.091)	.98
Northeast	.335	(.182)	1.4	.350	(.731)	1.4	.067	(.308)	1.1
South	−.503***	(.128)	.60	.213	(.729)	1.2	−.376	(.230)	.69
Socialization									
Proximity	.041	(.066)	1.0	.036	(.164)	1.0	−.054	(.117)	.95
Everyday discrimination	−.002	(.006)	.99	−.012	(.015)	.99	−.010	(.011)	.98
Major discrimination	.031	(.034)	1.0	.022	(.088)	1.0	.116*	(.057)	1.1
Constant	−1.03*	(.413)	.36	−4.55***	(1.18)	.01	−1.47*	(.687)	.23
N	2,044								
Pseudo R²	.138								

* $p < .05$, ** $p < .01$, *** $p < .001$

"underclass."[34] The results here suggest otherwise. The results in the first column of table 3.1 suggest that respondents with more education prefer "Black" to "African American." Vilna Bashi Bobb and Averil Clarke convincingly argue that it is not that those who identify as "Black" tend to do less well than those who embrace an ethnic identity label but rather that those who identify with African Americans have a stronger belief that race mediates the effects of education as a tool of social mobility.[35] Further, Sherri-Ann Butterfield reveals many Black immigrants use the term "Black" as a means to identify with African Americans and embrace their racial identity, not as a sign of "downward" assimilation.[36]

The results in the first column of table 3.1 also indicate that older Blacks are more likely to identify as "African American" than "Black."

Those who live in the South are less likely to prefer "Black" over "African American," and respondents who live in the Northeast are more likely to identify as "Black"; the p-value of this predictor is just at .06.

The second column of table 3.1 examines whether individuals prefer a country-specific term to "African American." Here, it is clear that those who are not from the U.S.—Caribbeans, Haitians, and Africans—are more likely prefer a term that is based on their country of origin over "African American." This is expected, especially among first-generation immigrants. This finding is corroborated by the remaining results in this analysis. Those in the second generation are less likely than those in the first generation to embrace a country-specific label. Finally, we see in the third column of table 3.1 that age is an important predictor of preferring some other racial label to "African American." This result is likely to be driven by older Blacks who prefer "Negro" to "African American."

Overall, the results indicate that the shifting demographics of and increased ethnic diversity among Blacks in the United States have made the meanings of "Black" and "African American" more ambiguous. Even though "African American" has a very specific connotation in the United States, it appears to be preferred by both native-born Blacks and African immigrants but not by West Indians or Haitians. The results also suggest that while "Black" and "African American" may be viewed as synonymous to African Americans, they mean very different things to newcomers. The information provided by the NSAL is incredibly rich, but these initial results leave us with more questions than answers: How do African Americans and Black immigrants define these terms? Do they view these terms as synonymous? Why do some groups prefer one term to the other? The interview respondents help to answer these questions in a more detailed way and put some meat on these quantitative bones.

Step 2: African American. Black. It's All the Same. Right?

While the preceding analysis allowed us to gain a sense of the underlying predictors of preferences, face-to-face interview data provide the opportunity to examine the rationale that individuals employ when making considerations about their identity. I asked respondents, "Is there a difference between 'Black' and 'African American'?" I also asked respondents which racial or ethnic labels apply best to them. Four themes became clear. The first theme concerns the notion of "political correctness"; African Americans, especially, are concerned with the extent to which both terms are viewed as pejorative by white Americans and how whites use these terms. They often select the label they feel has more positive use by white Americans. The second theme that arose was the notion that both African Americans and Black immigrants see these traditional racial terms—"Black" and "African American"—as both different from each other and evolving. Third, the respondents explain that they adapt their preferences for racial labels on the basis of their perception of what these labels signify. Finally, the narratives reveal that while African Americans tend to have very stable ideas about how to identify (largely because they rely on the "one-drop" rule to make determinations about their racial label selection), first- and second-generation immigrants tend to have more dynamic and contextual identity choices and selection processes.

I Was "African American" until . . .

African American respondents communicated that they tend to see "Black" and "African American" as interchangeable, but they, at times, also struggled with which label is most appropriate—especially if they felt that dominant-group members use "Black" in a derogatory way. Further, and perhaps more importantly, several of the respondents felt that although "African American" had been the term they used to describe themselves through childhood and adolescence, the term's connotation has evolved since then (not that long ago, considering these individuals were born in the late 1980s and early 1990s). That is, previously, they embraced the term "African American," believing that it signified pride in their heritage and connection to Africa, but due to a growing number of interactions with people from the African continent, "African American," from their point of view, has become a term that not only is too broad but also is an inaccurate descriptor of their lineage, which is actually many generations removed from direct African ancestry. Overall, their narratives show how ephemeral, equivocal, and unstable racial labels can be.

As mentioned, in 1988, Jesse Jackson argued that the term "African

American" puts Blacks in the United States "in our proper historical context."[37] The term "African American" became popular for native-born Blacks in the late 1980s. As such, some African Americans understand the term "African American" to mean those whose families were descendants of African slaves in the United States. Amir, an African American man from South Carolina, expressed this sentiment. Amir explained that because he attended a predominantly white institution where this issue frequently comes up, he prepared a small statement to use when his white peers asked him why Black people from the U.S. might want to be called "African American":

> It's because of the connection that we have with our ancestry and the struggle of African slaves in the Americas, and that's why people still like to be connected with that part of their history. And while I understand that people, you know, nowadays like to say, "Oh, I've never been to Africa. Africa's such a distance place," it connects you to the struggle, it connects you to your people, and that's why some people like to be called African American. And I believe that folks should just respect what people want to be called. There's some people who can't stand being called African American, and so you call them Black if they make that known to you. I mean, I don't think it's all that big a deal.

Amir explained, "I identify as Black, African American. The terms don't matter all that much to me." Like Amir, most of the respondents had thought about what the terms "African American" and "Black" entail but tended to used the terms interchangeably or situationally chose which term to use. Similarly, Elle, a dark-skinned African American woman from Illinois, stated, "But I would say, I guess, the definition for 'African American' is basically you were born in the United States, your parents were born in the United States, everybody was born in the United States. But I mean, we all start somewhere, so it gets muddy." Elle makes an argument that even though native-born Blacks have been in the United States for generations, "we all start somewhere," meaning Africa. "It gets muddy" because most African Americans do not know exactly from which countries their first African ancestors came, but, for Elle, "African American" describes someone like her—a Black person who is several generations removed from Africa.

Michael, an African American man from Washington State, also recognizes that there are people who do know exactly where in Africa their ancestors are from, but still he prefers to use the term "African American" to describe native-born Blacks:

> I think there is a difference [between the terms "Black" and "African American"], because you get Africans who come from Africa who come to America, and they're like, "Well, we're technically African Americans because we're from Africa, and now we're in America, so we're African American." It's just weird because you get people from the Caribbean who aren't from Africa, but they're Black, and then they come here and they're like, "Well, I'm not African American. I'm Caribbean American" or "I'm Haitian American," and they throw a nationality in front of it. Um, for me, I don't really like using the word "Black" just because like when you look at people, no one's black. I mean black is really . . . I mean this [points to his black notebook] is black. It's a really dark color, so I mean most people are brown. I mean, I'll use "Black," but most of the time I'll just use "African American." But I do understand that there's a difference depending on where you're from. I think that's a large part. I mean, I've always lived in America, and so I've just been African American.

Michael prefers the term "African American" to "Black" because for him, like several others, "Black" has a negative connotation. Nevertheless, Michael also communicates that he, too, is a person with African heritage who currently lives in America; he makes a claim for "African American" as an appropriate racial label for himself despite the fact that others might make a fighting claim for the term.

While my African American respondents tended to identify as "Black" or "African American," one challenge that respondents had in choosing whether to racially label themselves with one or the other term was negotiating the particular surroundings or context in which they sometimes found themselves. They noted that while most of the time they identified as "Black," they sometimes felt that white Americans tended used "Black" for derogatory jokes or references while "African American" was saved for more politically correct, academic, and polite usage. For example, Laura, a twenty-one-year-old woman from

Maryland, mentioned that how she identifies racially does not change depending on with whom she is speaking or where she is, but she said, "The only the thing that changes though is if I call myself 'Black' or 'African American' [*laughs*]." I ask her why this matters, and she explained: "Because if I'm around white people, I say 'African American' because I want them to call me 'African American' because I don't . . . [*pause*] Sometimes I hear other people use 'Black' in derogatory terms, so when I'm around white people I'll say 'African American,' you know. But when I'm around Black people, I'll just say 'Black,' like it's, you know, that's who I am."

Similarly, Carmen pointed out that she also struggles with various terms. Carmen is a college sophomore from Texas, and when I asked her with which racial groups she identifies, she answered,

> I check the "African American slash Black" box. [*Laughs*] Because that's what I feel like, that's what I've always said I am. And like, I'm not—I'm discovering this year that "Black" is okay with me. I know my grandfather does not like the term "Black," like I guess 'cause back in their time, "Negro" was the one that they would go with that wasn't derogatory or anything. So he would probably identify with the word "Negro" more.

Although most African American respondents identified as and called themselves "Black," respondents who felt that "Black" had a negative connotation were more inclined to avoid using that term in public or in white spaces, opting instead for a more "politically correct" term such as "African American." Again, these responses mirror that of the national African American population (see figure 3.1). Jeffery M. Jones also found that when African Americans were asked what they preferred to be called on a personal level, they showed a slight preference for "Black" over "African American," but when they were asked what they preferred the group to be called, they had a preference for "African American" over "Black."[38] The respondents here help us to see why this is the case.

Deciding whether to use "African American" or "Black" is not the only challenge respondents faced when choosing racial labels, however. African American respondents also struggled with the "African" portion of the term. For example, Carmen decided to embrace the term "Black," which she previously thought of as offensive, after she reassessed what "African American" might imply to others:

> It's not offensive to me to be called Black, and I think it's kind of like, kind of like . . . not politically incorrect but somewhat incorrect to call me African American 'cause like I don't know my ancestry back to Africa, whereas my friend who is from Nigeria, like he's actually African American 'cause he is—like his parents who gave birth to him are from Nigeria, not just like someone down the line.

The notion that "African American" is not the most appropriate label for Black people whose families are several generations American came up for ten of the seventeen African American respondents. Jason, for instance, grew up in a Maryland military town and briefly mentioned that this issue was one that he and his younger fourteen-year-old brother, who came along for the interview, had been thinking about. Jason explained, "When I first got [to college], I considered myself African American. And so I said it, and someone was like, 'Oh, what country are you from?' and I was like, 'Uh . . .' [*laughs*]." Jason, in turn, was prompted to rethink about his ancestry and to reconsider which racial label was most appropriate for him: "My ancestry, I would say 'Black.' I don't like saying 'African American' because I don't really know my ties to Africa besides the fact that I'm Black. So I prefer to just say 'Black.' And as far back—I know as far back as my great-great-grandfather, who lived in Maryland, and so it's like to me, my ancestry is traced back to Maryland [*chuckles*]." Candace, an African American college senior, explained that her view about using the term "African American" was challenged after visiting various African countries:

> I'd say yes, they [the terms "Black" and "African American"] are different. But it depends on . . . In popular societal, like political correct, usage, they're interchangeable, but I would say having been to Africa and interacting with students who are of Caribbean descent and who are of African descent and who still have family in other countries, I would say the term "African American" is like the term "Asian American." You

have a closer knowledge of your immigrant past. Whereas I don't have that knowledge, and so I feel more connected, I would say, to the term "Black." Because while I understand that my family connected at whatever point in our history to Africa or to the Caribbean, I don't identify with those places, so I prefer the term "Black" to "African American" for myself.

Similarly, Kimberly, whose family has lived in Chicago for several generations, mentioned that the connotation as well as the boundaries around the term "African American" changed for her; previously, she believed people like her, native-born Blacks, should be called "African American," but when she learned that "African American" might be used by others, perhaps even whites, she began to associate the term with a different group of people:

And I would say before I went to college, I just considered myself, you know, African American. And one time when I was working back at home, I was talking to one of my supervisors, and we had this whole discussion about what being Black is and what is African American. And he told me anybody can be African American. There are some whites that come from Africa, and they could be considered African American. And I was like, "Oh really?" So that's when I started to say, "I'm just Black."

When Kimberly learned that the term "African American" might include someone whom she did not consider part of her in-group, "whites that come from Africa," she moved to adopt a term that had more exclusive boundaries. Kimberly specifically said that she identifies as "just Black," which is not uncommon to hear among young people. In fact, there are terms among Black students at various universities that signal that a Black person is from the United States. Facebook groups such as "I'm a Regular Black" and "Sorry, We're Just Regular Black" are popular among native-born African Americans. Similarly, at an elite university in the Northeast, Blacks with American ancestors have given themselves the nickname "Legacies." One of my Black immigrant respondents employed this language, labeling African Americans as "JBs" or "Just Black."

The "New" African Americans

The topic of whether the term "African American" is an appropriate racial or ethnic label was not exclusive to the considerations of African Americans. It was also discussed among first- and second-generation immigrants, especially but not limited to first- and second-generation African students. There was a large range of attitudes concerning these debated terms. On one end of the spectrum of attitudes, some respondents applied the term "African American" in its most literal sense to describe themselves. Chinwe and Ahmad, both second-generation Black immigrants, utilized the same rationale to explain why they use "African American" as an appropriate label for themselves. Chinwe responded,

> I consider myself African American. I think that is the best describing word for me because I . . . I am an American, I was born in America and raised here, and this is what I feel is, you know, home for me, and I would never, you know, move somewhere else to live. But at the same time, I feel that I am also African in that it's my heritage. I'm closely connected to it. You know, my parents are immigrants, and so I consider myself African American.

Similarly, Ahmad, in a separate interview, explained, "I identify as African American, an African American Muslim to be exact. Let me explain it you. I've always thought about it that way, that I am African. You know, I accept that and I respect that and I admire that, but at the same time, you know, I am an American, kind of thing." Yet another respondent attempted to expand the definition of "African American" to include both people such as himself and Blacks from the United States. Antwon, who lived in Nigeria until he was six years old, took a position at the middle of the spectrum:

> When you say "African American," you automatically think of like slavery and people whose family originated—they came from Africa to the United States, but then they had kids here. I consider that African American. But then you have another type of African American, as in you're

legitimately African, like your parents or your grandparents' grandparents weren't born or didn't live in the United States. My parents or anybody from like in my family tree is all based in Nigeria. To me that's African American too.

For Antwon, the term "African American" could be used in multiple ways. One interesting thing that stands out, however, is that Antwon uses the phrase "legitimately African," which is in direct contradiction to Jesse Jackson's rationale for using the term "African American" in the first place. Antwon, and several others, imply that Blacks who have deep roots in the U.S. have no "legitimate" connection to Africa. Antwon, perhaps representative of others, is willing to share the term "African American" but not necessarily claims to a shared African homeland.

On the other end of the spectrum, some respondents recognized that while the term "African American" could be a descriptor for them, they also realized that in the U.S. "African American" has evolved to mean something very specific and has become associated with Black people whose families have lived in the United States over several generations. John, a first-generation South African immigrant, explained why he identifies as Black: " Black, yeah, 'cause to be honest, like, people say like, 'Oh yeah, African American,' but I don't really feel like an African American because I feel like there's a difference between African Americans and Africans—because of upbringing, because it's like different cultures, you know. And, yeah, so I just consider myself to be Black." Similarly, Daise, a first-generation Panamanian woman who identifies as "Black" and "Hispanic" does not identify as "African American" because, she said, "I feel like 'African American' carries so much more weight [*chuckles*] in the term. Like there is more of a history behind it in the United States." Her sentiments mirror those of Nym, a first-generation Nigerian, who explained,

"African American," for me, implies not just a reference but an identification with a past history of subjugation within the United States. . . . So "Black" could incorporate like an immigrant who just literally moved like a week ago into the U.S. from, I guess, African or Caribbean or, you know, darker-skin roots. And then "African American," as I said, references a particular history of subjugation within the U.S., which I guess we would think of slavery times, or just an identification with that, you know.

We have traditionally assumed or implied that those who identify as "Black" or "African American" are those individuals who are nth-generation Americans, but it is becoming increasingly clear that the boundaries of Black identity are expanding to include immigrants of African descent. African immigrants are just as likely as African Americans to assume an "African American" identity, while Caribbean immigrants are likely to embrace a "Black" identity. Demographic change will influence the meaning and connotation of these terms, and we see that Black immigrants also challenge traditional American racial categories by asserting alternative, less traditional identities and demanding to be recognized as such.

Stable and Dynamic Identities

The racial and/or ethnic labels that people select for themselves reflect not only how they think of themselves but also a sense of group belonging and awareness. As previously mentioned, however, social identities do not exist without public affirmation. The respondents' narratives show that they incorporate both their own ideas about what group they want to belong to with how other people see them. While African Americans and Black immigrants tended to identify as Black, it is clear that African Americans' choice of racial labels is primarily based on definitions conferred by the broader society. Black immigrants' identities, on the other hand, were more fluid, situational, and contextual. African Americans were more likely to call on the "one-drop" rule in explaining how and why they choose their racial label, while Black immigrants were more likely to determine which label they choose on the basis of the context.

I asked respondents, "How would you describe you ancestry? How do others perceive your racial identity? How do you identify?" While many of my African American respondents gave different answers to each of the three questions, not only did they articulate the power of the "one-drop" rule as part of their decision-making calculus in deciding which racial label was most appropriate for themselves, but they answered the self-identification portion of my question as if the answer was obvious: "Black or African American."

For example, Peter, a light-skinned man with long dreadlocks, explained, "I identify as Black even though I live with my mom [who is white]." He further explained that his mother emphasized that he should be proud of his Black identity. I asked him, "Do you change how you identify depending on the situation, maybe who you're talking to or where you are?" Peter replied emphatically, "No. It's never changed for me. It's always been Black. It's always—if it's an application for school, no matter who I'm around, it's always, I'm Black."

Nicole is a light-skinned Black woman from Boston with a mixed-race heritage. I asked, "Why is it that even though you have all of these different types of people in your family, you just identify as Black?" She responded as if I should have already known:

> Because I don't really identify with any of those other cultures. Like I've never been exposed to them. My grandfather is Austrian, but he died before I was born, so, you know, we don't . . . He quote-unquote hated "whities." So, you know, it was never anything. And then, my grandma is Native American, and she's—well, half Native American—and she's very proud of that. But if she's half, then what am I? And she's probably not even just half, you know. So it's just not something—I mean, now that I do have a Native American friend here, I look more into it, and she always laughs at me 'cause she's like, "You could tell there's Native American in your family." But I also feel like Natives are kind of exclusive. So if you're not, if you didn't grow up that way, you know, they kind of still keep you on the outside.

Nicole, like many others, described an array of races and ethnicities in her family, but felt like group boundaries are closed off to her despite her ancestry. In addition to the fact that certain boundaries were more rigid, African Americans also took into account how other people saw them. This was especially prominent among biracial respondents. Michael, who is a dark-skinned man with straight hair, explained that although he is biracial, he has had no other choice than to identify as Black. I asked him if being African American is an important part of his self-image, and he responded,

I think it is. I mean, it's sad, but it's always been my defining image, I guess. Not by choice. I've been thinking about it, taking all these classes. I think it's just 'cause everyone else has always labeled me as that. I never had an option to be anything else. Like, I actually had a conversation with my brother before I went to college, and I was trying to explain to him 'cause he's like, "Well, I'm African American. Like we have the same parents." And I'm like, "No, you're not. You're white. You've . . . We don't look the same, and you can turn it off and on. You can tell people that you have a Black father and get away with it, but you don't have to. So you have the option to, and I don't."

Here, we see two mechanisms at work. First, Michael identifies as Black because that is how other people see him; his main means for identifying himself and others (such as his brother) is primarily based on his perceptions of the majority of society and the types of interactions that might come along with these perceptions. This narrative is similar to that of other African Americans who articulate that "African American" and "Black" are not just racial terms but are also closely related to a set of experiences. Second, Michael is also policing the borders of his in-group. He bars his brother, who is phenotypically white, access to using "Black" as a racial label to describe himself because his brother can "turn it off and on."

Many of the African American respondents, including the three biracial students, explained that they were of mixed ancestry, but despite the variation in races and ethnicities among their ancestors, they identified as Black or African American. Here we see that racial labels are chosen due to people's experiences as well as due to a recognition of how others see them. Largely, the respondents felt that others saw them as Black and treated them that way, showing that social identities are influenced both by the way you see yourself as well as the way you believe others perceive you. All the African American respondents felt that their racial identity was central to their self-image, and this identity was stable, not fluctuating with context.

Through an analysis of first- and second-generation immigrants' interviews, I found that, in contrast to the African American respondents, who tended to consistently identify as Black or African American, the first- and second-generation Black immigrants were more likely to feel that their racial and ethnic identities fluctuated in salience, and in turn, the labels which they chose to describe their identities changed situationally and strategically, too. All but one of the Black immigrant respondents grew up surrounded by coethnics—people who share their culture and ethnic identity—but in times when there were only a few people who shared their ethnic identity, the respondents reported that their racial identity became more salient than their ethnic identity. Ten of the thirteen Black immigrant respondents suggested that they made decisions about which label to choose on the basis of the context. Ann is a second-generation Ghanaian woman who plans to study Shakespeare in graduate school. She explained,

> I mean, I know I'm Ashanti, but in general I just refer to myself as Black because I think that there's just more commonality, especially like even though I grew up around a lot of Ghanaian people—that's because like my parents had Ghanaian people back home that they knew were here. So like that was kind of like not artificial, but they already had the contexts. But especially at [PSU] and like in high school, so like I didn't, my own friends, you know—it was very rare to find Ghanaian friends, so I would just identify with Black people in general, like anyone who was Black. So that's how I identify myself, but I know specifically I'm Ghanaian.

Ann chooses to identify as Black—she uses a racial label—when her ethnicity makes her feel like a minority within a minority. Identifying as Black is also a means to unify her with other racially Black people rather than to distance herself through her ethnic identity. Several respondents noted that being around coethnics allowed them to feel like they could and should identify with their ethnicity, but when they were around native-born African Americans or a plethora of different types of Black people, they tended to choose a racial label in solidarity with those around them. Stacy, a second-generation Haitian, provided a clear illustration of this:

> Like I said before, I consider myself Black because I know that there are people who are actually, you know . . . Like I know that my ancestry, our ancestry originated in Africa. I'm aware of that; that's how I got my dark

skin. But I think because of the fact that I think that Caribbeans are different from people from Africa—you know, people from Haiti, people from Nigeria, people from Zimbabwe, Kenya, all those kind of things—like there's a certain pride that comes with that, and I would never want to take away from that pride by just restricting myself to being African American. So I identify as Black to kind of encompass all of that, you know.

Stacy provides an excellent example of diasporic consciousness. She communicates the idea that "Black" is a group composed of disparate ethnic groups: Caribbean, Nigerian, Zimbabwean, Kenyan, and American, as examples. She appreciates the differences that exist among these groups, but she also communicates a sense of solidarity that she has with these other groups by employing a pan-ethnic identity, "Black." She walks a tightrope between recognizing the differences among these groups and embracing an all-encompassing identity.

Another factor that influenced first- and second-generation Black immigrants' choice of a racial or ethnic label was how others viewed them. Ahmad provides an excellent example. Ahmad moved from place to place, growing up in Long Beach, California and then moving to San Jose and then, finally, Bellevue, Washington. Each city had a different racial makeup, and this seems to have played a major part in how people viewed Ahmad's identity:

So it's really, really interesting in that I was born in Southern California. And over there, in a predominantly Black community, I was not considered Black. I was considered African. And it's something I could never understand. And then when we went to San Jose, California, where the neighborhood that we lived in was predominantly Hispanic and Chinese or Asian, I don't know exactly which one, and it's actually really funny. At that point, I became Black to them. But at the same time, there were other Black families around. It wasn't as densely populated. But they actually . . . I was considered part of the group, but I was distinguished from African American, in that I'm not, obviously, I don't have, I guess you can say, the physical characteristics that would, you know, that somebody would in that area, would consider me African American, to a certain extent.

Ahmad then explained that when he moved to a majority-white neighborhood in Washington, the way others perceived him and how he perceived himself changed again: "And Bellevue—this is a very funny story—the first week we moved, I was taking out the garbage, and the next thing I know, somebody's driving by like, 'Oh, we have Black people here now.' And at that point is when I realized, 'Okay, I guess I'm Black now.'" Although Ahmad tended to identify as "African American, an African American Muslim to be exact," he was well aware of how others see him, and this shapes his identity as well as influences which racial label he chooses in any given environment. At times he was accepted into certain racial and ethnic boundaries, while at other times he was differentiated and excluded. What is more, at times his race was made more salient, while in other environments his ethnicity as Eritrean or African was a determinant of how people understood his identity. He, personally, embraces both his racial and ethnic identities, but he chooses various labels depending on his surroundings.

Most of the respondents felt that others viewed them as not being different from African Americans, but they noted that sometimes people would look more carefully at their physical features (e.g., hair texture, skin tone, facial features) or would hear them speaking another language, prompting observers to ask more questions about their identities. Daise, a first-generation Panamanian, explained how she navigates these situations:

In the United States, you always have to explain [your racial identity]. Like, most times people just said, "Oh, you're Black." And I never corrected them, and I still don't. I'm like, "Okay." And only when I randomly talk Spanish on the phone with my mom, like a semester or a year after they even know me, do they realize, "You're not just Black." You know, like, "No, I'm not, but I didn't tell you because I didn't think it mattered." So like, I'm Black, therefore [pause] . . . I look Black. I am Black. If you call me Black, I'm Black. But if you need me to qualify or tell you why, I'm like, "Well, I'm from Panama," and I will state that.

Daise explained that when she was growing up, she would vacillate between employing the terms "Black" and "Hispanic," but, she said, "I think Hispanic took over" and now uses "Hispanic" as a racial label because it makes it easier to explain why she is culturally different from other types of Black people. Daise went on to say, "I'm Black. I'm just not African American in the sense that you think, I guess. So like, I just chose Hispanic 'cause it's easier to explain why I was so, I guess, FOBy [fresh off the boat]. Sometimes I can't understand like some U.S. popular cultural terms. And like I grew up with this, so it was easier for me, I guess."

Vanessa is a Dominican woman with dark skin, curly hair, and small facial features, and from time to time people ask her questions about her identity. She described a typical situation:

> They ask me, "Are you Black?" And my immediate reaction just because I . . . I . . . I feel that that question is so ignorant, my immediate reaction is like, "Well, my skin is black; obviously I'm Black." And they're like, "No, but are you Black Black?" So then I'm like, "What does that mean?" And they're like, "Well, are you African American?" And then that's when I'm like, "Okay, no. I'm not African American. I was born in the Dominican Republic. I'm Hispanic."

The ways in which Black immigrants choose their racial and ethnic labels may at times be a form of racial distancing, but it may also be the case that using a different racial or ethnic label is also a way to communicate that while they understand that they have been placed into a Black racial category, there are also ethnic and cultural differences within a larger racial group. Among first- and second-generation Black immigrants, choosing a racial label is complex, is situational, and in some ways, is political. All these respondents made clear that their racial identities as Black people were central to their self-image, but the ways in which they communicated their identity through racial and ethnic labeling changed. First- and second-generation immigrants embraced both their racial identity and their ethnic identity, but they also found that one identity may become more salient than the other at times. Only two of the Black immigrant respondents identified solely with their ethnicity. Rose described herself as "Ethiopian-American," and Vanessa tended to identify as "Hispanic." John, a South African immigrant, identified primarily as "Black," and the remaining ten respondents used both racial and ethnic labels to describe their identities.

Step 3: From Group Membership to Group Identity

So far, we see that individuals do not select racial labels randomly or carelessly; they consider the connotation and meaning of the term and choose a label only after some degree of contemplation. These labels are important because they play a role in determining who is a group member, but we have to keep in mind that group membership is not synonymous with group identification. While group membership involves being placed into a category, group identification is a psychological attachment to the members who are in the category.

This section of the chapter explores the transition from group membership to group identity. After asking respondents how they characterized their own racial and ethnic identity, I asked respondents how they conceptualized who is Black and what kind of people constitute "the Black community."[39] I also queried about perceived similarities and differences between African American and Black immigrants from various places of origin. From the answers to these questions, I aimed to gain a sense of how African Americans and Black immigrants determine who is Black and, more importantly, the extent to which African Americans embrace an identity that is inclusive of Black immigrants as well as the extent to which Black immigrants do the same.

The respondents illuminate the fact that Black immigrants and African Americans tend to have a broad conceptualization of who is Black because the criteria that they have for racial group membership are primarily based on exposure to certain types of racialized experiences—be they historical or contemporary. The respondents also illustrate that the processes of developing a pan-ethnic identity are prone to intraracial tensions because those processes occur within a social system that stigmatizes its (potential) members. Overall, the narratives elucidate group members' agency in constructing both their own identities and the group's boundaries.

Expanding Contours of Black Identity

The boundaries of any racial group are politically important to map because there are material and psychological advantages or disadvantages distributed to each group's members. William Cross and his coauthors suggest that belonging to and connecting with a racial group offers fortification from "psychological harm that may result from daily existence in a racist society."[40] Additionally, social, political, and economic resources may be provided to certain people depending on their identity. Whether people feel that they share an identity with others may influence their opinions about who is deserving of any social, economic, political, or psychological resource.

African American respondents expressed a feeling of shared identity with Black immigrants in the United States, and first- and second-generation Black immigrants mirrored that feeling. But race on its surface is primarily a marker of phenotype and other physical features. It is the characteristics and stereotypes that are attached to these features that make race meaningful. A few respondents felt that they share a racial identity with various ethnic groups of African descent simply because they share the same physical features, but the overwhelming majority of respondents provided insight into what they thought it meant to be Black beyond phenotype.

Two major themes arose in respondents' explanations of who belongs to a larger (abstract) pan-ethnic Black community. The first is that although each ethnic group has had different experiences with racism and discrimination, they all share a historical legacy of marginalization. For them, Black identity is global because Blacks have been constructed as marginalized people all over the world. The second theme that arose was that Black people in America, despite their ethnicity, are still affected negatively by racism. These are all expressions of diasporic consciousness.

Both African Americans and Black immigrants were well aware of the various but shared histories of Black people around the world. Several respondents mentioned that these similar histories tied people in the African diaspora together. John, an immigrant from South Africa, explained, "I feel like 'Black' is like an all-encompassing idea." Again, like many other respondents, John has a very broad idea about who he believes is Black. I asked what, in his opinion, is the meaning of a shared Black identity, and he responded,

> Well, I think . . . I think it means we have a shared history, a shared experience. In a sense that like obviously racism happens everywhere—in

Africa, in Europe, and America. And all of us have been affected in one way or another by it. And I think in some ways it continues today, so I think it's like that shared sense of like being treated like second-class citizens of sorts. I think that's what makes us, you know, Black.

Michael, an African American from Washington State, provided a similar explanation concerning why he considers both African Americans and Black immigrants as pan-ethnic or racial group members:

I think so mainly just because like racism isn't just in America. It's not just an American concept. It's different in all parts of the world, but like, for example, like I was thinking of too many categories, people from Africa and people from the Caribbean. And so, you know, Haiti was the first nation to be like a free Black state, and that's a very large part of Haitian culture. So there's this understanding of, you know, "At one point we had to go through this struggle." And in Africa, I mean, colonization still plays a huge role in people's lives. So there's the understanding, too, of white people coming in, and so it's different in each part of the country. But I think there's the same understanding that, you know, racism affects us because we look different.

Both John and Michael suggest that while racism in Europe, Africa, the Caribbean, and the United States all look different, they have the same result of othering and marginalizing people, especially those of African descent. Their opinions mirror the commentary of Black diaspora scholars, who center notions of Black diaspora and identity around ideas of a global nature of anti-Blackness.[41] W. E. B. Du Bois suggested that the color line belts the world, so "the Negro problem in America is but a local phase of a world problem."[42] My respondents seemed to recognize that idea and in turn have developed a broader conceptualization of Black identity by looking beyond the frame of the nation-state to find ties that bind Black people around the world.

While some respondents stressed that a shared history of subjugation was important in determining who is Black and who is a member of a larger Black community, others emphasized ongoing effects of racism in determining who should be a group member. Respondents saw racism as a contemporary, consistent, and ongoing factor shaping Black identity. Alexis, an African American woman from Trenton, New Jersey, provides an example of this way of thinking:

> I feel like [the Black community is] everyone, whether it's—even people don't always identify. So I think that it's Black Americans, I think that's immigrant African Americans, I think that it's Black Latinos, I think that it's everyone that's in that group that has to ties to Africa at some point in time. As far, yeah . . . when I use it, I think of it as more inclusive, even though people don't always identify as that. I still think that society reacts to them in a certain way, even though I know there's like gray areas and people that you can't always tell and things like that. But I still think that if society treats you a certain way based on what you look like, that's what makes you Black.

Two things stand out here. One is that Alexis argues that being Black or belonging to a Black community is in some ways involuntary; that is to say, for Alexis, race is ascribed to you, thereby making you a member of the group. This is not unlike Michael, who identifies as Black because he feels like he has no other choice. Laura articulated a similar idea, when she argued that all people of African descent in the U.S. are Black, "just because that's how society has kind of, you know, constructed race." There is a sense that people's ability to move from one racial group to another is severely constrained because racial boundaries are so rigid in the United States.

This sentiment was not lost on first- and second-generation Black immigrants. Evelyn made a point that illuminates that being Black is not an essentialized identity but rather is one that arises from experiences of being a racial group member. Michael C. Dawson argues that the reasons why a Black counterpublic came into existence—constrained opportunity structures, racial discrimination in housing and employment markets, health and wealth disparities—remain the same reasons why a Black counterpublic exists now.[43] Evelyn, a second-generation Dominican, articulated Dawson's argument through an explanation of who is included within a Black community and why:

> When I think of "Black," I don't necessarily think of only "African American." I think of Black descendants, African descendants, and I guess

that's the [diversity] I find in that. But in general I think it's a community
that no matter what has been significantly, not oppressed, but like significantly marginalized and disadvantaged. And through that there needs
to be some community. . . . If there weren't a system of oppression, the
community would be unnecessary, is how I think of it.

Evelyn explained that she felt, for the most part, that African Americans and Black immigrants are treated similarly because of their shared
position in America's racial hierarchy. Most of the respondents, at some
point in their interview, discussed the notion that light is faster than
sound—or, in other words, people tend to judge others based on their
looks first and generally do not take the time to learn about a person's
background. It is only later, through verbal communication, that a person might analyze a another's identity more carefully and critically. But
many respondents argued that even after the ethnicity of a person of
African descent is known by others, chances are that the person will not
be treated any differently than an African American would be.

Happy Family? The Other Face of Diasporic Consciousness

The picture that I have painted so far has been one of mutual recognition and feelings of a shared sense of community. While most respondents tended to view Blacks of various ethnicities as encompassing
one racial group and, therefore, one pan-ethnic community, they also
pointed out instances of conflict and distancing on the part of African
Americans and Black immigrants alike. These conflicts and how people
respond to them are important because while respondents recognize
that they are lumped together by a dominant white American society, group members still have agency to determine whether they will
embrace the identity placed onto them or make an effort to distance
themselves from their ascribed racial group.

The following narratives illustrate the intragroup tensions that arise
as group members aim to construct a pan-ethnic identity. One major
issue that African Americans bring up is the idea that many Black
immigrants do attempt to distance themselves from African Americans. Actually, many African Americans are fairly tolerant of this strategy because they recognize that newcomers to the United States do

not understand the U.S.'s ethnoracial hierarchy, and they presume that when newcomers "see the light," then they can make a more informed decision. However, African Americans have their limits, primarily set at the border between embracing a Black identity due to group pride and using a Black identity for personal gain. In contrast, Black immigrants' tension in promoting a broad Black identity primarily arises from coethnic group members who want to distance themselves in the face of negative stereotypes that exist about African Americans.

When prompted, all the respondents were able to discuss times when they noticed African Americans and Black immigrants making an effort to communicate that they are different from the ethnic out-group members. Laura attends a school in Boston where, according to her, intraracial tensions are high. When she was the president of the Black Student Union, she found that student groups that aimed to serve Caribbean and African students avoided working with her organization. She described a situation that she contended is representative of the intraracial atmosphere at her college:

> And [African Americans and Black immigrants] seem to get along pretty well, but there were times when it was different. So, for example, [this] Black American boy and a Haitian boy got into an argument, and the Haitian boy said . . . Well, the Black boy said to him, "Oh, nigga, this blah blah blah." And the Haitian boy said, "What? Nigger. I'm not no nigger. You're a nigger," like that to him. So that just kind of like—whew!—that stirred it up. And them also, too, sometimes the Haitian students, you know, they say that Black Americans don't treat them the same. They say that Black Americans look down on them, make fun of their culture, their music, the foods they eat, you know.

Laura shows that both African Americans and Black immigrants participate in distancing. While the existing literature suggests that Black immigrants tend to distance or differentiate themselves from African Americans, Laura provides an example of how both African Americans and Black immigrants use negative stereotypes and derogatory terms to denigrate the other group.

One really interesting thing that stands out from these interviews is the notion that while many of the African American respondents

noticed that Black immigrants might make attempts to distance themselves, they seemed to understand why someone might try to do so.
Laura said, "Yeah. I think that what happens is that when Black people
are out of the U.S., in their own countries, the image that they see of
Black people is a stereotype. And so when they get here, they don't want
to associate with that at all. So it's like disassociate yourself from it; that
way you can be considered better." African Americans can understand
why Black immigrants who have learned negative stereotypes about
African Americans might want to distance themselves, but they are not
necessarily sympathetic. Instead, they communicate a "they know not
what they do" sentiment about Black immigrants, who not only will
eventually learn that these stereotypes are incorrect but more importantly will learn how easily stereotypes can be attached to any Black
person. Nicole expressed a sentiment similar to that of other African
American respondents and Black immigrants, too:

> I would say yes [Black immigrants and African Americans recognize the
> effects of racism] because when you—you might not come here thinking
> a certain way or you might think or you might place more blame on the
> Black community because of things that they've done, things that they
> haven't done. You know, 'cause it's definitely a two-sided issue. But then
> on the other hand, I think so—I think they're more critical, like more
> Black immigrants are critical with the things that the Black community
> does to perpetuate these things or not to change these things. But on the
> other hand, I think that once they're here for a while, you know, when
> a cop or whoever looks at you, they don't know if you're first or second
> generation, if your family's been here for forever, whatever. So you sort
> of get treated the same way. So they may be more successful or more
> whatever and think that "these issues don't affect me," but if you hap-
> pen to be in a situation where something like that might affect you, then
> you get treated the same way. So I think over time, their views and their
> experiences may change.

Many of the respondents felt that there was a learning curve that Black
immigrants encounter upon arriving the United States. For them, this
learning curve is climbed not only by gaining a better understanding

of structural racism and the U.S.'s racial hierarchy but also by personally experiencing negative personal interactions due to your race, which
African American respondents implied are almost inevitable. On the
other side of this coin, however, some African Americans communicated that while they understood that Black immigrants might feel a
connection to both their racial and ethnic identities, they felt that it
was unacceptable for Black immigrants to situationally distance themselves from their racial identity if that contributed to perpetuating the
racial hierarchy.

Peter told a story about a time when some of his Black teammates
were joking around about how Blacks in America were treated during
slavery or the Jim Crow era, and his Rwandan teammate said, "Man, I'm
from Africa. I didn't have to go through that like y'all. Like they brought
y'all on the boats over here or whatever, not me." Peter mentioned that
everyone laughed about it, but when he looked back at the situation, he
did not think that it was a joking matter:

> And so I kind of just realized that, you know, in some situations, people
> identify with certain groups or feel part of a group when it's convenient
> to and when it's easy to, but then when something bad happens or some-
> thing goes wrong and they can step out and distance themselves from
> it or anything like that . . . Like, "Oh, I'm not a lazy Black person. I'm a
> hardworking . . ." or whatever, or "I'm not, you know, violent or anything
> like that." When it's convenient to, they'll identify, but easily step out,
> like, "That's not me," and act like it has nothing to do with them at all or
> anything like that.

He went on to say, "Even though it was only a joke, and we all thought
it was funny, it was just like thinking back on it, it was like . . . I'm pretty
sure if it could happen like that, it happens with bigger situations,
with different things that people identify with or choose to pick and
choose what Blackness or what Black qualities or whatever you would
call it to attribute to themselves and what not to." African American
respondents were sympathetic if Black immigrants wanted to differentiate themselves because of pride in their culture, heritage, or country
of origin. African Americans' tolerance ran low, however, when Black

immigrants perpetuated negative Black stereotypes, ultimately serving to perpetuate the U.S. racialized hierarchy through adoption of "white racial frames."[44] This attitude was most prevalent when African American respondents observed Black immigrants expressing that racism was not "their" problem or that they were model minorities.

Almost all the Black immigrants responded that they had grown up hearing their parents and other coethnics espouse negative stereotypes about African Americans. The major battle in their efforts to develop an identity that included African Americans came in the form of combating negative stereotypes about Black people. My first- and second-generation Black immigrant respondents tended to eschew negative stereotypes and embrace a pan-ethnic identity for three major reasons. First, they understood or came to understand the structural nature of racism in the United States. Second, many experienced racist personal interactions or knew somebody who had. And third, they recognized that when people were talking badly about Black people, they too were implicated because they were seen as Black.

Nym was raised in Nigeria until he moved to the United States when he was about eleven years of age. He explained that immigrants tend to buy into racial stereotypes because they do not understand the nature American racism:

> I do believe there's tension in some situations, and there's perceptions on both sides that are wrong. Yeah, but I think that there is and in some cases a superiority complex on the immigrants' part because they tend to look at the African American—or the racial situation in the U.S. without . . . without you know, actually, without a good knowledge, you know, an in-depth knowledge of exactly like what the situation is and the historical implications of like things today and the actual reasons for injustices and inequalities in the U.S. They presume that it's because of these very stereotypical or currently or proverbial answers to like the problem, like Black people are lazy or African Americans are lazy or blah blah blah blah. You know, like they buy into a lot to the . . . to these normative ideas that are fueled in American society, and so they tend to, I guess, spew them out and imbibe them in the same way that like, I guess, a white American would because they don't have any idea of exactly what caused these, you know, what perpetuate and propagate them.

Similarly, Ahmad observed, "But definitely, when you're on the outside looking in, you don't see it as well. When you get here, you don't see it as a problem, 'cause you see the situation you're coming from is so much worse than you see this place as, you know. All you see are the opportunities, but once you . . . you're here long enough, you do." Ahmad also brings to the discussion the notion that Black immigrants see the United States as the land of opportunity, leading people to believe that the reason why African Americans are in their position in society is because they are lazy and rely on race and racism as excuses. However, Ahmad as well as others suggest that once "you're here long enough, you do" recognize that racism and discrimination toward Black people of various ethnicities is widespread and constricting.

What is more, the respondents also reported that they have either been on the other side of these stereotypes or know somebody who has been a victim of these negative stereotypes. Black immigrant respondents repeatedly mentioned that they believe white Americans really do not make a distinction between native-born and foreign-born Blacks. Some did point to the notion that perhaps a person with a distinct accent or way of dress may be treated differently from African Americans. Daise, for example, suggested, "There is a struggle with like, I guess, racism in general. I mean, it doesn't matter if you're not from the United States. If you look Black, you're probably going to be treated the same way, unless you have an accent. Then they'll treat you a little bit worse, I think." Like Daise, others mentioned that the fact of being an immigrant was a potential cause for being discriminated against. But beyond that, the Black immigrant respondents recognized the prospect of being discriminated against because of their race rather than their ethnicity, thereby reducing their chances of adopting negative stereotypes about African Americans.

The first- and second-generation Black immigrant respondents recognized that they were racialized as Black. However, because they felt a connection to other Black people, my respondents were intolerant of negative talk about African Americans, sometimes even confronting their loved ones about it. Stacy, a Haitian American woman, and Ahmad, a second-generation Eritrean, illustrate this. Stacy said, "Like even like in my own family, like sometimes like, you know, we'll be watching like BET, and like, you know, my grandmother, like my older, old-school aunts, 'Oh, look at those Black Americans just shaking their butt,' and I'm just like, 'We're all Black!'" Stacy points out that her grandmother and her aunts assume that the people in the music videos are African Americans because the actors are doing something that they do not approve of. Stacy, however, suggests that this distinction cannot be made so easily. She also makes the point that her grandmother, aunt, and herself share a racial identity with the people on the television. For Stacy, speaking harshly about African Americans and other Blacks is an affront to her personal identity. Ahmad provides another example: "I know African people, like African immigrants, who are racist against Black people. I hear that from people all the time. My mom's like, 'Why you saggin' your pants,' you know. There's a saying like, 'the hoodlums,' it's in our language. It's like, 'Why you being like the hoodlum?' I'm like, 'Mom, you're considered Black too.'"

Through these responses, we are able to see racial formation at work. That is, we see how Black immigrants become racialized. The respondents suggest that even though some immigrants want to distance themselves from African Americans, society has grouped Black immigrants and African Americans and responds to them in the same ways. But we also see that there are complicated internal group dynamics involved as well in this identity-formation processes. Native- and foreign-born Blacks both participate in shaping their own identities within a social system that marginalizes them.

* * *

Racial group boundaries change. They may become more permeable or more rigid, and groups may become more inclusive or exclusive. The racialization processes that shape Black people's identities have been taken for granted; it is assumed that the power of top-down, macro processes will place all Blacks within an undifferentiated Black category and that group membership will automatically evolve into a racial identity. This study recognizes these processes, but this chapter, in particular, highlights the role that individuals within that group have in shaping Black identity in the face of increasing ethnic diversity among Black people in the United States.

Proper nomenclature for Blacks in the U.S. has been debated over decades, but with a growing influx of African and Caribbean immigrants to the United States, the term "African American" has become a focus of debate among both native-born Blacks and foreign-born Blacks. "African American" was introduced as a means to appropriately describe the cultural roots of Black people in the United States and has gained popularity over the past two decades, eventually appearing on the U.S. Census for the first time in 2000. While most American-born Blacks have adopted this term, it has also become contested due to the increased ethnic diversity within the racial group.

This chapter shows that Blacks who have deep roots in the United States tend to employ two racial labels—"African American" and "Black"—to describe themselves, with a preference for "Black." But we also see that "Black" and "African American" are not the only terms embraced by people of African descent. Those who are newcomers to the U.S. tend to use a larger range of racial and ethnic labels to describe themselves. The quantitative results show that socialization in the U.S., feelings of closeness to Blacks, education, and age are major factors in determining one's choice of racial labels.

Meanwhile, the qualitative data paint a richer, more complex picture about Blacks' preferences, rationalizations, and meaning-making processes. Both the quantitative and qualitative data show that African Americans use the traditional racial labels of "Black" and "African American," but it is only through the interviews that we see that this limited choice is muddled with ambivalence. On the one hand, African Americans want to embrace a term that puts them in their "proper historical context," as Jackson suggested, but they also see their group being less credible claimants of this label. Interestingly, they see "Black" as a term that is a tool for discrimination but also as the more appropriate available term for their group. Black immigrants have similar, ambivalent attitudes about these racial labels, especially around "African American," leading them to be careful about how they choose to identify. In all, we have seen that instrumentalism, boundary policing, the structural constraints of the "one-drop" rule, and optimal distinctiveness (especially on the part of older Black immigrants) are all mechanisms that shape the boundaries of Black identities.

What is intriguing about the narratives, particularly of the Black immigrants, is the notion of embracing a Black identity not because society wills the respondents to do so but because they see Black identity as a political and personal affirmation. We see that even though Black identity in the U.S. is associated with negative characteristics and stereotypes, Black immigrants, who in many ways have a choice, still choose to embrace this identity. I recognize that this "choice" is in many ways constrained, but the narratives show that the awareness of the link between one's racial identity and one's opportunity structure ironically leads the newest group members to coalesce around that Black identity in the same way that awareness has done for African Americans historically. Thus, we see many of the stages described by William Cross's nigrescence model when we examine Black immigrants, too.

The narratives presented here compel us to move beyond the singular characterization of racial formation processes as macro driven or top-down when examining Black identities. While the ways in which society determines who is Black play an incredibly important role in shaping how Black people see themselves, we see from the respondents that Black identity is also shaped by group members—new and old, native- and foreign-born. Black immigrants have the opportunity to distance themselves from African Americans, especially in a time when the space for claiming nontraditional identities is growing. In all, the results confirm the need to take into account the ways in which Black people see themselves and have agency in shaping their groups' boundaries.

This chapter has focused on the ways in which Black people of various ethnicities seek to participate in developing their own self-identity as well as their group identity. It has also homed in on the intragroup tensions that arise as group members have different strategies for navigating a racialized social system. The narratives, for the most part, show that African Americans and first- and second-generation immigrants recognize the fact that they have been placed in the same racial category and, consequently, have embraced a shared group identity. How this shared identity will influence Black politics is examined in the subsequent chapters. The extant Black politics literature shows that African Americans tend to incorporate their feelings for their racial group into their political decision-making calculus. While this chapter shows that

Black immigrants tend to have a shared identity with African Americans, it is unknown whether they will similarly consider their racial identity and racial group when they are making political decisions; that question is examined in chapters 5 and 6. The next chapter analyzes data from the NSAL to get a broader picture of the determinants of African Americans' and Black immigrants' identities.

4

Broadening Black Identity

Evidence in National Data

Both Roy Simon Bryce-Laporte and Milton Vickerman, writing at very different times, explain that upon arrival to the United States, Black immigrants must balance and negotiate what they have garnered from the racial socialization processes they experienced in their country of origin with the reality of race as it functions in the United States; they describe this state of being as "cross-pressured."[1] This balancing act is clearly illustrated in the previous chapter, but chapter 3 also shows that in general, Black immigrants' ethnic identity—their identity as it relates to their (or their parents') country of origin—is generally a matter of cultural expression; meanwhile, in recognizing that light is faster than sound, Black immigrants realize that it is their racial identity rather than their ethnic identity that is most likely to influence their life chances.

The aim of this chapter is to provide a broader perspective on what drives the development of various aspects and dimensions of Blacks' racial identity. More specifically, this chapter addresses two major questions: What are the underlying determinants of Black immigrants' racial identification? And how do these determinants compare to those of native-born African Americans? I focus on racial identity rather than ethnic identity because, as Stephen Cornell and Douglass Hartmann explain, race has been the most powerful and persistent group boundary in American history, distinguishing, to varying degrees, the experiences of those who are classified as nonwhite from those who are classified as white.[2] Racial classification, therefore, is both a symbol of social status and a boundary of exclusion. Further, racial categories represent systems of power and hierarchy, and "racial classification has implications for a person's life chances because racial stratification is a social hierarchy."[3] While differences among and between ethnic groups matter, it is largely the differences between racial groups rather than ethnic groups that structure opportunities and experiences in a racialized social system such as the United States.[4]

A theory of diasporic consciousness predicts that while there may be differences in the extent to which African Americans and Black immigrants feel close to other group members, racialized experiences will be a major determinant of racial identity. Structural constraints have a homogenizing effect. Additionally, since this theory emphasizes the need to explain differences, it should also be expected that while experiences with discrimination will similarly influence African Americans' and Black immigrants' identity, Black immigrants are also likely to be influenced by levels of acculturation and ethnic differences as well. Race is conceived of differently in the U.S., the Caribbean, Latin America, and African countries, too, and we should expect these differences to crop up as the racial identities of various subgroups of Blacks (continue to) develop during their time in the United States.

Measuring Black Identity

The National Survey of American Life (NSAL) includes a battery of questions to measure various dimensions of Black identity. This battery of questions was adopted from Robert Sellers and his colleagues' Multidimensional Inventory of Black Identity (MIBI).[5] The MIBI is based on this group of scholars' theoretical framework known as the Multidimensional Model of Racial Identity (MMRI). The MMRI "focuses on the significance and the nature of an individual's racial identity at a given point in time"; that is to say, the "MMRI assumes that identities are both situationally influenced as well as being stable properties of the person."[6] The MMRI identifies four dimensions of Black racial identity. The first dimension, racial salience, concerns the extent to which one's race is a relevant part of one's self-concept at a particular moment or in a particular situation. The second dimension is racial centrality, which "refers to the extent to which a person normatively defines himself or herself with regard to race."[7] These first two dimensions reflect the significance that individuals attach to race in defining themselves.

The third and fourth dimensions are racial regard and ideology. Racial regard "refers to a person's affective and evaluative judgment of his race in terms of positive-negative valence."[8] There are two types of racial regard. The first is public regard, which concerns respondents' perception of how members of other racial groups think of Blacks. The second, private regard, reflects whether an individual feels positively (or negatively) toward other Blacks as well as if he or she feels positively about being Black. Finally, ideology is the dimension that corresponds to "individuals' beliefs, opinions, and attitudes with respect to the way she or he feels that members should act."[9] This dimension is composed of nationalist, oppressed minority, assimilation, and humanist philosophies.

What is particularly intriguing and valuable about the MMRI is that Sellers and his colleagues allow for "the fact that the significance and the meaning that individuals place on race are likely to change across their life span."[10] The NSAL includes variables for two of the three measurable dimensions outlined in the MMRI (salience cannot be measured). As such, we are able to get a snapshot of how a national sample of Blacks see themselves, how they feel about other racial group members, and how they perceive out-group members' assessments of Blacks, on average. The models estimated in this chapter explore the determinants of racial centrality, public regard, and private regard. These dimensions are likely to be highly influenced by racialized experiences such as discrimination for African Americans and Black immigrants alike. In addition to these experiences, Black immigrants' racial identity is likely to be influenced by their level of acculturation and their ethnic background.

Traditional Predictors of Black Identity

The interviewees' responses to questions concerning their identity in the previous chapter bring to light the very important influence that experiences with discrimination and racism have on their racial identity. Whether they experienced discrimination themselves or whether they recognized the structural and ubiquitous influences of racism, discrimination, and prejudice on the lives of average Black people in the United States, these perceptions affected the way they viewed their identity. The NSAL allows for an assessment of the extent to which various forms of discrimination influence each of the measured dimensions of Black racial identity.

The NSAL also provides the ability to gain a better understanding of other important and well-documented determinants of Black racial identity. Early studies of Black identity primarily focused on how African Americans felt about being Black and the social-status determinants of these feelings.[11] Through these studies, scholars were able to outline some of these central determinants of Black identity. For example, Clifford Broman, Harold Neighbors, and James Jackson found that where one resides (i.e., rural versus urban areas or which U.S. region one lives in), income, and age are just a few factors that affect Black racial identity.[12] Richard Allen, Michael Dawson, and Ronald Brown also found that socioeconomic status and frequency of church attendance affect the ways in which African Americans come to understand and develop a sense of racial identity and group consciousness.[13] Later studies added to these findings, further suggesting that childhood socialization, feelings about in-group members, and feelings about out-group members are also important determinants of racial identity development among African Americans.[14] The National Survey of American Life provides the opportunity not only to gauge the role of these factors on African Americans but also to assess the extent to which these factors might also influence Black immigrants, which, to my knowledge, has not been previously analyzed.

New Determinants to Consider

When engaging in conversation about immigrants and identity, we must also think about assimilation and acculturation processes. Previously, white ethnic immigrant groups such as Italians, Irish, and Jews, to some extent, melded into a larger white racial group through social mobility and intermarriage. Moreover, "race was an achieved rather than ascribed status" for white immigrants, perhaps because at the time a rigid Black-white dichotomy ruled social relations; white ethnic immigrants were viewed as nonwhite rather than Black.[15] White immigrants gained access into the boundaries of whiteness, but the "traditional," "straight-line" path of assimilation into the American mainstream has

GARY PUBLIC LIBRARY

not been an option for post-1965 immigrants of color. Taking this into consideration, it becomes clear that we have to consider additional factors that may influence the racial identity of immigrants of color during their time in the U.S.'s unique racial landscape.

Acculturation is the process of adapting to one's surrounding environment and the dominant culture.[16] But acculturation processes are "not a matter of one's individual strategy where one has the free choice to unproblematically integrate the values of the host culture and one's own immigrant group."[17] Acculturation processes are shaped by variables such as where immigrants settle or whether coethnics surround new immigrants; these processes are also shaped by the receiving country's response to their nationality, race, gender, and class.[18] The acculturation and assimilation processes for first-generation immigrants are quite different from those of second-generation immigrants, and obviously, these factors have little to nothing to do with the ways in which African Americans' identities develop.

The literature on first-generation Black immigrants' identity, assimilation, and acculturation processes primarily focuses on immigrants' efforts to distance themselves from African Americans and a Black racial identity. There are four explanations for why Black immigrants may want to distance themselves from African Americans or Black racial identity. The first is captured by the notion that one's ethnic identity may be used as a means to distance oneself from African Americans because many first-generation Black immigrants hold negative stereotypes about African Americans.[19] Nancy Foner finds that her Afro-Caribbean respondents tend to think of themselves as being more ambitious, harder workers, and greater achievers than African Americans.[20] Similarly, Mary Waters reports that her respondents express the same stereotypes about African Americans that many white Americans have historically harbored.[21] For example, her respondents suggest that African Americans are lazy and have wasted the opportunities that have been presented to them as American citizens; this sentiment is not very different from the one that underlies contemporary forms and expressions of racism, such as "racial resentment" or "symbolic racism," which ultimately prevent (white) Americans from supporting policies aimed to ameliorate racial disparities.[22]

A second explanation for why Black immigrants might distance

GARY PUBLIC LIBRARY

themselves from a Black racial identity is that the use of one's ethnic identity during residence in the United States may be viewed as a psychological coping mechanism in the face of (overt) racial discrimination.[23] Black immigrants may use their ethnic identity as a buffer against some of the negative effects of their racial identity.[24] Reuel Rogers finds that when Black immigrants have been treated poorly because of their race, they often retreat to a "myth of return" to their country of origin, an option—real or imagined—that African Americans do not have.[25]

Yet another reason for racial distancing on the part of Black immigrants may be characterized as strategic or instrumental. It is well documented that some employers prefer Black immigrants to African Americans.[26] Distancing may derive real economic benefits. Tatishe Nteta also suggests that some Black immigrants differentiate themselves from African Americans in an effort to achieve sociopolitical incorporation in a similar fashion as Irish, Italian, Polish, and Jewish immigrants did in their efforts to become white.[27] As shown in chapter 1, there are times when Black immigrants embrace a racial identity, but there are also instances when ethnic identity has been turned into a political wedge and placed in between African Americans and Black immigrants by political entrepreneurs.

The three reasons just outlined dominate the literature as explanations for Black immigrants' distancing from African Americans, but I want to suggest a fourth explanation. Foreign-born Black immigrants have their own sensibilities about their racial and ethnic identity.[28] Black immigrants' socialization processes and cultures, just to name a couple of attributes, differ from those of African Americans. First-generation immigrants tend to remain focused on their home country; for example, some first-generation immigrants continue to read their home country's newspapers and vote in home elections as well.[29] Therefore, the communication of an ethnic identity by Black immigrants may be a means to explain a fact (e.g., "I am Nigerian") rather than a means to racially distance themselves (e.g., "I am *not* Black").

The previous chapter provided evidence for the three dominant reasons, but the respondents' answers primarily centered on the fourth explanation. That is, making known one's ethnic identity did not preclude feeling a sense of closeness with a larger racial group. Beyond that, it is also important to keep in mind that racial identity—the feelings of connectedness with other racial group members—is flexible and contextual and changes over time. Black immigrants who choose to come to the United States arrive in a society where their racial identity places them on the bottom of the social hierarchy, largely because of their phenotype and ancestry. Over time, many Black immigrants come to identify with African Americans. Research shows that the longer Black immigrants reside in the U.S., the more likely they are to experience racial discrimination; each experience pushes them to realize that race trumps ethnicity in the United States.[30] First-generation Black immigrants are apt to change many of the negative opinions they hold about African Americans as well as to feel closer to African Americans over time because they come to gain a broader perspective on the structural constraints that Blacks—from all country of origins—face in the United States.

What about second-generation Black immigrants? The research on the children of first-generation Black immigrants provides more nuanced theories about the development of racial identity. Unlike their parents, who come to the U.S. with a clearer and more defined identity, second-generation immigrants straddle at least two different cultural worlds.[31] Those of the second generation have to reconcile their parents' understanding of race and ethnicity with their own realities in America.

Alejandro Portes, Ruben Rumbaut, and their colleagues' oft-cited works propose that second-generation immigrants of color, generally, and Black immigrants from the Caribbean, specifically, are likely to experience "segmented assimilation."[32] The theory of segmented assimilation is rooted in the idea that post-1965 immigrants will acculturate and assimilate differently than their European immigrant predecessors did. Portes and his colleagues have found that second-generation immigrants have more complicated identity choices, and they explain that these choices are dictated by the "direction" of the assimilation path.[33] More specifically, these scholars maintain that second-generation Black immigrants may take a "straight-line" path into the white middle-class majority; face "downward assimilation" into an undifferentiated Black, inner-city "underclass"; or experience a combination of upward mobility and heightened ethnic awareness. These paths have consequences on the identities of members of this group, such that those who experience "downward" assimilation will identify racially—as African American or

Black—while those who take "upward" assimilation path will identify with an ethnic or a hyphenated American identity.

Mary Waters also develops an alternative theory of assimilation for second-generation Afro-Caribbean immigrants in her seminal text *Black Identities*. Waters similarly proposes three identity trajectories or paths for second-generation West Indians: identifying as African American, identifying as an ethnic or hyphenated American, or maintaining their parents' ethnic identification. Waters finds that these "choices" are influenced by class and gender.[34]

A number of scholars have critiqued Portes's and Waters's theories. Stephen Steinberg, for instance, argues that the theory of segmented assimilation erroneously implies the following:

> Immigrants who live in close proximity to African Americans adopt their "adversarial stance" toward white society, including a devaluation on education "as a vehicle of advancement." Stated another way, the children of West Indian immigrants run the risk of assimilating "the wrong way," forsaking the rich and positive cultures of their parents for the aberrant culture of African Americans.[35]

On the same note, Vilna Bashi Bobb and Averil Clarke show that it is not that those second-generation immigrants who identify as Black tend to do less well than those who maintain an ethnic identity but rather that those who identify with African Americans have a stronger belief that race mediates the effects of education as a tool of social mobility—which it does. Successful African Americans also hold such an attitude.[36] Alford Young provides evidence that among African American males, those who recognize the constraints of race tend to be more successful than those who do not realize that they have to navigate a racialized social system.[37]

Portes's and Waters's work also deserves criticism because they have a "culture of poverty" tinge to them, erroneously suggesting that African Americans are in the position that they are in primarily because they do not behave well. What is more, these theories tend to highlight the supposed benefits of culture rather than the constraints of structure. Philip Kasinitz and his colleagues, for example, point out that Black immigrants who live in racially segregated, low-income neighborhoods are just as likely as white Americans to engage in rebellious behaviors that may get them arrested; what is different between the two groups is the way society reacts to them, as second-generation immigrants of color are more likely to face harsher penalties and have less resources to deal with the repercussions.[38] Finally, segmented assimilation theories imply that identifying as Black or African American is a "reactive" or "adversarial" identity instead of considering the possibility that Black immigrants might come to adopt such an identity because they feel that they share similar experiences with African Americans or because they feel a sense of pride in this identity; embracing a racial identity may also help Blacks of various ethnicities to navigate racist personal interactions. Segmented assimilation models and the notion of "downward assimilation" ignore the usefulness that the Cross Model brings to bear on understanding the identity development of Blacks, including newcomers.[39]

Suffice it to say, many scholars point out that there is not necessarily a struggle between second-generation Black immigrants' ethnic and racial identities. Second-generation Black immigrants tend to feel connected to and identify with people from their parents' country of origin (or ethnic identity) as well as with African Americans (racial identity), showing that these identities are not mutually exclusive.[40] Sherri-Ann Butterfield titles one of her articles "We're Just Black" because she finds that her second-generation Black immigrant respondents identify as Black and see "Black" as an identity that encompasses all people of African descent, despite their ethnicity. The interview respondents in my study also expressed this sentiment.

Gender and class also influence identity development, assimilation patterns, and acculturation strategies of second-generation Black immigrants.[41] Waters explains that poor and male Afro-Caribbeans are more likely to identify as African American, while the well-to-do and female respondents are more likely to identify with their ethnicity. Butterfield finds that middle-class second-generation Afro-Caribbeans tend to distance themselves from lower-class Blacks in general, including coethnics.[42] Several scholars also find that male second-generation Black immigrants are more likely to identify with their racial identity because they recognize that they are often followed in stores, harassed by the police, and otherwise discriminated against because they are

Black men.[43] These studies on second-generation Black immigrants are largely qualitative studies focused on those who live in New York, but the National Survey of America Life provides the opportunity to assess the influence of generational status, class, gender, and region on Black immigrants' racial identity with greater statistical power and to assert conclusions with more confidence.

Expectations and Hypotheses

African Americans and first- and second-generation Black immigrants have different relationships to America's racial history and racial politics. What is more, they each have their own ideas about what race means to their self-identity and to their life chances. Nevertheless, the theory of diasporic consciousness suggests that African Americans and first- and second-generation Black immigrants will similarly be influenced by the U.S.'s racial hierarchy. To be clear, I am not making an essentialist argument, but rather I am suggesting that because African Americans and Black immigrants share a similar position in America's racial hierarchy, they are likely to have similar experiences, which will shape their identity. However, we should also expect variation in ethnic identities to mitigate a total homogenizing effect. Black immigrants experience American racism from a different perspective, from a lens quite different from African Americans'. In turn, while racialized experiences might influence African Americans and Black immigrants to move in the same direction, the range of movement will also be influenced by ethnicity.

Racialized experiences, especially those related to racial discrimination, are likely to influence the extent to which Black people of various ethnicities will view their race as important to their life and to their self-image, but we should also expect some differences between African American and first- and second-generation Black immigrants. More specifically, I hypothesize the levels of racial centrality to differ by nativity and generational status. I expect the results to reveal that first-generation immigrants' racial identity is not as central to their self-image as African Americans'. However, we can safely predict second-generation Black immigrants' racial identity to be as central to their self-image as it is to African Americans, as suggested by scholars such as Butterfield who show that second-generation Black immigrants recognize the role of their race on their chances of success.[44]

I also expect differences in levels of public regard by nativity and generational status. Since first-generation Black immigrants reportedly tend to feel that race is not an important influence on their lives, I expect that they will have higher levels of public regard than African Americans do; that is, first-generation Black immigrants will feel that outsiders think more positively about Blacks than African Americans do. Again, because second-generation Black immigrants have been socialized within the U.S. context, I do not expect a difference in levels of public regard between African Americans and second-generation Black immigrants to appear.

Similarly, we should expect differences in private regard by nativity and generational status. Private regard concerns the way that people feel about their racial group members. Since many first-generation Black immigrants hold negative stereotypes about African Americans, I predict members of this group to have lower levels of private racial regard. Meanwhile, I anticipate second-generation Black immigrants' levels of private racial regard will be similar to African Americans', as the previous chapter showed that many second-generation Black immigrants tend to defend African Americans because they feel closely tied to them.

Diasporic consciousness centers people's experiences as major influences on their identity and their political attitudes. I expect that experiences with racial discrimination will lead African Americans and Black immigrants to enhance their feelings of racial centrality (increase racial centrality) and to dampen public regard. I also expect that experiences with discrimination might highlight structural barriers (rather than individual failures) as a major influence on the social position of Blacks in the U.S.; in turn, I expect those who report experiences with discrimination to have a higher sense of private regard.

Modeling Identity

While the factors that determine the ways in which one chooses to identify are infinite, I focus on a few that are most relevant to this study: ethnicity, generational status, and experiences with discrimination. Additionally gender, socioeconomic status, region, and racial socialization processes arise as some of the most salient determining factors for racial identity among African Americans and Black immigrants.[45]

Racial Identity

Racial identity is a multidimensional construct, which entails not only the extent to which you feel your racial identity is central to your self-image but also the way you feel about people in your group as well as how you think non-group-members perceive your group. The NSAL provides three of the MIBI scale's dimensions: centrality, public regard, and private regard. Centrality is measured with statements such as "Being a Black person is a large part of how I think of myself" and "What happens in my life is largely the result of what happens to other Black people in this country." Private regard is the extent to which people feel positive or negative about their in-group. The private regard measure corresponds to the respondents' level of agreement with statements such as "I feel good about other Black people" and "I am proud to be Black." Public regard measures how a person perceives out-group members' feelings about the in-group. Public regard is measured using a series of statements such as "Other racial and ethnic groups in this country think of Blacks as intelligent and competent" and "White people in this country do not think of Black people as important contributors to this country."

Immigrant Status and Ethnicity

The model accounts for whether respondents are first- or second-generation immigrants. The comparison group is African American in the models that include all Blacks. There are four "ethnic" groups: African American, West Indian, Haitian, and African. In models that include all Blacks, African Americans are the reference group. Meanwhile, in models that only examine Black immigrants, first-generation immigrants and West Indians are the reference groups.

Discrimination

I measured two types of discrimination: major and everyday. The first measure, major discrimination, is a scaled measure, which includes items probing whether respondents believed they were unfairly fired from their job; whether they believed they were unfairly stopped, searched, or abused by police; and whether they believed a realtor or landlord refused to sell or rent them a home. Everyday discrimination is also a scale that aggregates how frequently respondents were reportedly treated with less courtesy than other people, if people acted as if they were dishonest, if they were followed in stores, and the like.

Demographic Variables

As mentioned, racial identity is heavily influenced by one's gender, one's (family) income, one's level of education, and where one lives. The values of the income measure are formed by a ten-point income scale from $0–$20,000 to $180,000–$200,000+, in $20,000 increments. Education level was coded into four categories: (1) zero to eleven years of school; (2) earned a high school diploma; (3) some college; (4) college degree or more. Finally, I account for region. I create dummy variables for whether one lives in the South, in the Northeast, or elsewhere.

Racial Socialization

Racial socialization is the process by which people learn about their race and what it means to the larger society.[46] I use the measures provided by the NSAL that best approximate racial socialization. First, I measure how often respondents' parents talked about race and racism. Second, I measure the extent to which the respondent interacts or has come into contact with other Blacks. Respondents were asked to think about if the spaces they commonly frequented, including grammar school, junior high school, high school, the neighborhood where they grew up, and their present neighborhood, were occupied by a range of individuals who were mostly white (1) to mostly Black (5). I averaged the responses to create a variable called "proximity," where higher values indicate that respondents interacted more with Blacks than with whites.[47] Finally, I measure whether respondents participate in some sort of Black organization. It is in these counterpublics where Blacks are likely to continue to learn about their racial group.[48]

Descriptive Results

The descriptive results in table 4.1 illustrate the distribution for each of the three dimensions of racial identity examined in this study: racial centrality, public regard, and private regard. Table 4.1 provides the means and standard deviations. In general, there is little difference between the extent to which African Americans and Black immigrants feel that their race is central to their identity, the way they believe whites feel about Blacks, or their feelings about their racial group members. Interestingly, differences surface when the Black immigrant group is disaggregated into more specific ethnic categories and by generational status. First, the results show that Haitians tend to view their race as less central to their self-image than African Americans do. We see another difference between African Americans and Haitians in the last column, as well. Not only do Haitians have lower levels of racial centrality, but they also feel less positive about other Blacks.

Intriguingly, table 4.1 reveals that second-generation Black immigrants tend to have higher levels of racial centrality than African Americans do. There is also a difference here between first- and second-generation Black immigrants: first-generation Black immigrants tend to have lower levels of racial centrality than second-generation Black immigrants do. This latter result is expected; extant literature shows that second-generation Black immigrants are more aware of the role

Table 4.1. Summary Statistics of Centrality, Public Regard, and Private Regard by Ethnicity and Nativity

	Centrality			Public regard			Private regard		
	Mean	SD	N	Mean	SD	N	Mean	SD	N
African American	2.74	(.69)	2,048	2.17	(.78)	2,053	3.81	(.43)	2,069
Black immigrant									
(composite)	2.74	(.68)	600	2.21	(.77)	605	3.79	(.44)	608
West Indian	2.77	(.69)	511	2.17	(.74)	514	3.8	(.43)	516
Haitian	2.58*	(.65)	71	2.33	(.84)	72	3.69*	(.49)	73
African	2.74	(.73)	19	2.70*	(.92)	20	3.65	(.49)	20
First generation	2.67	(.68)	414	2.26*	(.81)	421	3.80	(.43)	423
Second generation	2.89*†	(.67)	183	2.11†	(.65)	181	3.75	(.47)	182

* Significantly different from African American (95% confidence level)
† Significantly different from first generation (95% confidence level)

that their race plays in their lives than their first-generation counter-parts are.

The results also indicate that first-generation immigrants and African immigrants have higher levels of public regard than African Americans do. That is to say, in comparison to African Americans, African immigrants and first-generation immigrants tend to feel that out-group members (whites and other non-Blacks) have a more positive view of Blacks. Again, we see a generational difference; second-generation Black immigrants tend to feel that out-group members have less positive view of Blacks than first-generation Black immigrants do.

Multivariate Results

The results shown in table 4.1 allow us to get a general sense of the differences in racial identity that exist between African Americans and Black immigrants as well as differences among Black immigrants. But in order to develop more specified knowledge about these differences, multivariate analysis is required. Tables 4.2, 4.3, and 4.4 provide more thorough analyses of racial centrality, private regard, and public regard, respectively.

Racial Centrality

I hypothesized that nativity and generational status as well as experiences with discrimination will influence the extent to which people define themselves with regard to their racial identity. The results of this hypothesis test are shown in table 4.2. Model A, in the first column, shows that among all Black respondents, everyday and major experiences with discrimination have significant effects on the extent to which Black people feel their race is important to their self-image, with experiences of major discrimination having a larger effect on the likelihood of respondents reporting enhanced levels of racial centrality. Both forms of discrimination seem to serve as mechanisms that prioritize race as a prominent identity among Black people in the United States. Scholars of social identity theory explain that identities that are viewed negatively by mainstream society or affect one's life negatively

Table 4.2. Determinants of Racial Centrality

	Model A: All Black respondents		Model B: African Americans vs. Black immigrants		Model C: Black immigrants	
	OR	SE	OR	SE	OR	SE
Perceived Discrimination						
Everyday discrimination	1.02***	(0.01)	1.02***	(0.01)	1.03**	(0.02)
Major discrimination	1.07**	(0.03)	1.07**	(0.032)	0.93	(0.07)
Generational Status						
First generation	—	—	18.46	(36.88)	—	—
Second generation	—	—	26.25	(52.52)	1.52*	(0.35)
Ethnicity						
West Indian	—	—	0.05	(0.09)	—	—
Haitian	—	—	0.04*	(0.07)	0.79	(0.26)
African	—	—	0.02*	(0.036)	0.45	(0.29)
Demographics						
Gender (male = 1)	1.16	(0.11)	1.18*	(0.11)	0.85	(0.19)
Age	0.99***	(0.003)	0.98***	(0.003)	0.99	(0.01)
Education	1.21***	(0.06)	1.23***	(0.06)	1.26**	(0.13)
Income	0.98	(0.03)	0.99	(0.03)	1.037	(0.07)
Region						
South	1.27**	(0.15)	1.27**	(0.15)	2.17	(1.29)
Northeast	1.21	(0.17)	1.27	(0.19)	2.17	(1.25)
Racial Socialization						
Proximity	1.05	(0.06)	1.08	(0.06)	1.09	(0.15)
Black organization	1.45***	(0.21)	1.45**	(0.21)	1.89*	(0.69)
Parents talk	1.24***	(0.06)	1.23***	(0.06)	1.56***	(0.21)
N	2,016		2,016		410	
Pseudo R^2	0.031		0.033		0.056	

Notes: Coefficients based on ordered logistic regression. P-values based on two-tailed tests.
*** $p < 0.01$, ** $p < 0.05$, * $p < 0.1$

are also likely to be more salient to an individual than are identities that are viewed positively or neutrally.[49]

Model A, which could be considered a baseline model, also shows that older Blacks have lower levels of racial centrality than do younger Blacks, as noted by an odds ratio of less than one. This is counterintuitive. Recent polls and some studies have shown that African Americans have become more optimistic about the role of race in their lives, which I suspect is due to cohort replacement. These polls led me to predict that younger Blacks, who are further removed from the Civil Rights

Movement, may feel that race is less central to their lives, but the findings here suggest otherwise. Further, the results in Model A indicate that as education levels increase, the odds of reporting higher levels of racial centrality do as well. Model A shows that Blacks in the South are 1.27 times as likely to report higher levels of racial centrality as those living in other parts of the country.

Finally, racial socialization plays a significant role in racial centrality. Those who belong to an organization with the mission to improve the status of Blacks in this country have higher levels of racial centrality than do those who do not belong to a Black organization. Parental talk about one's race also increases the odds of respondents viewing their race as central to their identity.

Model B allows us to gain a sense of the differences in racial centrality between African Americans and Black immigrants of various ethnicities. The extant literature suggests that because Black immigrants generally come from countries where their racial identity is not perceived to be central to their day-to-day lives or opportunity structure, their racial identity is not central to the way they think of themselves.[50] Contrary to those expectations, the model shows that generational status has little effect on the extent to which Black immigrants feel that their racial identity is central to their self-image, or at least we can determine from the model that first- and second-generation immigrants' racial centrality does not differ significantly from African Americans', once we control for other important variables.

The results revealed for second-generation immigrants were expected nonetheless. Second-generation immigrants' levels of racial centrality are not significantly different from African Americans' once you control for important factors. Second-generation Black immigrants tend to identify as Black in addition to identifying with an ethnic identity, and they tend to see their racial identity in the same way that many African Americans do.[51] Model B, however, does reveal differences by ethnicity. West Indians report similar levels of centrality as African Americans do; they may be driving the "generational" results. Haitians and Africans, on the other hand, are much less likely than African Americans to report high levels of centrality.

The third regression, Model C, is an analysis of Black immigrants alone; this will allow us to examine similarities and differences within the group and to gain a sense of whether African Americans are driving the previous results. Model C shows that everyday experiences with discrimination are a major influential factor in determining levels of racial centrality among Black immigrants, but the same is not necessarily the case for major experiences with racial discrimination. It is also shown that second-generation immigrants have higher levels of racial centrality than do their first-generation counterparts. This is expected; literature shows that second-generation Black immigrants tend to identity with their racial identify more than their first-generation counterparts do.[52] But there appear to be few differences between ethnic groups. West Indians are the reference group in Model C.

Finally, some of the control variables help us to better understand racial identity development among Black immigrants. As Black immigrants attain more education, they are also more likely to see their racial identity as central to their self-image. Furthermore, both parental racial socialization and participating in an organization designed to improve the well-being of Blacks bolster the levels of racial centrality among Black immigrants.

Private Regard

Private regard is the extent to which you feel close to and positive about your racial group members. I predicted that African Americans should have a higher private regard than first-generation Black immigrants do, but the levels of private regard should be similar between African Americans and second-generation Black immigrants. The hypotheses also asserted that experiences with discrimination should increase racial private regard. The results of the hypothesis tests for private regard are reported in table 4.3.

Overall, the models actually provide very little information about the determinants of private regard, and the information that is garnered does not provide support for the stated hypotheses. Nonetheless, the results provide some helpful material. The first observation to note is that the two models that include African Americans, Models A and B, show that parental talk about racial issues serves to diminish private regard among respondents. This is counterintuitive, as we might expect parents to explain the influence that racial discrimination has on

Table 4.3. Determinants of Private Regard

	Model A: All Black respondents		Model B: African Americans vs. Black immigrants		Model C: Black immigrants	
	OR	SE	OR	SE	OR	SE
Perceived Discrimination						
Everyday discrimination	0.99	(0.01)	1.00	(0.01)	1.00	(0.02)
Major discrimination	0.98	(0.04)	0.98	(0.04)	0.89	(0.09)
Generational Status						
First generation	—	—	41.68	(78.96)	—	—
Second generation	—	—	21.26	(40.29)	0.71	(0.22)
Ethnicity						
West Indian	—	—	0.03*	(0.05)	—	—
Haitian	—	—	0.01**	(0.03)	0.52	(0.22)
African	—	—	0.004***	(0.008)	0.19**	(0.15)
Demographics						
Gender (male = 1)	1.20	(0.16)	1.24	(0.17)	1.02	(0.31)
Age	1.00	(0.004)	0.99	(0.004)	1.02	(0.01)
Education	1.10	(0.07)	1.12*	(0.076)	0.84	(0.12)
Income	1.09	(0.05)	1.09*	(0.05)	1.42***	(0.16)
Region						
South	1.13	(0.17)	1.14	(0.18)	1.86	(1.35)
Northeast	1.08	(0.19)	1.29	(0.28)	1.81	(1.27)
Racial Socialization						
Proximity	0.94	(0.07)	0.95	(0.08)	1.38*	(0.25)
Black organization	1.31	(0.28)	1.34	(0.29)	1.44	(0.73)
Parents talk	0.85**	(0.057)	0.84**	(0.06)	0.86	(0.15)
N	2,029		2,029		414	
Pseudo R^2	0.0121		0.0212		0.0752	

Notes: Coefficients based on ordered logistic regression. P-values based on two-tailed tests.
*** $p < 0.01$, ** $p < 0.05$, * $p < 0.1$

Blacks' social status, but we also know that Blacks in the U.S. also use "white racial frames" and semantic mechanisms of colorblind racism to explain the position of their group in society.[53] That is to say, parents may explain to their children that Blacks, in general, are in the position they are in because they behave poorly, do not value education, or the like. Anecdotally, one theme I found among my interview respondents was the tendency to associate "poor" and "Black" when I asked them such questions as "What issues do you think are important to Black people?" One of my African American respondents relayed a memory she had of her father, who would point to Blacks in desperate situations, in an effort to provide "teachable moments" of how poor decisions and disreputable behavior could negatively and perpetually influence one's life. Carmen briefly mentioned,

> My parents would always—not [intentionally]—take me down there [to a low-income neighborhood in Dallas]. . . . That's where I went to school, and that's the same area, Oak Cliff, [where our church is]. . . . They never spoke down about people who lived there. They would say—they would use things like teachable moments. Like if a wino [an obviously drunk person] was on the street or whatever, like my dad would be like, "See, he probably made one bad decision in life and kept making bad decisions and kept making bad decisions, and ended up where he is now." Or he'll say like of people who come into his store [a family-owned pharmacy], like they wander, the drug addicts who wander into the store would, you know, how life is just a vicious cycle for them. He would always use that as a teachable moment.

This language mimics the abstract liberalism frame that serves to perpetuate a colorblind ideology. This frame uses "ideas associated with political liberalism (e.g., "equal opportunity," the idea that force should not be used to achieve social policy) and economic liberalism (e.g., choice, individualism) in an *abstract* manner to explain racial matters."[54] We might expect Black parents' talk about race to center around structural constraints, but they may also rely heavily on discussions of proper, respectable behavior, or the lack thereof, to explain the social status of Blacks in the United States, as Blacks are also susceptible to endorsing the frames of colorblind racism.[55]

Model B in table 4.3 is a comparative model. When we look at differences between ethnic groups, the results show that West Indians, Africans, and Haitians have lower levels of private regard than do African Americans. This was expected, as the extant literature suggests that Black immigrants often tend to think poorly of other Blacks, particularly of African Americans. The results of this model also indicate that those who have higher levels of education and higher incomes also tend to feel closer to or more positive about their group members, which is consistent with findings in much of the Black politics literature.[56]

Finally, Model C allows us to examine Black immigrants in isolation.

The results also show that African immigrants have lower levels of private regard than do West Indians. But income and proximity to other Blacks increases the odds of one reporting higher levels of private regard. The latter finding, concerning proximity, also goes against the grain of longstanding sociological literature. Portes and Zhou's initial development of "segmented assimilation" is largely derived from their observations that Black immigrant parents were especially wary of their children associating with Africans Americans when they lived near African Americans and sent their children to predominantly Black schools.[57] Here, we see that those Black immigrants who had plenty of interactions with other Blacks were more likely to feel positively toward other Blacks.

Public Regard

Public regard measures how one perceives out-group members' evaluations of one's racial group. I made three predictions about this dimension of racial identity: first-generation Black immigrants would have a higher sense of public regard than African Americans do; African Americans and second-generation Black immigrants would have similar levels of public regard; and discrimination will dampen public regard among Black respondents. The results for public regard are presented in table 4.4. All three models in table 4.4 provide support for the hypothesis concerning discrimination but not for the hypotheses concerning nativity or generational status. What is most clearly illuminated is that as Blacks experience major and everyday forms of discrimination, they are more likely to express that non-Blacks do not value Blacks or view Blacks positively.

Model B allows us to compare levels of racial public regard between African Americans and Black immigrants. This model shows that there are no significant differences in public regard between African Americans and Black immigrants. In fact, adding ethnicity and immigration status did not add much predictive ability to the baseline Model A. Interestingly, across the two models that included African Americans, men were more likely to express higher levels of public regard than women were, and all three models show that those who live and work in predominantly Black environments have lower levels of public

Table 4.4. Determinants of Public Regard

	Model A: All Black respondents		Model B: African Americans vs. Black immigrants		Model C: Black immigrants	
	OR	SE	OR	SE	OR	SE
Perceived Discrimination						
Everyday discrimination	0.96***	(0.01)	0.96***	(0.006)	0.97**	(0.01)
Major discrimination	0.84***	(0.03)	0.85***	(0.03)	0.84***	(0.06)
Generational Status						
First generation	—	—	1.04	(1.81)	—	—
Second generation	—	—	0.84	(1.46)	0.80	(0.18)
Ethnicity						
West Indian	—	—	1.08	(1.87)	—	—
Haitian	—	—	1.29	(2.27)	1.30	(0.42)
African	—	—	1.42	(2.59)	1.56	(0.96)
Demographics						
Gender (male = 1)	1.44***	(0.14)	1.42***	(0.14)	1.40	(0.29)
Age	0.99***	(0.003)	0.99***	(0.003)	1.00	(0.007)
Education	1.07	(0.05)	1.07	(0.052)	1.08	(0.11)
Income	1.02	(0.03)	1.02	(0.03)	1.07	(0.06)
Region						
South	1.00	(0.11)	1.00	(0.11)	0.70	(0.40)
Northeast	0.89	(0.12)	0.87	(0.13)	0.69	(0.39)
Racial Socialization						
Proximity	0.87**	(0.05)	0.86***	(0.05)	0.79*	(0.11)
Black organization	1.02	(0.15)	1.03	(0.15)	0.61	(0.22)
Parents talk	0.93	(0.05)	0.93	(0.05)	0.97	(0.13)
N	2,017		2,017		413	
Pseudo R²	0.0319		0.0324		0.0348	

Notes: Coefficients based on ordered logistic regression. *P*-values based on two-tailed tests.
*** $p < 0.01$, ** $p < 0.05$, * $p < 0.1$

regard than do those who spend their lives in mixed-race or predominantly white environments.

* * *

Overall, the results here corroborate the predictions of a theory of diasporic consciousness. The results indicate that experiences with discrimination affect two of the three measured dimensions of racial identity. These results are telling because they show that negative racialized experiences and interpersonal interactions play a significant role in shaping racial identity among African Americans and Black immigrants. As mentioned, some researchers suggest that Black immigrants should, in a time of declining discrimination, be able to claim an ethnic identity, rather than an all-encompassing racial identity, since the constraints of racism are loosening. While the results here do not speak to ethnic identities, per se, they do suggest that everyday and major experiences with discrimination bolster rather than diminish various dimensions of racial identity. Discrimination serves to reinforce the salience of racial identity, and these experiences with discrimination also serve to highlight the negative feelings that out-group members have about Black people; consequently, Blacks who have these negative interpersonal experiences have lower levels of public regard.

What is more, the findings in this chapter show that while Black immigrants and African Americans have very different legacies of racism in their countries of origin, contemporary experiences of racial discrimination within the borders of the United States influence the ways in which Black people of various ethnicities identify. Black immigrants, in a sense, are a helpful marker of racial progress in the United States. Here we see that those who are relatively new to the United States are influenced by ongoing racism in the same ways that African Americans are affected, but there are still some differences. While we see that experiences with racism influence Black immigrants' self-image and ideas about what others think about their racial in-group, these effects are weakly mitigated by ethnicity. In comparison to African Americans, Haitian and African immigrants have lower levels of racial centrality, all things being equal; and all three immigrant groups have lower levels of private regard from the outset.

The previous chapter showed that African Americans and Black immigrants feel that the boundaries of Black identity include various ethnic groups, and this chapter has shown that African Americans' and Black immigrants' racial identities are similarly influenced by discriminatory experiences. These chapters reveal how diasporic consciousness might be shaped among native- and foreign-born Blacks. In other words, the effects of racism influence Black identities among the subgroups' members in a similar way, but ethnic attachments constrain these experiences from homogenizing Black identities.

5

Politicizing Identities

Linking Identity to Politics

Group consciousness is a critical explanatory variable of African American political attitudes and behavior.[1] Gabriel Sanchez asserts, "group consciousness is a resource that generates political activity through an individual's attachment to a group."[2] Dennis Chong and Reuel Rogers further explain that racial group consciousness "potentially heightens awareness and interest in politics, bolsters group pride and political efficacy, alters interpretation of group problems, and promotes support for collective action."[3] Michael Dawson calls the psychological process that triggers these behaviors the "black utility heuristic."[4] African Americans have developed this heuristic—or mental rule of thumb—and employ it when making political decisions because of past and present racialized experiences in the United States. Historically, African Americans have been treated as group members rather than as individuals, and this race-based treatment has contributed to a tendency for African Americans to act in solidarity in the political realm. The black utility heuristic leads African Americans to use the well-being of their racial group as a proxy for their own well-being when making political decisions. Dawson further predicts that as long as the U.S. continues to be a society where one's race is inextricably linked to one's life chances, we should continue to see Blacks in the United States act as group members.[5]

What we see empirically, however, yields an interesting puzzle. We know Black immigrants are subject to the same discriminatory institutions, behaviors, and attitudes that have contributed to high levels of linked fate among African Americans.[6] But we also know that the reality of racial discrimination is not sufficient to develop a sense of group consciousness.[7] The findings in chapters 2 and 3 suggest that

Black immigrants' racial identity is salient at some points in time while at other times their ethnic identity is more salient. Furthermore, we know there are instances when Black immigrants distance themselves from Blacks Americans and ignore the role racism plays in the lives of minorities.[8] Chapter 1 also revealed that Black immigrants' identities may be translated into political action exclusively on behalf of their ethnic group, or their racial identities may be mobilized toward Black, pan-ethnic political matters, especially when they are threatened due to their racial group membership. What these very sensitive and contextual identities mean for Black immigrants' political behavior and attitudes—as well as for a united, pan-ethnic Black politics—raises a number of empirical questions, which will be addressed and answered in this chapter.

More specifically, this chapter tackles a number of issues concerning a key mechanism in the identity-to-politics link. First, this chapter seeks to answer a series of very basic but foundational questions: Do Black immigrants have a sense of racial group consciousness as we have seen it among African Americans? If so, which Black immigrants are likely to have a (strong) sense of racial group consciousness? One cannot assume that this concept, which has primarily and specifically been applied to African Americans, will pertain to other racial minority and ethnic groups—even Black immigrants.

The descriptive statistics actually show that African Americans and Black immigrants have quite similar levels of group consciousness, but that observation raises another set of questions that may best be answered with the help of qualitative interview data: Do African American and Black immigrants similarly recognize that Blacks in the United States are in a unique position in America's racial hierarchy? And does this awareness lead them to feel that something should be done about the status of Blacks in the United States via the political realm? In order to answer these questions, I primarily analyze respondents' answers to a line of questions that begins with "Does your identity influence your political attitudes?" Not only do we get a sense of how Black immigrants and African Americans connect their identity to their politics from the interviews, but their answers also provide clues as to what the major determinants of group consciousness are and help us develop a sense of which political attitudes are influenced by this politicized identity.

In an effort to paint both a larger and more detailed portrait of Black political behavior, I draw on data from the National Survey of American Life (NSAL) in addition to the responses of the thirty informants. The final set of analyses in this chapter will answer the following questions: What are the determinants of group consciousness for Black immigrants? How do these determinants compare to the factors that influence African Americans? Will racial identity have different influences on Black immigrants' political attitudes and behaviors in comparison to African Americans'? Finally, what are the limits of racial group consciousness in predicting Black immigrants' policy attitudes and political behaviors?

What We Know about Racial Group Consciousness

There are several steps between being placed in a racial category and mobilizing that ascribed identity toward political action. "Acquiring a group identity and a sense of common fate is therefore just the first step toward a fully developed group consciousness."[9] That is to say, group consciousness starts with a shared identity or sense of closeness with group members. Racial group consciousness is an "in-group identification *politicized* by a set of ideological beliefs about one's group's social standing as well as a view that collective action is the best means by which the group can improve its status and realize its interests."[10]

Group Consciousness among African Americans

The role that racial identity plays in African Americans' political behavior is clearly viewed through the notions of group consciousness and linked fate.[11] More specifically, political scientists explain that African Americans tend to consider the status of their racial group as an important variable when making political decisions because of past and present racialized experiences in the United States.[12] Group consciousness may be triggered by the perception of discrimination against one's group as well as a sense of belonging to a group with a lowered status in society.[13] Historically, African Americans have been treated as group members rather than as individuals; in turn, a very unique set of political attitudes and political behaviors developed among the group's members, and group consciousness has shown to be an important mechanism in shaping the ways in which African Americans think about politics and how they respond to the American political system.

To be more precise, African Americans have not only developed a set of schemas around racial issues, but more importantly, they have developed a racial belief system. Schemas organize information in our memory; provide categories to label things; group information into "larger, more meaningful, and more easily retrievable categories"; allow individuals to make inferences from incomplete data by filling in missing information; and supply heuristics that aid in simplifying the problem-solving process.[14] Belief systems, on the other hand, require a breadth and depth of knowledge. "While cognitive schemata actively process and store information and generate expectations about future events and actions, belief systems help the social participant access and process information and make decisions heuristically."[15] Belief systems are concerned with the existence of conceptual entities, such as God, ESP, and racism; they present representations of "alternative worlds," principally, how the world is, in contrast to how the world should be; they rely on evaluative and affective components, defining large categories of concepts as "good" or "bad"; and they include episodic material from personal experience.[16] Belief systems come into being over time. African Americans' belief system concerning the role of race has developed due to historical interactions with race and racism in the United States, and these systems are reinforced by racial socialization processes (particularly certain ongoing experiences within a racialized social system).

Concerning political attitudes, African Americans have traditionally been fairly liberal on issues such as social welfare, government spending, and affirmative action. Black public opinion has historically been marked by homogeneity, with a slight exception for more conservative attitudes among the affluent.[17] Racial group consciousness has been credited for liberalizing African Americans' attitudes. The theory suggests and empirical evidence supports the notion that since African Americans view themselves as group members and use the well-being of the group as a proxy for what is good for the individual, they tend to support policies that will help most group members.[18] For example,

African Americans tend to be more supportive than white Americans of a bigger government due to the expectation that a larger government is likely to enforce antidiscrimination and ameliorative policies such as affirmative action and to ensure the stability of social safety-net programs. In general, African Americans have historically tended to "support an activist welfare state as a form of racial redress."[19]

Similarly, group consciousness influences African Americans' political behavior. One of the most striking attributes of Black political behavior is the tendency for African Americans to act in solidarity and behave homogeneously as group members in the political realm. For instance, acting in accordance with their political attitudes, African Americans tend to vote for the political party that best represents the average group member's political, social, and economic interests.[20] Group consciousness exerts influence on the levels and rates of participation among African Americans as well. Those individuals with a strong sense of group consciousness are more likely to participate in the political realm, but Chong and Rogers show that not all forms of political participation are equally influenced by group consciousness; they also suggest that group consciousness may even direct some people away from some political activities.[21]

There is some dissent concerning the role of group consciousness in contemporary Black politics.[22] For example, Lawrence Bobo and Franklin Gilliam suggest that "political empowerment" rather than group consciousness is what drives African Americans' political behavior in a post–Civil Rights era.[23] Nevertheless, many more political scientists have determined that group consciousness is a powerful indicator and predictor of political behavior and attitudes among African Americans, and further, they predict that we should continue to see African Americans act as group members in the political realm because the U.S. remains a racialized social system, or a society where one's race is inextricably linked to one's life chances.[24]

Group Consciousness among Black Immigrants

The literature on the extent to which Black immigrants identify with African Americans is mixed, so we cannot be certain whether and to what extent Black immigrants' racial identity will be politicized in the same way it is for African Americans. On the one hand, empirical studies show that even though Black immigrants tend to have a higher socioeconomic status than African Americans, Black immigrants experience the same levels of, if not higher levels of, racial discrimination in the employment and housing markets as African Americans.[25] Scholars also show that racial discrimination negatively affects Black immigrants' health outcomes just as it does African Americans'.[26] Overall, the factors that help maintain a sense of linked fate among African Americans are also a reality for Black immigrants. However, the reality of racial discrimination is not sufficient to develop a sense of group consciousness.[27] Other scholars find that Black immigrants tend to distance themselves from African Americans and a Black racial identity.[28] Reuel Rogers finds that most Black immigrants do feel close to—or have a sense of shared racial identity with—African Americans, but he still predicts this identity may not be politically mobilized in the same way as African Americans' racial identity.[29]

The existing literature does provide some hints as to whether Black immigrants have a sense of racial group consciousness and how this might affect their political attitudes. As mentioned, racial group consciousness is predicated on a sense of closeness with group members, perceptions of group discrimination, and the idea that collective action could be and should be employed to improve the status of the group. Concerning closeness, Rogers's study on the political incorporation of Black immigrants finds that a solid proportion of his first-generation West Indian informants feel close to African Americans, but he also finds that first-generation immigrants are likely to ignore the role of race in interpersonal interactions, often blaming African Americans themselves for the status of the group.[30] The latter finding—blaming African Americans—is a sign that a sense of racial group consciousness among this group may be hindered from fully developing; while Afro-Caribbeans may at times attribute the status of African Americans to institutional barriers, first-generation Black immigrants generally focus on individual characteristics and negative stereotypes of African Americans to explain the group's position in society. Arthur Miller and his colleagues suggest that "system-blame," or explaining a group's position as due to systemic or institutional factors, is important for developing group consciousness.[31] However, several scholars who study Black immigrants find that they may be more prone to blame individuals' behaviors for the group's well-being rather than structural constraints,[32] thereby weakening the type of feelings of group consciousness that we observe among African Americans.

Nonetheless, the extant literature also shows that over time and over generations, Black immigrants' ideas about the role of race as well as their own racial identity change. Sherri-Ann Butterfield as well as Teceta Tormala and Kay Deaux find that second-generation immigrants are likely to perceive racial discrimination in their day-to-day experiences, while those in the first generation are less likely to do so.[33] Moreover, Butterfield finds that even though second-generation Black immigrants identify with their ethnicity, they also find solidarity with African Americans. Second-generation Black immigrants have been socialized in the United States, and thus, they tend to recognize the influence that their group membership has on their opportunity structure, similar to the way African Americans do.[34] Additionally, Milton Vickerman, who interviewed male Jamaican immigrants, found that the longer immigrants are in the U.S., the more empathetic they become with African Americans' struggle against racial inequality.[35]

Furthermore, historians illuminate examples when racial identity has been clearly politicized among Black immigrants. Recall some of the accounts explicated in chapter 1. Susan Greenbaum described how Afro-Cubans' racial identity and sense of group consciousness became more salient as they recognized that their life chances were inextricably linked to their racial identity rather than their ethnicity.[36] Similarly, Ginetta Candelario explained that in Washington, D.C., during the 1960s and 1970s, Dominicans' racial identity became more central to their self-image and more politicized as they recognized that a raised racial group consciousness was necessary to garner the social, political, and economic benefits that African Americans were attaining.[37] Also, recall that in New York, Black immigrants developed political relationships with African Americans as they became cognizant of the fact that much of their treatment derived from out-group members' perceptions and stereotypes of them as Black rather than as Afro-Caribbean, Haitian, or the like.[38] Black immigrants' sense of racial group consciousness seems to be contextual, primarily being triggered when they feel that their racial identity will heavily influence their life chances. That is to say, Black immigrants' attitudes and behavior are at times more influenced by their ethnicity, while at other times their racial identity has a more salient influence.

Black immigrants must negotiate their racial and ethnic identities while living in the United States, but very little is known regarding how these identities influence their political behavior. Jane Junn and Natalie Masuoka suggest that the existence of group consciousness among Latinos and Asians should be "treated as a hypothesis rather than an assumption," because students of race and politics are still unsure how identity and political behavior are linked for non-Black minority groups, "*particularly those whose population growth is attributed to new immigration.*"[39] A significant portion of Black population growth is attributed to new immigration as well. This chapter tests this hypothesis. The following set of analyses will help us to gain a better sense of whether Black immigrants' identity-to-politics link follows a similar pattern to that of African Americans'.

Levels of Group Consciousness

Taking Junn and Masuoka's warning seriously, I assess whether Black immigrants have a sense of racial group consciousness, in the first place. As mentioned, the racially discriminatory institutions and interactions that influenced the development of group consciousness for African Americans are very real for Black immigrants as well. One might assume that Black immigrants, therefore, will have a sense of racial group consciousness, but here I will test that assumption. I measure group consciousness with the survey item, "Do you think what generally happens to Black people in this country will have something to do with what happens in your life?" The respondents can answer no, or they can respond in the affirmative and describe the intensity of that feeling: "yes, a little," "some," or "a lot." While some scholars are concerned with using linked fate as a measure for group consciousness,[40] Paula McClain and her coauthors make a convincing case:

> Perhaps, as a sophisticated and parsimonious alternative, racial group consciousness may best be operationalized through the measure of linked fate . . . , as linked fate appears to capture simply the complex

decision algorithms (heuristic processes) used by most voters . . . , incorporates the feelings of in-group identification and an awareness of having a similar status with other group members, and helps us to understand better the links between group membership, identification and political behavior and attitudes.[41]

In summary, even though group consciousness is understood to be a multidimensional construct,[42] I use the linked fate measure because it addresses the cognitive component of group consciousness; in other words, linked fate captures whether respondents use the status of the group as a proxy for the well-being of the individual.[43] This measure is also the best available measure of group consciousness in the survey.

Figure 5.1 shows the distribution of levels of group consciousness among African Americans and Black immigrants. We see that for the most part African Americans and Black immigrants tend to share a similar sense of group consciousness. About 38 percent of African American and 37 percent of Black immigrant respondents reported that they do not feel a sense of linked fate with other Black people in the United States. Among the roughly 60 percent who do feel a sense of linked fate, 10 percent of African Americans feel their fate is linked to other Blacks but only "a little"; this feeling is shared by about 11 percent of Black immigrants. Approximately 34 percent of African Americans and 31 percent of Black immigrants reported that they feel that what happens to other group members will have "some" effect on their own lives. Finally, 17 percent of African Americans feel their fate is very much linked to the lives of other Blacks, while 20 percent of Black immigrants reported this feeling.

When Black immigrants are disaggregated by ethnicity and by nativity, we see subtle differences. African immigrants tended to respond in the affirmative to the linked fate question. Only 23.4 percent of African immigrants reported that they do not feel a sense of linked fate with other Blacks in America, leaving the great majority of Africans to respond in the affirmative. Among Black immigrants, Haitians were the most likely to report that they do not feel a sense of linked fate with other Black people in the United States.

Finally, figure 5.1 shows that second-generation Black immigrants have the highest levels of group consciousness, even higher than

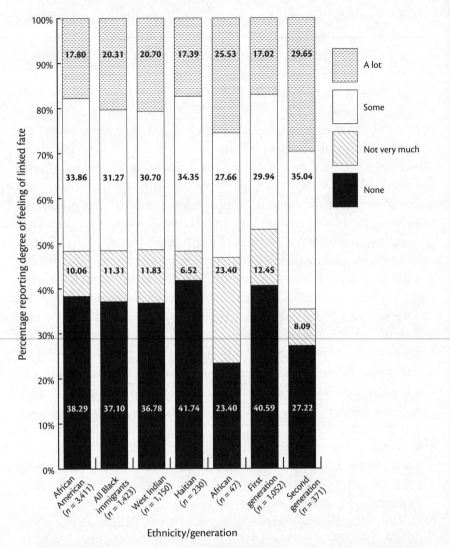

Figure 5.1. Levels of group consciousness among African Americans and Black immigrants

African Americans".[44] About 73 percent answered in the affirmative, in comparison to approximately 62 percent of African Americans, which is significantly different at a 95 percent confidence level. This is both a counterintuitive and interesting finding. Scholars who focus on second-generation Black immigrant identity development suggest that even though members of this group are exposed to two worlds—their parents' country of origin and the United States—they tend to be very aware of the ways in which their life chances are uniquely influenced by America's racial hierarchy.[45] Perhaps the results here illustrate the effects of second-generation immigrants comparing their parents' nostalgic narratives of their "colorblind" countries of origin and the reality of race in the United States. This comparison may bring about a heightened awareness of one's racial identity and the ways in which this group membership affects one's opportunity structure. Historically, the racial consciousness of African Americans, especially soldiers who were exposed to societies where their race did not matter as much as it did in the United States, became incredibly heightened.[46] The results here may reflect the effects of second-generation immigrants' cross-country comparisons. Overall, the data in figure 5.1 indicate a fair amount of similarities between African Americans' and Black immigrants' sense of group consciousness on average, but the following analyses—starting with the interview data—will discern whether this politicized identity is triggered by the same stimuli, and furthermore, it will help us determine whether group consciousness influences the political attitudes and behaviors of Black immigrants as it does African Americans'.

"I'm a Democrat Because I'm Black"

The descriptive statistics shed just a bit of light on this very important mechanism—group consciousness—in the identity-to-politics link. What we are able to gather thus far is that both African Americans and Black immigrants do share a politicized identity, but the descriptive statistics do not clarify whether Black immigrants and African Americans conceptualize the notion of group consciousness similarly. They agree that their fates are linked, but how does this translate into the political realm? I engaged my respondents on how their identity influences their political attitudes and behaviors. The face-to-face interviews were semistructured, so I did not ask everyone the exact same questions, but often the conversations veered toward the relationship between how people see themselves and how they view politics. To be more precise, I directly asked about half the respondents, "How, if at all, does your racial identity influence your political attitudes?"[47]

African Americans' Responses

I was able to ask nine out of the seventeen African American respondents if and how their racial identity influences their political attitudes, and 77.8 percent (or seven) of them responded that their racial identity is a very important factor in the way they view politics. Among the nine African American respondents, two mentioned that their racial identity does not influence their political attitudes.

One of the respondents, Michael from Spokane, Washington, claimed that his racial identity does not affect his political attitudes. He explained his position this way: "I've always been very liberal not because I was Black but because I was poor, really." For Michael, his economic position is a more important factor than his race in shaping his political decisions and attitudes. While many scholars note that race is the modality by which class is lived,[48] Michael has made an effort to disentangle the two forces. The other person who answered that her race does not affect her political behavior is Elle, who is from Chicago. She explained that she is a Democrat not because of feelings of connectedness with other Blacks but instead because her parents, who are also Black, are Democrats.

Nevertheless, a great majority of the respondents were more like Peter, an African American from Rochester, New York, who explained, "I think my racial identity is very important in just how I look at politics and different views in politics. And just to go back to the whole underprivileged thing and life for Black people and stuff like that, I'm more big on stuff like that, that's going to affect underprivileged Black people to making things better for them." Peter grew up in a poor, predominantly Black neighborhood and explained that he feels a connection to poor, Black people in particular. In turn, when he makes political decisions, he considers how underprivileged Black people will be affected. Similar to Peter, Laura made the point that because her experiences have been shaped by her racial identity, her view of the political world is influenced by her racial identity. She explained, "I think my racial identity is kind of what shaped me as being more liberal because I recognize that these things exist because I've experienced them, and I know social injustice is there because it's something I deal with on a regular basis." Alexis, an African American woman from New Jersey, mentioned that she feels strongly about issues surrounding education, criminal justice, poverty, and health care. When I asked her how her racial identity influences these attitudes, she answered, "A lot. Even with the four that I named, they come from . . . the issues that I have with them come from either personal experience or the way that Blacks are treated when it comes to these different issues—when it comes to criminal justice and education and the unequal opportunities that people have." Arthur Miller and his colleagues explain that in addition to group identity and polar affect—or having a preference from one's in-group—polar power and system-blame are also two important dimensions of group consciousness.[49] Polar power can be described simply as dissatisfaction with one's group's current status, power, or resources in relation to another group. System-blame, as previously mentioned, is the belief that a group's social status is attributable to structural inequalities. Peter's and Alexis's responses highlight the latter two components in particular. These respondents make mention of the notion that Blacks tend to be in "underprivileged" positions in society due to social injustices such as unfair access to quality education and bias in the criminal justice system.

The theme of partisanship also came up when I asked the question of whether the respondents' identity influences their attitudes. Joshua, an African American man from Dallas, responded this way to my question: "I'm a Democrat because I'm Black." We then had this exchange, in which Joshua elaborated on his position:

> JOSHUA: I mean, that's what I thought when I was younger. I've gotten a lot more politically savvy obviously, but I think that my complete, you know, ideology, everything political up until I started taking classes [in college], was because my parents were [also Democrats]. And my mom, God bless her heart, always said, "If you were a Black conservative, you hate yourself." And so . . .
>
> CANDIS: What do you think she meant by that?
>
> JOSHUA: I think that she meant that like the Democratic Party, in her opinion, has policies that help Black people. And by helping Black people, you help yourself. So if you don't want policies that help Black people, then you don't like yourself. And so . . .
>
> CANDIS: And what's your thought on that now?

JOSHUA: Ridiculous, I think. I think that, you know, there are things from the Democratic Party where I'm like, uhhh, no. I just don't agree with, you know . . . I mean, more often than not I'm pretty liberal, and I can say that because I know what liberal means. . . . I mean, now that I'm politically savvy and I know what's going on, I still have that very, very Democratic mind-set about things.

Although Joshua's initial response seems very elementary, his response also manages to get from one side of the identity-to-politics link to the other in an efficient manner. Joshua explains that even though he does not quite agree on everything that his mother has to say about the subject, nor does he agree with everything the Democratic party stands for, he tends to support that party because, from his perspective, it tends to stand for policies that will positively influence the lives of Blacks.

Amir, an African American college student from South Carolina, provided a similarly emphatic response to the question concerning the extent to which his racial identity influences his political attitudes: "I think that I'm more conscious of how people who look like me, Black people, have struggled in this country. And so, I *can't* support, I *can't* support a party or an individual who doesn't support those issues that will positively affect change in the Black community." I asked Amir if there is a political party that he does tend to support. He answered,

Because historically, it has been—the Democrat Party has really worked, I think, on behalf of Black people. And I understand, you know, Lincoln Republicans and all that stuff, yada, yada, yada. However, the party is much different today than it was back then. People when they argue more about economics and all that stuff, and "We can't afford, you know, to support a welfare program that, you know, makes people sit at home and become lazy," as the lieutenant governor of my state [South Carolina] said—I can't support a party that believes in stuff like that and who has people in the party who say stuff like that. That's why I don't support the Republican Party. I actually agree with a number of things the Republican Party says with regard to national security and stuff like that, but social issues trump [*chuckles*]—and this is unfortunate for some—but social issues trump issues of national security in my book because I see these [Black and poor] people on a daily basis. And I'm disconnected more so from issues of national security than I am from seeing people struggle. So I can't support the Republican Party in that regard. But I do stand with them for other issues.

Amir's response, like that of several others, shows how one's racial group identity influences not only which issues one believes are important but also one's partisan affiliation and candidate vote choice. Moreover, we see that even though Amir agrees with the Republican Party on some policy domains—"national security and stuff like that"—he is more inclined to support the Democratic Party because it touts a policy platform focused on helping Blacks improve their status as a group. Amir, as many African Americans do, prioritizes issues that directly and positively influence Blacks' life chances and opportunity structure over other issues such as foreign policy or national security.

Black Immigrants' Responses

African American respondents were not the only ones who felt that the issues important to them are central because of their racial identity. I asked seven Black immigrant students the same question: "How, if at all, does your racial identity influence your political attitudes?" Six responded that their racial identity influences their political attitudes. Ann, the one woman from this group who said she does not see the link between her racial identity and political attitudes, explained, "I don't, I mean, I don't know. For some reason, I just separate them."

Contrarily, when I asked Antwon, a 1.5-generation immigrant from Nigeria, if and how his racial identity influences his political attitudes, he responded, "Huge. It's my experience. If you had interviewed a white guy, he would have a completely different story. 'Cause I've lived it. So because I'm Black, I'm going to be able to speak from a Black perspective, be able to relate and have distinct stories of why I feel a certain type of way." In our two-hour conversation, Antwon, who grew up in a poor, Black neighborhood in Marietta, Georgia, told me a number of stories of times when he felt discriminated against because of his race. For example, he recalled a time when he was very well dressed in Manhattan; he was doing an internship for a prestigious investment bank. He went up to a white man to ask for directions to his new workplace, and as he approached the man, the man extended his arm and waved his hand, as one would to dismiss someone. Antwon realized this man thought he was a vagrant despite the fact he had on a suit and had recently got a haircut. D. L. Hughley, a Black comedian, once joked that although it is highly unlikely that a Black man dressed like Antwon would be homeless, it is not unlikely that a sartorial-minded man would indeed be well dressed on his *first day* of being homeless; but this, of course, was not the case for Antwon.

Another of Antwon's experiences occurred on PSU's campus. He explained that he was assumed to be the janitor by another student's parent. Antwon's experience as a Black person—as a Black male—has shaped not only how he sees himself but also how he sees the world. He realizes that despite the fact that he was a student at an elite university or that he was well dressed and on his way to a prestigious internship, he was treated as a group member rather than as an individual. Further, even though Antwon's mother, according to him, repeatedly told him, "You're not just a Black guy. You're Nigerian," he still recognizes the ways in which his fate is linked to his racial—rather than just his ethnic—group membership, and he responds accordingly in the political realm.

Ashley, a woman of Ethiopian descent, answered my question of whether her racial identity influences her political attitudes this way:

> I think it . . . it . . . it [my race] affects it [my politics] a lot. Because I know that if there are—because I am Black and if there are policies or decisions or things like that, that will directly impact Black people in general, that is going to affect . . . that is going to affect like my political radar. Like I'm not that involved in politics that much. I know the big names. I know, and I try to get involved with like local politics and who are the people in that, but to be quite honest, I'm just not that involved compared to some students here. But again, like that definitely—issues that do involve Black people, and especially those who are disenfranchised, which sometimes is Black people, I pay attention.

Ashley identifies as both Black and Ethiopian, but it is clear that she has a strong sense of racial group consciousness. Ashley's response raises three important issues. The first is that her racial identity influences what issues she thinks are important; she named two: health care and social equality. The second is that she is more likely to pay attention to the issues that influence her racial group members. The third is that Ashley most clearly explicates the idea of the black utility heuristic. She uses the group's well-being as a proxy for her own well-being and consequently pays attention to issues that affect the larger racial group because she feels those issues will influence her just the same.

Claire, a second-generation Nigerian woman, displayed a similar attitude. When I asked her how her identity influences her political attitudes and behaviors, she answered,

> I think that the reason why I identify with the Democratic Party is because I see . . . I think as of late, especially, I think politics has become very racially divided along partisanship lines, maybe inherently or unconsciously. Well, consciously . . . I think the fact that I identify as a Black American kind of defines where my partisanship lies. And I guess maybe more so with, you know, the election of Obama, maybe I feel more like the Democratic Party is more in tune with some of the issues that are of value and importance to the Black community.

Claire's response is very similar to Joshua's; she feels there is a strong link between her racial identity and partisanship. She chooses the party she perceives as being sensitive to issues of members of her racial group.

Overall, the respondents who answered in the affirmative explained that their racial identity influences what issues they think are important, and they explained that they could only support political candidates, parties, and platforms that work toward the well-being of the racial group. While there were members of both groups who claimed their racial identity does not influence their political attitudes, the majority (about 81 percent) do feel their race matters.

Black immigrants' sentiments concerning the link between their racial identity and their political attitudes and behaviors were quite similar to African Americans'. In addition to respondents from both groups showing that they have an affinity for their group members (polar affect), they also illustrated other dimensions of group consciousness. African Americans and Black immigrants are aware of and dissatisfied with the inequalities between racial groups (polar power), and they generally expressed the notion that they feel their group's members face structural inequalities (system-blame) that could be remedied through the political system or with the help of certain political parties. Some of the respondents suggested their personal experiences—growing up in poor, predominantly Black neighborhoods or being treated unfairly even after attaining a higher level of education—influences them to think about their racial identity when making political judgments. Further, it is clear that many of them employ the black utility heuristic when thinking about politics. That is to say, they think about the group when making political decisions for themselves as individuals.

Determinants of Racial Group Consciousness

So far, we have seen a number of similarities surface between African Americans' and Black immigrants' sense of group consciousness. But what are the underlying determinants of racial group consciousness among Black immigrants? Are these determinants similar to or different from those of African Americans'? It is well known that African Americans' sense of group consciousness is influenced by a plethora of factors including closeness with one's in-group, experiences and perception of discrimination,[50] socioeconomic status,[51] socialization, and interracial interactions.[52]

Previous research on African Americans' political attitudes and behaviors has not been compelled to focus on generational status (as it relates to the immigrant experience), levels of acculturation, or citizenship, but the increasing ethnic diversity among Blacks in contemporary America has changed the criteria for developing a fully specified predictive model for Black political behavior. To what extent should we expect "traditional" factors (e.g., socioeconomic status or parental socialization) to also influence Black immigrants' sense of group consciousness? How might accounting for "new" factors such as generational status or acculturation help us to better understand Black immigrants' racial group consciousness?

Building on the literature of African American politics as well as the literature concerned with Black immigrants' identity formation, a theory of diasporic consciousness predicts that while Black immigrants do not have a shared historical legacy with race and discrimination in the United States, the factors that initially led African Americans' racial identities to be politicized still exist today. As such, I hypothesize that contemporary experiences with discrimination will politicize Black immigrants' racial identity just as they do for African Americans. I also predict that there will be additional factors such as generational status, socialization in the United States, and gender that will influence Black immigrants in ways that do not affect African Americans. The hypotheses can be most simply stated as follows:

H_1: Black immigrants of various ethnicities will have similar levels of group consciousness as African Americans, ceteris paribus.

H_2: Black immigrants who identify with other Blacks will have a higher sense of linked fate than those who do not feel as close to racial group members.

H_3: Experiences with racial discrimination will increase the extent to which Black immigrants feel a sense of group consciousness, as they do for African Americans.

H_4: Black immigrants who are more acculturated to the United States, especially second-generation Black immigrants, will have a higher sense of group consciousness than do Black immigrants who are foreign-born.

Ethnicity is the first independent variable of importance; by accounting for ethnicity in addition to the other independent and control variables, we get a more sophisticated rendering of the findings in figure 5.1, thereby allowing a more accurate test of the first hypothesis. I created dummy variables for West Indian respondents, Haitian respondents, and African respondents. African Americans are the comparison group in the models that include all Blacks. West Indians are the comparison group in the models that include Black immigrants only.

In order to test the second hypothesis, I account for racial identity with both traditional and newly developed measures. As for the traditional measure, I employ a measure typically referred to as "closeness"; respondents are asked, "How close do you feel in your ideas and feelings about things to Black people in this country?" This measure "emphasize[s] the facet of black identity that most closely resembles classic definitions of group identity."[53] I also employ the three dimensions of racial identity captured in chapter 4—racial centrality, private regard, and public regard. Arguably, one can feel close to a group yet not identify as a group member; by including a measure such as centrality, the model will discern whether feeling close to Blacks and identifying oneself as Black, or both, will influence the extent to which a respondent feels a sense of group consciousness.[54] There are multicollinearity problems neither among these four measures nor between these four measures and the dependent variable.

To test the third hypothesis, the models include a measure to capture respondents' exposure to racial discrimination. Experiences with discrimination are measured in the same way they are in the previous chapter. Both major and everyday experiences with discrimination are included in the analyses. In order to test the fourth hypothesis concerning acculturation, I include a measure for generational status, accounting for whether the respondent is a first-generation immigrant. Finally, I include a number of control variables. The models control for racial socialization, measured by the proximity variable as well as the extent to which respondents' parents discussed issues of race with them. I also include socioeconomic (income and education) variables as well as demographic variables (age and gender).

Results

Table 5.1 includes five models, each of which tests at least one hypothesis. All of the models are ordered logistic models; odds ratios and 95 percent confidence intervals are reported. Model A is a baseline model that includes all Black respondents. Here we see that some aspects of racial identity are statistically significant variables in determining a sense of group consciousness. That is, those who feel close to other Blacks and those whose racial identity is central to their self-image also tend have a sense that their fate is linked to other Black people in the United States. Additionally, Model A shows that both everyday and major experiences with discrimination are significant determinants of racial group consciousness.

The control variables in Model A also provide interesting information. First, the results reveal that Blacks with higher levels of education tend to feel a higher sense of group consciousness. But those respondents who were socialized around more Blacks feel a lower sense of

Table 5.1. Determinants of Group Consciousness

	Model A: All Black respondents OR (95% CI)	Model B: African Americans vs. Black immigrants OR (95% CI)	Model C: African Americans OR (95% CI)	Model D: Black immigrants (comparative model) OR (95% CI)	Model E: Black immigrants (full model) OR (95% CI)
Identity					
Closeness	1.55***	1.55***	1.49***	1.87***	1.85***
	(1.37–1.76)	(1.36–1.76)	(1.29–1.72)	(1.43–2.46)	(1.40–2.42)
Centrality	1.47***	1.46***	1.50***	1.33*	1.28
	(1.29–1.67)	(1.29–1.66)	(1.30–1.74)	(0.98–1.78)	(0.95–1.72)
Public regard	0.91	0.92	0.90	0.96	0.99
	(0.81–1.02)	(0.81–1.03)	(0.79–1.03)	(0.74–1.24)	(0.76–1.29)
Private regard	0.88	0.90	0.95	0.67*	0.69
	(0.72–1.08)	(0.72–1.09)	(0.76–1.19)	(0.41–1.07)	(0.43–1.12)
Perceived Discrimination					
Everyday discrimination	1.02***	1.02***	1.02***	1.03**	1.03*
	(1.01–1.03)	(1.01–1.03)	(1.01–1.03)	(1.01–1.06)	(1.00–1.06)
Major discrimination	1.13***	1.13***	1.15***	1.04	1.03
	(1.07–1.19)	(1.07–1.19)	(1.08–1.22)	(0.91–1.19)	(0.89–1.18)
Demographics					
Income	1.01	1.01	1.04	0.95	0.95
	(0.96–1.08)	(0.95–1.07)	(0.96–1.12)	(0.84–1.07)	(0.84–1.07)
Education	1.16***	1.15***	1.17***	1.09	1.09
	(1.06–1.27)	(1.05–1.26)	(1.05–1.29)	(0.89–1.33)	(0.88–1.33)
Age	1.00	1.00	1.005	1.00	1.00
	(0.99–1.01)	(0.99–1.01)	(0.99–1.01)	(0.99–1.01)	(0.99–1.01)
Male	1.15	1.16	1.14	1.19	1.22
	(0.96–1.38)	(0.96–1.39)	(0.93–1.39)	(0.79–1.79)	(0.81–1.85)
Socialization					
Proximity	0.86***	0.88**	0.88**	0.77**	0.88
	(0.77–0.96)	(0.79–0.98)	(0.78–0.99)	(0.60–0.99)	(0.67–1.16)
Parents talk	1.01	1.01	1.01	1.06	1.06
	(0.92–1.11)	(0.92–1.12)	(0.91–1.12)	(0.82–1.38)	(0.82–1.38)
Ethnicity					
West Indian	—	1.62***	—	—	—
		(1.17–2.24)			
Haitian	—	1.51	—	—	0.91
		(0.74–3.11)			(0.47–1.76)
African	—	2.18	—	—	1.29
		(0.66–7.16)			(0.40–4.13)
Acculturation					
First generation	—	0.52***	—	—	0.52***
		(0.35–0.78)			(0.34–0.80)
N	1,966	1,966	1,566	400	400
Pseudo R²	0.0475	0.0497	0.0482	0.0558	0.0651

Notes: Coefficients based on ordered logistic regression. *P*-values based on two–tailed tests.
*** $p < 0.01$, ** $p < 0.05$, * $p < 0.1$

group consciousness than those who were more likely to interact with whites, as shown by an odds ratio of less than one. These findings indicate that those who are exposed to a racially diverse array of individuals are likely to see racial disparities even when individuals are similarly qualified, and thus they more readily recognize how race privileges some and disadvantages others, in comparison to those who have a larger set of racially homogeneous experiences.[55]

Model B is the first effort to test the first hypothesis. The results provide mixed support for the hypothesis, which predicted that there will be no major differences in levels of group consciousness among various groups of Black immigrants and African Americans. What we see is that West Indians are much more likely than African Americans to report high levels of group consciousness; however, there is no statistical difference when we compare African Americans to Haitian or to African immigrants, all other things being equal. However, one thing that must be mentioned is that first-generation Black immigrants have much lower levels of group consciousness than do African Americans or second-generation Black immigrants.

Models C, D, and E help us to better parse out the determinants of group consciousness for African Americans and for Black immigrants, separately. I included Model C, which focuses on African Americans only, as a comparative model; this model also helps us to gain a sense of whether African Americans are the primary drivers of any of the determinants in Models A or B. The results in Model C indicate that African Americans' sense of closeness to other Blacks and racial centrality, their experiences with both major and everyday discrimination, and levels of education all play important roles in developing group consciousness. Nonetheless, proximity to other Blacks tends to decrease a politicized identity.

What is important about Model C is that it is not very different from Model D, which is exclusive to Black immigrants, but the differences are illuminating. The first item to note is that in addition to closeness and centrality, private regard also plays a role in group consciousness for Black immigrants (although not in an intuitive way). Those Black immigrants who feel positively about other Blacks seem to have lower levels of group consciousness; this variable is just significant though, at a p-value of .09. The second difference to note is the fact that everyday discrimination bolsters Black immigrants' racial group consciousness, but major discriminatory experiences do not. Perhaps, everyday experiences serve as micro-aggressors, which upon reflection and aggregation may be easier to understand as racial discrimination for Black immigrants in comparison to major experiences with discrimination, which happen with less frequency.

Finally, Model E is a fully specified model that allows us to test H_4, which predicts that one who is more acculturated to the U.S. will have a higher sense of group consciousness than a Black immigrant who is new to the this country. The model indicates that levels of acculturation do matter in developing a sense of group consciousness; those of the first generation are shown to have a lower sense of group consciousness than their second-generation counterparts.

The asserted hypotheses are largely supported. All things being equal, African Americans, Haitians, and African immigrants have similar levels of group consciousness; West Indian immigrants bypass African Americans, but this finding is likely to be driven by second-generation Black immigrants. African Americans and Black immigrants who feel close to other group members and whose racial identity is central to their self-image are more likely to report high levels of group consciousness. Experiences with racial discrimination bolster both native- and foreign-born Blacks' sense of group consciousness. Finally Black immigrants who have been socialized in the U.S. are more likely than those who are relative newcomers to have a high sense of group consciousness, as expected.

What we have seen so far is that there have been relatively few differences between the levels of group consciousness and the extent to which racial discrimination plays a critical role in developing a politicized identity across ethnic groups. The last portion of this chapter takes us one step further in the identity-to-politics link and tests the extent to which Black immigrants' sense of group consciousness influences their political behaviors and attitudes.

Political Effects of Racial Group Consciousness

Black immigrants and African Americans report similar levels of group consciousness, and members of both groups are in agreement, for the most part, that since their life chances are influenced by their racial identity, they should consider this identity and their group members when making political considerations. However, the historical analysis presented in chapter 1 suggests that while ethnicity does not preclude group consciousness, it does mediate its effects. Black immigrants' racial identity tends to be more salient when policies affect them due to their racial group membership, and this identity is mobilized in instances when there is a sense of racial threat.[56] Thus, the underlying theory driving this final analysis is that if group consciousness is relevant for Black immigrants' political attitudes, it is most likely to influence attitudes in policy areas that affect Black immigrants because of their racial group membership. That is to say, we should expect Black immigrants' racial identity to be politicized in racially salient policy areas.

H₅: Group consciousness will influence Black immigrants' political attitudes but only in racially salient policy areas.

Even though this chapter is primarily concerned with the role that racial group consciousness plays for Black immigrants, it is important to compare this group with African Americans to gain a sense of the extent to which the contours of Black politics are influenced by ethnic differences. Black politics literature generally implies that group consciousness can influence group members' attitudes in a broad array of policy areas, including areas with little or no noticeable racial content. African Americans tend to be uniquely influenced by policies that are not racialized, or associated with one particular racial group—such as education, unemployment, and healthcare—and consequently, they tend to have very different attitudes than white Americans.[57] For example, African Americans tend to be less supportive of war efforts than whites are; this is a policy domain that has no noticeable racial content, but one explanation for the lack of support derives from the fact that Blacks are cognizant that their racial group members are likely to bear a disproportionate amount of war causalities.[58] Relatedly, Alvin Tillery explains that Black elites have historically been interested in foreign policy, especially when they calculate that U.S. involvement would "shift the national discourse about the capacity of the black race for U.S. citizenship."[59] African Americans' matured racial belief system allows them to recognize the link between a nonracialized policy area such as foreign policy (or health or education policy) and the group's well-being; this has developed over a long history of interactions with the American political system. In turn, African Americans are keen to engage even when seemingly nonracial policies will influence their group differently than other groups. With this consideration, I propose the following hypothesis:

> H_6: While Black immigrants' racial group consciousness will influence policy areas that are clearly racialized, African Americans' sense of group consciousness will influence attitudes in both racially salient policy areas and those policy arenas with no noticeable racial content but that are perceived to influence Blacks differently than other groups.

In addition to gaining an understanding of how group consciousness influences political attitudes, this study also aims to illuminate how group consciousness might influence Black immigrants' political behavior. Black immigrants tend to naturalize at very low rates and tend to focus on the politics of their homelands because they imagine that they will return someday.[60] Moreover, Rogers also reveals that Black immigrants tend to shy away from nontraditional political participation such as contacting a political official, participating in a political campaign, or the like because these are not typical modes of political behavior in the home countries of many Black immigrants.[61] Taking this information into consideration, one would expect Black immigrants to participate at lower rates than African Americans, especially in nontraditional modes of participation.

> H_7: Participation rates among Black immigrants will be lower than they are for African Americans.

However, because Black immigrants face very similar racial constraints as African Americans and are likely to develop a sense of racial group consciousness that mirrors African Americans', I contend that we should expect group consciousness to enhance Black immigrants' political behavior, as seen among African Americans. We should expect group consciousness to bolster participation, particularly those

participatory methods that are less traditional to respondents or require more resources (material or psychological), such as contacting a
representative or participating in a political campaign. To address the
question of whether group consciousness influences Black immigrants'
political behavior, I hypothesize the following:

> H_8: Group consciousness will play an influential role in participation rates
> for Black immigrants and African Americans, especially in nontradi-
> tional areas of participation.

In order to test these four hypotheses (H_5-H_8), I investigate the role
that racial group consciousness plays in shaping Blacks' attitudes in five
policy areas, which serve as dependent variables. Three of the policy
areas are racially salient issue areas (government's role in improving the
status of Blacks, minority voting districts, and reparations to Blacks).[62]
The other two policy areas are general issue areas (abortion and allowing lesbian or gay people to adopt children). This array of dependent
variables allows me to gain a sense of whether racial group consciousness has a greater influence on some policy areas than others.

The first general issue is abortion, and the dependent variable is
based on the survey item "A woman should always be able to obtain
an abortion." The other general issue dependent variable is based on
the survey item "Homosexual, gay or lesbian, couples should be legally
permitted to adopt children." The respondents could choose among
four options on a Likert scale from "strongly disagree" (1) to "strongly
agree" (4).

The three racially salient issues were chosen because they clearly
affect Blacks in the United States at both the local level and the national
level. One of the racially salient questions concerns the extent to which
respondents believe the government has a role in improving the status
of Blacks; the survey item is worded, "The government should make
every effort to improve the social and economic position of Blacks living in the United States." Second, given that the ability of Blacks to be
placed in districts where they can have a substantial influence in choosing a representative has long been of importance among Blacks in the
United States,[63] I utilize a survey item that refers to this constant struggle: "Political districts need to be formed so that more racial minority

candidates can be elected." Finally, I utilize a question concerning reparations, which is clearly racialized as Black: "The government should give reparations (compensation, payback) to African Americans for historical injustices and slavery." Again, the respondents could choose among four options: "strongly disagree" (1), "somewhat disagree" (2), "somewhat agree" (3), or "strongly agree" (4).

The second set of dependent variables concerns political behavior—or political participation. Respondents were asked if they had campaigned for a political party, contacted a representative, or voted in a previous election. Respondents answered either in the affirmative or the negative.

In addition to testing for the role of group consciousness, I include variables concerning political orientation. Here, I measure partisanship, which is represented by a dummy variable for Democrat (1). Independents and Republicans are combined and compared against Democrats in this model.[64] Further, I measure ideology on a seven-point scale from "extremely liberal" (1) to "extremely conservative" (7).

I include a very similar set of control variables as I did in the previous series of analyses: family household income, level of education, age, and gender. I also include variables concerning the extent to which respondents have had political and racialized experiences. I include a binary variable that measures whether a respondent belongs to a group that works toward improving the well-being of Blacks in America. I utilize this variable because scholars provide evidence that participation in these racially aimed mobilizing structures serves to bolster a psychological attachment to a racial identity.[65] I also account for experiences with discrimination. Finally, since levels of acculturation are likely to influence Black immigrants' political outcomes, I include generational status and citizenship when appropriate.

Political Attitudes: Multivariate Results

For each policy domain, I run two models. The first model includes only variables relevant to both African Americans and Black immigrants. The second of each pair includes an additional variable—generational status—to gain leverage on the extent to which levels of acculturation influence Black immigrants' political outcomes. Since the dependent variables—policy attitudes—are based on a Likert scale, I used ordered logistic regression, and the tables report the odds ratios and 95 percent confidence intervals, which allow for a more intuitive interpretation of the results.[66]

The first stage of the analysis is to assess the role of racial group consciousness on the general and racially salient policy areas for Black immigrants. The first hypothesis asserted that racial group consciousness should play a role in racialized policy areas for Black immigrants but not necessarily in general issue areas. The results in table 5.2 illustrate the influence of group consciousness on racialized policy area attitudes, while the results in table 5.3 focus on general policy area attitudes for Black immigrants.

The results in table 5.2 provide mixed support for the stated hypothesis. Concerning racialized policies, linked fate affects policy attitudes related to reparations but not the policies concerning the government's role in improving the status of Blacks or creating districts where minorities could be more easily elected. Those respondents with a higher sense of linked fate expressed more support for reparations for African Americans. Through the analysis of a series of face-to-face interviews, Rogers shows that Black immigrants share feelings of respect for African Americans' struggles in the United States, and perhaps the results here corroborate those findings.[67] Additionally, as Black immigrants experience more discrimination, they are more supportive of reparations for African Americans. This, however, is the only issue area influenced by linked fate for Black immigrants.

Only generational status influences levels of support for creating districts that allow for minorities to be more easily elected. Second-generation immigrants are more supportive of policies aimed to create such districts. Perhaps second-generation immigrants are more likely to recognize the importance of descriptive representation than first-generation immigrants are because they have been socialized in the United States. Table 5.2 also illustrates determinants of feelings concerning the role of the government in improving the status of Blacks. This policy attitude is only influenced by partisanship among Black immigrants. Again, Democrats are more supportive of such ideas. Second-generation immigrants are not significantly different from those in the first generation in this domain.

Table 5.2. Determinants of Black Immigrants' Racialized Policy Attitudes

	Improve position		Minority districts		Reparations	
	Comparative model	Full model	Comparative model	Full model	Comparative model	Full model
	OR (95% CI)	OR (95% CI)	OR (95% CI)	OR (95% CI)	OR (95% CI)	OR (95% CI)
Group Consciousness						
Linked fate	1.094	1.077	1.116	1.089	1.178**	1.155*
	(0.930– 1.287)	(0.914– 1.269)	(0.950– 1.310)	(0.926– 1.282)	(1.005– 1.381)	(0.983– 1.356)
SES/Demographics						
Income	0.918	0.917	0.962	0.962	0.955	0.950
	(0.813– 1.037)	(0.812– 1.036)	(0.865– 1.070)	(0.865– 1.071)	(0.854– 1.069)	(0.849– 1.064)
Education	0.981	0.981	0.876	0.874	0.935	0.937
	(0.807– 1.193)	(0.807– 1.194)	(0.724– 1.061)	(0.721– 1.059)	(0.775– 1.128)	(0.777– 1.131)
Gender (male = 1)	0.807	0.824	1.106	1.152	0.772	0.792
	(0.541– 1.202)	(0.552– 1.229)	(0.754– 1.621)	(0.784– 1.693)	(0.528– 1.130)	(0.541– 1.160)
Age	0.997	0.999	1.005	1.007	0.993	0.994
	(0.985– 1.010)	(0.986– 1.012)	(0.993– 1.018)	(0.994– 1.020)	(0.980– 1.005)	(0.982– 1.006)
Political Orientation						
Partisanship (Dem = 1)	1.991***	1.973***	1.422	1.393	1.425*	1.405
	(1.291– 3.073)	(1.278– 3.046)	(0.928– 2.178)	(0.909– 2.137)	(0.939– 2.162)	(0.926– 2.132)
Ideology	0.897*	0.905	0.909	0.923	0.991	1.005
	(0.793– 1.015)	(0.799– 1.025)	(0.805– 1.026)	(0.817– 1.043)	(0.882– 1.114)	(0.893– 1.132)
Political Activity/Experience						
Black organization	0.618	0.599	0.760	0.733	1.618	1.591
	(0.332– 1.150)	(0.320– 1.118)	(0.412– 1.402)	(0.396– 1.356)	(0.895– 2.925)	(0.879– 2.881)
Minor discrimination experience	1.006	1.004	1.000	0.998	0.989	0.988
	(0.979– 1.033)	(0.977– 1.032)	(0.974– 1.026)	(0.973– 1.024)	(0.964– 1.015)	(0.962– 1.013)
Major discrimination experience	1.072	1.066	1.018	1.008	1.149**	1.137*
	(0.932– 1.233)	(0.926– 1.227)	(0.892– 1.162)	(0.882– 1.151)	(1.004– 1.314)	(0.993– 1.302)
Generational Status						
Second generation		1.319		1.469*		1.404*
		(0.864– 2.014)		(0.975– 2.213)		(0.938– 2.102)
Observations	443	443	431	431	432	432
Pseudo R^2	0.0261	0.0281	0.0123	0.0156	0.0177	0.0202

Notes: Coefficients based on order logistic regression. P-values based on two-tailed test.

*** $p < 0.01$, ** $p < 0.05$, * $p < 0.1$

Table 5.3. Determinants of Black Immigrants' General Policy Attitudes

	Abortion		LGBT adoption	
	Comparative model	Full model	Comparative model	Full model
	OR (95% CI)	OR (95% CI)	OR (95% CI)	OR (95% CI)
Group Consciousness				
Linked fate	1.094	1.087	1.075	1.007
	(0.936–1.278)	(0.929–1.271)	(0.919–1.258)	(0.857–1.183)
SES/Demographics				
Income	1.178***	1.178***	1.045	1.039
	(1.050–1.322)	(1.050–1.322)	(0.934–1.168)	(0.930–1.162)
Education	1.171*	1.169*	1.095	1.100
	(0.975–1.405)	(0.974–1.403)	(0.909–1.320)	(0.912–1.327)
Gender (male = 1)	0.642**	0.646**	0.565***	0.608**
	(0.440–0.936)	(0.442–0.944)	(0.383–0.832)	(0.412–0.898)
Age	0.983***	0.984***	0.982***	0.985**
	(0.971–0.995)	(0.972–0.996)	(0.970–0.994)	(0.973–0.998)
Political Orientation				
Partisanship (Dem = 1)	1.627**	1.618**	1.288	1.219
	(1.088–2.432)	(1.081–2.420)	(0.850–1.951)	(0.800–1.857)
Ideology	0.847***	0.850***	0.945	0.971
	(0.753–0.953)	(0.756–0.957)	(0.837–1.066)	(0.859–1.097)
Political Activity/Experience				
Black organization	1.192	1.183	0.769	0.708
	(0.669–2.122)	(0.664–2.108)	(0.416–1.422)	(0.381–1.316)
Minor discrimination experience	1.008	1.007	1.018	1.013
	(0.982–1.033)	(0.982–1.033)	(0.992–1.043)	(0.987–1.038)
Major discrimination experience	1.026	1.021	1.005	0.989
	(0.900–1.170)	(0.895–1.166)	(0.881–1.146)	(0.867–1.129)
Generational Status				
Second generation		1.125		2.395***
		(0.761–1.663)		(1.606–3.573)
Observations	432	432	434	434
Pseudo R²	0.0446	0.0449	0.0283	0.0447

Notes: Coefficients based on order logistic regression. *P*-values based on two-tailed test.
*** $p < 0.01$, ** $p < 0.05$, * $p < 0.1$

Moving to table 5.3, which includes the results for determining Black immigrants' "general" policy attitudes, we see that racial group consciousness does not influence either Black immigrants' abortion policy attitudes or policy attitudes concerning LGBT adoption, as predicted by the first hypothesis. Instead, abortion attitudes are primarily influenced by socioeconomic and demographic characteristics as well as political orientation.[68] Several of the control variables are statistically significant and in the expected direction. While individuals with higher incomes and education levels as well as Democrats have more liberal attitudes on this policy issue, older Black immigrants and males are more likely to be against abortion, noted by an odds ratio of less than one. The results also reveal that those respondents who are ideologically more conservative are also less supportive of abortion. Similarly, the policy area concerning the ability of lesbian or gay people to adopt is primarily influenced by demographic characteristics rather than linked fate among Black immigrants. Males and older Black immigrants expressed more conservative attitudes in this policy area. Second-generation immigrants are more supportive of the issue of LGBT adoption but not abortion. Overall, Black immigrants' sense of linked fate influences a restricted set of racial policies but not any of the tested general issue areas. Next, we turn to African Americans' attitudes.

The second hypothesis asserted that the role of group consciousness for African Americans will not be restricted to only racialized policies as it is for Black immigrants, but rather we should expect African Americans' politicized identities to influence attitudes in both racialized and non-racially-salient policy domains. Table 5.4 provides the results of the second hypothesis's test. As expected, we see that racial group consciousness influences both racialized policy attitudes and general issue policy attitudes for African Americans. African Americans' sense of group consciousness influences more policy domains than Black immigrants' sense of group consciousness does.

The results in table 5.4 indicate that in addition to linked fate, African Americans' income and political orientation influences attitudes concerning the role of the government in improving the status of Blacks in this country. African American Democrats are more supportive of each of these policies. However, those with higher levels of income are less supportive of the government improving the status of Blacks. Actually, this pattern shows up across each of the racially salient policies; as one's income increases, there is less support for the government improving the position of Blacks, providing reparations, or creating districts where minority candidates have a greater chance of getting elected. These findings run against the grain of the expectations of classical Black politics literature, which tend to anticipate that as income and education increases, Blacks are likely to be more supportive of policies aimed

Table 5.4. *Determinants of African Americans' Policy Attitudes*

	Racialized policies			General policies	
	Political districts	Improve status	Reparations	Abortion	LBGT adoption
	OR (95% CI)	OR (95% CI)	OR (95% CI)	OR (95% CI)	OR (95% CI)
Group Consciousness					
Linked fate	1.162***	1.125**	1.143***	1.121***	1.071*
	(1.063–1.269)	(1.028–1.231)	(1.047–1.248)	(1.031–1.219)	(0.984–1.166)
SES/Demographics					
Income	0.927**	0.905***	0.929*	1.034	0.964
	(0.863–0.997)	(0.840–0.975)	(0.862–1.001)	(0.964–1.109)	(0.896–1.037)
Education	0.936	0.921	1.002	1.182***	1.063
	(0.837–1.048)	(0.821–1.033)	(0.896–1.121)	(1.062–1.316)	(0.955–1.183)
Gender (male = 1)	0.951	0.849	0.867	0.938	0.771**
	(0.768–1.177)	(0.682–1.057)	(0.700–1.074)	(0.765–1.150)	(0.625–0.951)
Age	1.004	1.006*	1.014***	0.994**	0.982***
	(0.997–1.010)	(0.999–1.013)	(1.007–1.021)	(0.987–1.000)	(0.976–0.989)
Political Orientation					
Partisanship (Dem = 1)	1.574***	1.601***	1.343**	1.331**	0.936
	(1.243–1.993)	(1.264–2.026)	(1.065–1.694)	(1.063–1.666)	(0.746–1.174)
Ideology	1.031	0.965	1.003	0.903***	0.898***
	(0.962–1.105)	(0.900–1.035)	(0.936–1.074)	(0.845–0.964)	(0.840–0.960)
Political Activity/Experience					
Black organization	1.205	1.455**	1.148	1.451**	1.366**
	(0.883–1.645)	(1.056–2.003)	(0.843–1.564)	(1.083–1.945)	(1.017–1.835)
Minor discrimination experience	1.009	1.013**	1.022***	0.999	1.004
	(0.997–1.022)	(1.000–1.027)	(1.009–1.035)	(0.987–1.011)	(0.992–1.017)
Major discrimination experience	1.025	1.061*	1.116***	0.993	0.955
	(0.962–1.092)	(0.993–1.135)	(1.044–1.192)	(0.934–1.055)	(0.896–1.017)
Observations	1,446	1,484	1,470	1,468	1,463
Pseudo R^2	0.0124	0.0201	0.0236	0.0170	0.0171

Notes: Coefficients based on order logistic regression. P-values based on two-ailed test.
*** $p < 0.01$, ** $p < 0.05$, * $p < 0.1$

to improve the status of Blacks.[69] These findings, which are based on newer data, speak to Katherine Tate's more recent study that suggests African Americans, in general, are becoming more conservative.[70]

African Americans' sense of linked fate also plays a role in nonracial policy areas. Linked fate is an important predictor of abortion attitudes ($p < .10$). The odds of supporting abortion rights for women increase as linked fate increases. Along with linked fate, the results illuminate that as African Americans' level of education increase, their attitudes about abortion rights become more liberal. Further, those who are Democrats and are liberal in their political ideology are more supportive of a woman's right to choose abortion. What is more, older African Americans are less supportive of abortion and lesbian and gay adoption, as expected from what we see in the American population as a whole. Similar to abortion attitudes, linked fate also positively influences attitudes about LGBT adoption, but just outside the traditional upper cutoff, where $p = .11$.

In many ways, these findings are counterintuitive, especially as they relate to LGBT adoption. African Americans are, on average, quite conservative about these types of issues, and we see that ideologically conservative African Americans are less likely to support LGBT adoption. Cathy Cohen notes that gay members of Black communities often face the consequences of "secondary marginalization"; instead of receiving support, gay and lesbian African Americans are ostracized.[71] But there have been signs of a shift in African Americans' opinions about issues of gay rights and marriage equality. Near the end of President Barack Obama's first term, he reported a shift in his own attitudes toward equal rights for gay and lesbian citizens. Later in 2012, the board of the National Association for the Advancement of Colored People (NAACP) supported a resolution calling for marriage equality—although not without some pushback from some of its members. The NAACP's resolution also "commits the group to fight against any effort to write discrimination against lesbian, gay, bisexual and transgender community into law."[72] By referencing the Fourteenth Amendment, the NAACP in many ways makes a parallel between African Americans' struggle for equality and that of LGBT community members.

This sentiment also resounded among my African American interview respondents. For example, Amir mentioned in his interview, which preceded both the president's change of heart and the release of the NAACP's resolution, "Giving equality to people who are gay or lesbian is important to me just because I feel a connection with that community based on the struggle that Black folks have gone through." Similarly, Laura, an African American woman, stated, "I really think we need social justice for everyone, you know. I believe in gay rights, immigrant rights, everything. So anything that will promote the full and equal and equitable participation of all people in society." The notion of "injustice anywhere is a threat to justice everywhere" seems to be prevalent among African Americans, as marked by the effect of racial group consciousness on these issues of fairness and equality for women and member of LGBT communities.

To summarize, the hypothesis that African Americans' sense of group consciousness will influence more domains of policy—including policy areas without clear racial content—than Black immigrants' is supported here. African Americans' sense of linked fate has a broad influence on their policy attitudes, while Black immigrants' sense of racial group consciousness only influences a clearly racialized policy area.

Political Behavior: Descriptive Results

In order to compare rates of participation, difference in proportions tests between African Americans' and Black immigrants' participation rates were executed. The results reveal expected differences between groups. Each Black immigrant group was compared to African Americans to test the third hypothesis, which predicted that Black immigrants tend to participate at lower levels than African Americans.

Table 5.5 reveals that African Americans tend to vote at higher rates than immigrants of West Indian, Haitian, and African descent, as expected. The results, however, show that second-generation Black immigrants tend to vote at higher levels than their first-generation counterparts but at the same levels as African Americans. The second and third rows illustrate rates of participation with political campaigns and contacting a representative, respectively. In comparison to voting, there is a major drop-off in these two less traditional forms of participation. African Americans and second-generation Black immigrants tend to work with political parties and campaigns at the same rate. When

Table 5.5. African American and Black Immigrant Rates of Political Participation

	African Americans	All Black immigrants	West Indian	Haitian	African	First gen.	Second gen.
		Black immigrants					
Voted in previous election (%)	62.9	50.3*	51.1*	52.1*	25.0*	43.8*	65.4
	(n = 2,064)	(n = 603)	(n = 511)	(n = 73)	(n = 20)	(n = 418)	(n = 182)
Campaigned for a political party (%)	16.2	11.6*	12.6*	5.4*	10.0	9.6*	16.6
	(n = 2,065)	(n = 602)	(n = 509)	(n = 74)	(n = 20)	(n = 418)	(n = 181)
Contacted a representative (%)	26.2	25.3	26.0	23.0	15.0	21.0*	35.2*
	(n = 2,069)	(n = 604)	(n = 511)	(n = 74)	(n = 20)	(n = 419)	(n = 182)

* Significantly different from African American sample, 95 percent confidence level, one-tail.

looking at differences between ethnic groups, the results provide evidence for the fact that African Americans tend to work with political parties more often than Black immigrants, generally, and more often than West Indians and Haitians, specifically.

The third row reveals that African Americans and Black immigrants of various ethnicities tend to contact their representatives at about the same rates. The major differences surfaced when Black immigrants are disaggregated by generational status. The last two columns show that first-generation Black immigrants contact their representatives at lower rates than African Americans, but interestingly, second-generation Black immigrants tend to contact representatives more often than African Americans.

We might gain a better understanding of the results showing that second-generation Black immigrants tend to participate at levels on par with or exceeding African Americans' by using the Asian and Latino politics literature, which centers differences in ethnicity and levels of acculturation in its analyses. Within this literature, we see that second-generation immigrants tend to participate at higher levels than first-generation naturalized immigrants.[73] The results presented here indicate that second-generation immigrants mirror African Americans' political behaviors. Perhaps the differences between first- and second-generation immigrants reveal the differences in political socialization, particularly as this socialization relates to shaping attitudes toward the role of the government and the relationship between constituents and political representatives. The results may also derive from the fact that members of the second generation have very high levels of group consciousness.

Political Behavior: Multivariate Results

Tables 5.6, 5.7, and 5.8 report odds ratios and 95 percent confidence intervals, based on logistic regression analyses, for the effect of linked fate on voting, contacting a representative, and campaigning for a political party or representative, respectively. For each area of participation, I present a model for African Americans and an identical one for Black immigrants; then, I include an additional model, which allows us to discern the influence of citizenship and generational status on Black immigrants' political behavior. Overall, these models show, on the one hand, that group consciousness does have a significant effect on the political behaviors of Black immigrants and African Americans, but on the other hand, the results reveal that linked fate influences African Americans and Black immigrants in different ways.

Table 5.6 reveals the role linked fate has on voting for African Americans and Black immigrants. The models suggest that group consciousness does not have an influence on whether African Americans or Black immigrants vote. The question wording of the "vote" question asks respondents if they voted in a previous election, but it does not specify whether the election was local, national, or in some other country. Nonetheless, the results in the last column of table 5.6 show that American citizenship plays an important role in Black immigrants' voting behavior. Additionally, the results suggest that acculturation matters a great deal as well; second-generation respondents are much more likely than their first-generation counterparts to vote.

Table 5.7 summarizes the effects of the independent variables on whether respondents have ever called or written a public official about a concern or a problem. Here, linked fate is a significant determinant of both African Americans' and Black immigrants' interactive behavior with their political representatives. For a standard deviation increase in linked fate, the odds of contacting a representative are 1.2 times greater

Table 5.6. Determinants of Political Participation:
Voted in Previous Election

	African Americans	Black immigrants (comparative)	Black immigrants (full)
	OR (95% CI)	OR (95% CI)	OR (95% CI)
Group Consciousness			
Linked fate	1.013	1.068	1.071
	(0.918–1.118)	(0.901–1.267)	(0.865–1.327)
SES/Demographics			
Income	1.135**	1.298***	1.316***
	(1.029–1.252)	(1.134–1.487)	(1.104–1.569)
Education	1.485***	1.113	1.151
	(1.303–1.694)	(0.904–1.371)	(0.891–1.488)
Gender (male = 1)	0.674***	0.796	0.749
	(0.529–0.857)	(0.523–1.210)	(0.442–1.270)
Age	1.034***	1.043***	1.047***
	(1.026–1.042)	(1.029–1.058)	(1.028–1.066)
Political Orientation			
Partisanship (Dem = 1)	2.289***	2.249***	2.696***
	(1.788–2.931)	(1.433–3.529)	(1.563–4.649)
Ideology	1.004	1.095	1.091
	(0.929–1.085)	(0.959–1.249)	(0.927–1.285)
Generation/Citizenship			
Second generation			52.80***
			(21.47–129.8)
Citizen			58.29***
			(24.22–140.3)
Observations	1,646	490	490
Pseudo R^2	0.107	0.132	0.402

Notes: Coefficients based on logistic regression. *P*-values based on two-tailed test.
*** $p < 0.01$, ** $p < 0.05$, * $p < 0.1$

for African Americans and 1.3 times greater for Black immigrants. In addition to group consciousness, African Americans with higher levels of education and those who are older are more likely to contact a public official. What is more, those African Americans who are more liberal in their political ideology are more likely to contact a representative. Among Black immigrants, both socioeconomic indicators—income and education—as well as age are important determinants of this aspect of participation in addition to linked fate. The results here also show that citizenship status and generational status significantly influence Black immigrants' political behavior; those who are citizens

Table 5.7. Determinants of Political Participation:
Contact a Representative

	African Americans	Black immigrants (comparative)	Black immigrants (full)
	OR (95% CI)	OR (95% CI)	OR (95% CI)
Group Consciousness			
Linked fate	1.185***	1.344***	1.303***
	(1.068–1.315)	(1.113–1.622)	(1.075–1.579)
SES/Demographics			
Income	1.032	1.227***	1.212***
	(0.947–1.124)	(1.081–1.394)	(1.065–1.380)
Education	1.860***	1.300**	1.317**
	(1.631–2.121)	(1.035–1.634)	(1.045–1.659)
Gender (male = 1)	1.018	0.792	0.823
	(0.793–1.306)	(0.502–1.251)	(0.517–1.309)
Age	1.041***	1.020***	1.020***
	(1.033–1.049)	(1.005–1.035)	(1.005–1.036)
Political Orientation			
Partisanship (Dem = 1)	1.030	1.350	1.314
	(0.771–1.376)	(0.799–2.281)	(0.771–2.240)
Ideology	0.925*	0.997	1.018
	(0.852–1.004)	(0.864–1.151)	(0.879–1.180)
Generation/Citizenship			
Second generation			3.054***
			(1.654–5.639)
Citizen			1.865**
			(1.012–3.439)
Observations	1,646	491	491
Pseudo R^2	0.123	0.0805	0.105

Notes: Coefficients based on logistic regression. *P*-values based on two-tailed test.
*** $p < 0.01$, ** $p < 0.05$, * $p < 0.1$

and second-generation Black immigrants are more likely to contact a representative.

Finally, table 5.8 provides insight into the determinants of the third form of participation: campaigning for a political candidate or working for a political party. Here, there are some differences between African Americans and Black immigrants. Linked fate does not play a significant role in African Americans' participation with political parties, but Black immigrants are motivated by a sense of group consciousness in this area of participation. Among African Americans, levels of education, age, partisanship, and ideology influence this mode of participation. Among Black immigrants, the influence of linked fate is joined by education and age as determinants of this form of behavior. Here, generational status influences outcomes, but citizenship does not. Those in the second generation are two times more likely to engage with a political party than those in the first generation.

While many scholars have shown the important influence that group consciousness has on African Americans political behavior, Chong and Rogers found that when we disaggregate modes of participation, group consciousness only influences some types of participation.[74] In their analysis of the 1984 National Black Election Study, Chong and Rogers

Table 5.8. Determinants of Political Participation: Campaign for a Political Party

	African Americans OR (95% CI)	Black immigrants (comparative) OR (95% CI)	Black immigrants (full) OR (95% CI)
Group Consciousness			
Linked fate	1.095	1.344***	1.296**
	(0.972–1.234)	(1.113–1.622)	(1.004–1.673)
SES/Demographics			
Income	0.982	1.227***	1.003
	(0.891–1.082)	(1.081–1.394)	(0.845–1.192)
Education	1.686***	1.300**	1.390**
	(1.457–1.952)	(1.035–1.634)	(1.025–1.885)
Gender (male = 1)	1.049	0.792	1.684*
	(0.790–1.394)	(0.502–1.251)	(0.940–3.019)
Age	1.023***	1.020***	1.033***
	(1.014–1.032)	(1.005–1.035)	(1.013–1.052)
Political Orientation			
Partisanship (Dem = 1)	1.699***	1.350	1.059
	(1.180–2.447)	(0.799–2.281)	(0.535–2.098)
Ideology	0.876***	0.997	1.029
	(0.797–0.963)	(0.864–1.151)	(0.849–1.247)
Generation/Citizenship			
Second generation			2.023*
			(0.953–4.296)
Citizen			0.903
			(0.409–1.994)
Observations	1,645	489	489
Pseudo R²	0.0787	0.0676	0.0849

Notes: Coefficients based on logistic regression. *P*-values based on two-tailed test.
*** *p* < 0.01, ** *p* < 0.05, * *p* < 0.1

found that group consciousness has only a modest effect on voter turn-out among African Americans, but a politicized racial identity has significant effects on African American participation in campaign activities, petitioning government officials, and participation in boycotts and protests.[75] The models here, which employ new data, not only allow us to update what we know about African Americans, but new data also allow us to make more nuanced conclusions about how ethnicity, acculturation, and citizenship influence Blacks' political behaviors and to advance this previous work. For example, the results show that group consciousness does not affect either African Americans' voting behavior or participation with political campaigns, as previously reported. Perhaps, this shift is to be expected; Bobo and Gilliam have suggested that as African Americans gain more control in the political realm, we should see a decline in the influence of group consciousness on their political behavior.[76] Nonetheless, group consciousness does influence African Americans' behavior as it concerns contacting a political representative, and group consciousness leads Black immigrants to contact political officials and campaign for a political party. Overall, the results show that group consciousness does not influence all behaviors equally and, more importantly, that it does not influence all groups of Blacks in the same way.

* * *

A number of scholars have put forward a warning, stating that we may not be able to superimpose what we know based on the analysis of African Americans on other racial and ethnic minority groups, especially those groups that are immigrant replenished.[77] The goal of this chapter has been to examine group consciousness, which is an incredibly important step in the identity-to-politics link, but to do so in a way that allows us to determine if ethnic differences preclude group consciousness or simply modify it. More specifically, the goals of this chapter have been to establish whether Black immigrants have a sense of racial group consciousness, to capture the determinants of the construct, and to assess if Black immigrants link their racial identity to their political attitudes and behaviors in the way we have historically seen African Americans do. By analyzing data from the NSAL and from face-to-face interviews, this chapter has provided insight into the many similarities between African Americans' and Black immigrants' levels, determinants, and effects of group consciousness as well as has shed light on the important differences that arise.

Taken together, the results reveal that a lot of what we know about African American racial group consciousness can be extended to Black immigrants. Feelings of closeness to group members, racial centrality, experiences with discrimination, and racial socialization work to develop and heighten a sense of group consciousness among African Americans and Black immigrants alike. But there are some differences among Black immigrants and African Americans, which demonstrates that there is a need for a more flexible theory such as diasporic consciousness. For example, the analyses tell us that we should consider the generational status of Black immigrants when trying to understand or explain the extent to which identity is linked to politics for this group. Generational status and, therefore, socialization and acculturation in American society affect the development of racial group consciousness. The results in this chapter suggest that second-generation immigrants tend to have a higher sense of racial consciousness than first-generation immigrants. Since African Americans have been in the U.S. for several generations, generational status has not been an important factor in the previous Black politics literature, but these results compel us to consider the notion that as the immigration of Afro-Caribbeans, Afro-Latinos, and Africans remains a factor in the growth of the Black population, factors such as generational status and acculturation will need to be considered.

Although the policy areas and the various modes of political participation analyzed in this chapter are by no means exhaustive, they do help to provide answers to the questions presented at the beginning of the chapter. The results show that Black immigrants' political attitudes and behaviors are influenced by a sense of racial group consciousness but not necessarily in the same way as we have seen group consciousness influence African Americans. The results indicate that Black immigrants' sense of group consciousness plays a role in their political attitudes in some racially salient policy areas, and the number of policy domains affected by Black immigrants' sense of linked fate is much smaller than what we see for African Americans. Black immigrants' sense of group consciousness has a significant influence in their attitudes about reparations to African Americans but not in other racialized areas such as shaping voting districts that would allow minorities to be more easily elected or calling for the government to improve the status of Blacks in the United States. African Americans' sense of group consciousness, in comparison, influences all the tested racial policy domains as well as the nonracial policy areas of abortion and, to some extent, lesbian and gay adoption rights.

Additionally, this study illuminates differences in the way linked fate influences African Americans' and Black immigrants' political behaviors. Linked fate is an important determinant for African Americans' interactive political behavior. Interestingly, linked fate seems to have broader influence on Black immigrants' political behavior than it does on African Americans'. The results may reflect two sides of the same coin. Historically, group consciousness has tended to influence African Americans in nontraditional participation such as protesting or boycotting.[78] The fact that we see narrow influence of group consciousness on African American political behavior may suggest that as Blacks in the U.S. have gained more access to the political realm, they need less additional impetus, such as group consciousness, to participate in methods beyond voting. On the other side of the coin, Black immigrants are new to the U.S. and thus are less accustomed to the American political system; group consciousness may serve as the additional motivation needed to interact with a system that is more familiar to their African American (and second-generation) counterparts.

This chapter provides evidence for the idea that the ethnic diversity among Blacks in the United States may lead to an increase in the diversity in political attitudes and behavior among this group, which could have consequences for intragroup relations. Consider again the possibilities illustrated in figure 2.2. If Black immigrants and African Americans do not prioritize the same issues, we may see fissures in potential intraracial coalitions. The next chapter will delve into this issue more deeply.

6

Perspectives on Intraracial Coalition and Conflict

The color line mandates racial solidarity under all circumstances.
—Tunde Adeleke

It is . . . clear that the time for undiscriminating racial unity
has passed.
—Toni Morrison

A theory of diasporic consciousness rests on a bed of tension. On
one hand, we see that among African Americans and Black immigrants, shared discriminatory experiences not only help foster a shared
grouped identity but also politicize this identity, and in turn, this politicized identity is mobilized into political action that is geared toward
ameliorating racial disparities and improving the group's status. On the
other hand, ethnic diversity, like any other type of diversity, promotes
a miscellany of ideas about how to accomplish goals. This is not much
different from the ideological diversity that has existed among African
Americans for a century and a half.[1] The tension underlying a diasporic
consciousness derives primarily from the fact that while native- and
foreign-born Blacks embrace a shared racial identity, they also maintain
separate and distinct ethnic identities.

Michael Dawson notes, "the relative homogeneity of black public opinion has been generally considered one of the few certainties
of modern American politics,"[2] but this certainty is based on a partial
truth. African Americans' perspectives, attitudes, and behaviors are not
monolithic. There are some major divisions among African Americans'
political attitudes related to economic, ideological, and gender-based
divisions, and these divisions have made a unified Black agenda difficult to develop. Moreover, the prospects for a unified Black political

agenda may be further complicated by the fact that ethnic diversity among Black people is increasing.

Adolph Reed challenges scholars to first construct a more appropriate conceptualization of Black identity before attempting to decide what issues are or should be on a Black political agenda.[3] As previously mentioned, while African Americans and Black immigrants debate who can be called Black and who is considered a member of the Black community, it seems clear that both groups have a very broad conceptualization of who is Black (see chapter 3). This broader definition of Black identity could also influence what issues African Americans and Black immigrants consider important. The questions this chapter seeks to answer, then, are as follows: African Americans view Black immigrants as racial compatriots (and vice versa), but do native-born African Americans deem the political issues of Black immigrants important? Have the contours of the Black political agenda expanded to include issues that may be of particular import to Black immigrants? That is, has the Black agenda expanded in a manner that is consistent with the recognition of the increasing ethnic diversity among Blacks in the United States? What are the prospects for an intraracial coalition? A theory of diasporic consciousness helps us to recognize that at the end of the identity-to-politics link, there is the possibility that the policy matters of importance to one ethnic group may be quite different from, and even contradictory to, the matters of importance to another group, thereby troubling the potential unity among Blacks.

While Black political elites play a major role in developing and framing the Black political agenda,[4] I am interested in how ordinary African Americans and Black immigrants develop their own political agendas. I rely on my informants' responses to a series of questions aimed to gauge opinions concerning the issues that of are importance to African Americans and Black immigrants. Their answers also elucidate the extent to which native- and foreign-born Blacks agree or disagree on various policy matters. Finally, the respondents shed light on the range of opinions African Americans and Black immigrants have concerning the prospects of and their desire for an intraracial political coalition and a shared pan-ethnic political agenda.

Before examining the responses, I take a step back to briefly discuss how "the" Black agenda has been conceptualized and depicted in the existing research on Black politics and then move on to discuss what ethnic diversity might mean for the prospects of a unified Black agenda. Next, I outline hypotheses concerning what issues Blacks feel are important, and finally, I analyze the in-depth interview data that illuminate Blacks' prescriptions and proscriptions for Black pan-ethnic coalitions.

"The" Black Agenda

Among African Americans, there is widespread agreement on political and social goals and objectives for the group.[5] While it has been shown that the African American identity-to-politics link—or the influence of group identity on political attitudes—is strong,[6] the extent to which a "universal" Black political agenda exists is contested. For example, William Raspberry argues quite simply that "there is no black agenda"; but he goes on to assert that if there ever was one, it is shrinking and now only includes "affirmative action, incarceration rates of African Americans, and the sentencing disparities between crack and cocaine charges."[7]

There are others who very much disagree. Matthew Platt, for example, argues, "Black agenda setting in the post-[Vietnam] war era is fundamentally a story about change."[8] In the 1950s, the primary item on the Black agenda was voting rights, but after voting rights were attained and segregation was legally dismantled, there remained a set of core issues that affected Black people disproportionately that had not yet been remedied, including "full employment, guaranteed income, national health insurance, federal funding of education, and affirmative action."[9] Arguably, these issues are still on the table. Dona Hamilton and Charles Hamilton argue that the Black agenda includes issues of civil rights and also social welfare.[10] Similarly, Hanes Walton and Robert Smith suggest that the Black agenda is a "broad-based policy agenda encompassing both rights and material based issues."[11] For these scholars, the existence of a Black political agenda is taken as a given, but as Chryl Laird explains, "the contention surrounding how to define the Black Agenda is often related to changes that have occurred in the Black community and society over time."[12]

While a shared racial identity and group consciousness makes Blacks look to improve their position, there are differences that cannot be explained by linked fate.[13] Even though many Blacks have a high sense of linked fate, there still exists an incredible amount of diversity among African Americans' political attitudes and ideologies. Homogeneity in political behavior belies the diversity of African Americans' political attitudes; this homogeneity also serves to perpetuate the myth that Black people in the United States have been (and will continue to be) in political lockstep with one another. There have always been some differences in the political choices, opinions, and claims of Blacks in this society, and with diversity comes dissent. As such, "the" Black agenda has always had some fractures.[14] Ideological diversity and class bifurcation are two important sources of diversity, but a broadening set of Black identities also serves to increase the array of Black political agendas that may exist.

Potential Implications of Ethnic Diversity on "the" Black Political Agenda

The broadening set of identities to which Blacks are now allowed to make claim has caused considerable dissent among African Americans. The rise of the multiracial "Mark One or More" movement, for example, has sparked debates concerning "the" Black agenda.[15] The Mark One or More movement was an effort to create a multiracial category in the U.S. Census. Although some individuals desired the opportunity to communicate that being multiracial shaped their reality in a legitimating document such as the U.S. Census, Black civil rights leaders largely opposed the movement, claiming it would impede ongoing efforts to gauge progress in the fight against disparities between "traditional" racial (i.e., white, Black, Asian, American Indian) and ethnic (i.e., Hispanic) groups. This debate about "who is Black" is important because it has as much to do with individual Americans' self-identification as it does with allocating financial resources, civil rights, and political representation in African American communities across the country.

We might also consider the ways in which the increasing ethnic diversity of Blacks may influence Black political agenda setting. Black immigrants share with African Americans similar experiences of discrimination and racism in housing and employment markets as well as in day-to-day interactions. However, Black immigrants, especially first-generation immigrants, not only bring a different set of issues to the table (issues such as immigrant rights and homeland politics, which speak more to U.S. foreign policy than domestic policy) but also may see these issues from a different perspective than African Americans do. For example, Haitian immigrants may feel that the United States should provide more foreign aid to Haiti, while African Americans may feel that resources currently devoted to foreign aid should be used instead to improve schools in their communities. Similarly, issues surrounding immigrant rights and immigration policies may also be important for both African Americans and Black immigrants but in different ways. Black immigrants may feel that being able to immigrate into the United States should be made easier, while African Americans may feel that rates of immigration should decline.

Although Black immigrants share a racial group status with African Americans, it is unclear whether and to what extent African American elites and ordinary citizens will look superficially at the interests of Black immigrants, include their particular issues on a larger Black political agenda, or oppose policies to the detriment of Black immigrations, such as policies involving the development of less arduous paths to citizenship or increasing immigrant rights. Historically, Black immigrants have tended to blend into African American communities, but today the space to make claims to alternative identities has grown, thereby allowing more room for African Americans and Black immigrants to distance themselves from each other in the political realm. What is more, in the face of enhanced communication technologies and a decline in the cost of travel, today more immigrants can be characterized as transnational, which might also work to maintain or increase distance between native- and foreign-born Blacks.

Overall, it is difficult to predict the ways that African Americans may react to Afro-Latinos, Afro-Caribbeans, and African immigrants in today's racial, political, and economic climate. Nevertheless, African Americans share a long history with immigrants of various racial groups, and this history helps to shed light on the various possibilities for intraracial coalition or competition. For example, the issue of immigration as it relates to Black political agendas, attitudes, and behaviors is one that has changed over time. African Americans' attitudes have largely been influenced, on the one hand, by feelings of competition and threat and, on the other hand, by the desire not to participate in white hegemony through racist anti-immigration movements since Blacks, too, have been persecuted by white supremacy.

David Hellwig explains that historically African Americans have been wary of European immigrants, feeling that European immigrants had contributed to worsening the condition of Blacks.[16] Prior to World War I, white immigrant workers displaced Blacks, and white immigrants were intentional in distancing themselves from African Americans. Hellwig explains, "Despite their treatment in America, blacks were committed to the ideas of the nation and were uneasy about breaking a heritage of welcoming the oppressed of the world."[17] African Americans, elites and common citizens, wanted to curtail immigration during this time, but they had difficulty in devising a policy that did not clash with their principles.

Jeff Diamond explains that this dilemma arose again for African Americans after the enactment of the Hart-Cellar Act in 1965 and again after the U.S. government's "unsuccessful entanglement in Southeast Asia."[18] During the 1970s, Southeast Asian refugees sought asylum in the U.S., and almost every major Black leader endorsed a statement urging the government to admit these refugees. These leaders felt that even though Blacks continued to face political and economic constraints, the struggle of the refugees was linked to their own struggle for power and freedom. Ironically, many African Americans began to resent Southeast Asians because they perceived these immigrants as getting preferential treatment over African Americans, but Black leaders continued to defend a liberal asylum policy.[19] Diamond also explains that Black leaders and organizations are not monolithic on the issue of immigration. During the late 1990s, the Congressional Black Caucus was considered the most liberal block in Congress with respect to immigration policy, even more so than the Hispanic Caucus, although some Black leaders such as Frank Morris and Barbara Jordan had called for decreasing the numbers of immigrants to the United States.[20]

Today, African American citizens continue to be conflicted on the issue of immigration. Survey research reveals that while African Americans tend to feel that immigration should be decreased rather than increased or maintained at current levels, they do so less than whites do. When the issue of immigration is presented as an economic threat to African Americans, however, they are more likely than whites to espouse restrictionist attitudes.[21] This shows that the way immigration is framed—either as a matter of freedom and liberty for immigrants or as costly to Blacks—influences African Americans' attitudes. Due to their position in society, African Americans' feelings have always been, at best, ambivalent toward immigration policies and immigrants themselves.[22]

Both Niambi Carter's theory of racial mediation and Cathy Cohen's theory of secondary marginalization help to better understand how African American citizens think about immigration policies.[23] Carter, who is primarily concerned with African Americans in the South, explains that African Americans tend to feel uncertain about immigration because of their own sense of "racial insecurity"; that is to say, African Americans have learned over time that "their status as American citizens is not a guarantor of equal status in American society."[24] The arrival of immigrants of color revives the traumatic feelings they experienced when white European immigrants overtook them in America's social, political, and economic hierarchies.

Although Carter is concerned with African Americans' feelings about Latino immigration, her theory of racial mediation may help us to understand African Americans' feelings about Black immigrants and immigration as well. The expanding diversity among Blacks may also lead African Americans to see Black immigrants as political and economic threats and therefore cause them to eschew the issues facing Black immigrants. For instance, Lani Guinier suggests that Black immigrants represent a threat to African American educational interests, stating, "I don't think, in the name of affirmative action, we should be admitting people because they look like us, but then they don't identify with us."[25] Douglass S. Massey and his coauthors found that among Black people aged eighteen to nineteen in the U.S., about 13 percent are first- or second-generation immigrants, but these Blacks make up 23.1 percent of Blacks in public colleges and up to 40.6 percent of Blacks in Ivy League institutions.[26] Black scholars such as Guinier and Henry Louis Gates Jr., in reaction to this phenomenon, suggest that Black immigrants may receive preference over American-born Blacks. With this threat in mind, ordinary African American citizens and elites are attempting to "protect" the label of "African American"—that is, to restrict membership into the group—in an effort to make civil rights gains less accessible to Black newcomers. Aside from college admissions, in some cities, African Americans also perceive that Black immigrants increase competition for jobs as well.[27] These examples lead me to predict that even though ordinary African Americans may embrace an identity that includes Black immigrants, they may ignore the issues of Black immigrants or even support anti-immigrant stances.

Further, Cohen's theory of secondary marginalization asserts that while there are a number of so-called consensus issues among African Americans, there are also a number of pressing issues that are not prioritized by African American political leaders or a significant number of community members. As Cohen explains, consensus issues are the "political issues understood or defined in ways that tap into a racial group framework, initiating feelings of linked fate and the perception of advancing interests of the entire black community."[28] Cohen critiques the notion of a unified Black agenda because such an agenda inevitably will not include "cross-cutting" issues that affect smaller, marginal portions of the group. She presents the theory of secondary marginalization, the notion that within Black communities, some subpopulations are "denied access to dominant decision-making processes and institutions; stigmatized by their identification; isolated or segregated; and generally excluded from the control over the resources that shape the quality of their lives."[29]

Cohen brings to light that not all members of Black communities are allowed to participate in the development of any one Black agenda.[30] For example, although Black immigrants have a multiplicity of identities, many African Americans may assert that Black immigrants must prioritize their racial identity over their ethnic identity if they want to be formal participants in Black communities and Black politics.[31] This process of secondary marginalization may lead African Americans to relegate the issues most relevant to Black immigrants to the bottom of the list or to keep these issues completely off the list of policy priorities among African American masses and elites.

Determining Black Agenda(s)

A theory of diasporic consciousness allows us to consider and predict the circumstances under which African Americans' and Black immigrants' identity-to-politics links will result in similar or dissimilar political outcomes. African Americans and Black immigrants have a number of similarities concerning identity and political attitudes. The previous chapters confirm that both African Americans' and Black immigrants' sense of racial identity is central to their self-image and that a sense of group consciousness affects both groups, although at times differently. We should expect that due to shared racialized experiences, issues related to racial disparities will be of import to African Americans as well as to Black immigrants. Put simply,

> H_1: The issues that will gain the most attention of African Americans and Black immigrants will be issues that disproportionately affect Blacks.

But we must also expect and predict differences that arise from these groups, especially as issues relate to Blacks' group membership in distinct ethnic groups. For example, we should expect Black immigrants to be interested in issues that directly affect them because of their immigrant status, such as issues of American foreign policy as they relate to their country of origin or issues of citizenship. African Americans, on the other hand, may be ambivalent about certain "Black" issues, such as immigration, or they may be apathetic to those issues that more directly confront their immigrant counterparts. More specifically,

> H_2: Issues of immigration will not be important to African Americans but will be of utmost importance to first- and second-generation immigrants.

Finally, we must consider how the tension that inundates diasporic consciousness shapes the prospects for an intraracial political coalition. It is likely that African Americans and Black immigrants will support the notion of a Black pan-ethnic political coalition, but only inasmuch as this coalition's overall mission does not compromise the issues that are of priority to any particular subethnic group.

H₃: Black immigrants and African Americans will support a pan-ethnic political coalition insofar as their ethnic group's issues are prioritized.

Issues of (Un)importance

To address the hypotheses presented in the preceding section, I asked respondents an open-ended question: "What political issues or policy matters are important to you?" The respondents were able to provide as many or as few policy matters as they desired.[32] I analyzed the number of times policies were mentioned, and I examined the content of the responses. I believe the answers to this question reveal that the issues identified by my respondents are not just issues that are of importance to Black people, but more importantly, the responses show that Black people perceive these issues as being linked to their racial group, thereby constituting "Black political agenda items." Figure 6.1 provides the distribution of responses to this question.

Among African Americans, issues of education and social welfare were by far the most named issues of importance. In some ways, these

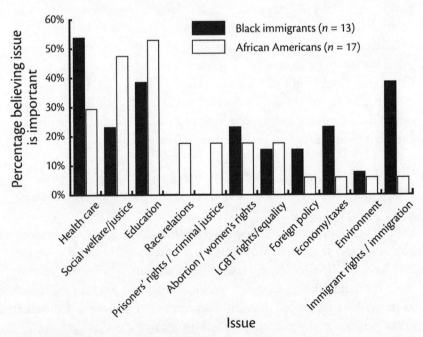

Figure 6.1. Political issues of importance to African Americans and Black immigrants

findings meet our intuitive expectations. We know that, for example, approximately 42 percent of the homeless are Black.[33] It is also well known that African Americans have lower rates of high school graduation than whites do, and African Americans more often have restricted access to better technology in their schools than do their white counterparts.[34] These are issues that disparately affect Blacks. The policy concern of education, in particular, came up often during the interviews: 53 percent of my African American respondents named education, specifically, as an issue that was important to them. This issue was clearly racialized as a Black issue in the minds of some of my respondents. For example, when I asked Naomi what issues were important to her, she answered,

> I would say educational-political issues. I feel like the No Child Left Behind Act was retro-productive [*laughs*]. . . . Because what I noticed is, they would take the schools that didn't make the annual progress report, and they would let the kids go to another school, but the only thing that would happen is that they would go to a different school, a different building with the same teachers. So they were getting the same education, and it seemed like the schools were overcrowding, which was also a bad thing, I think, because the classroom sizes were bigger. I think that was not beneficial for—more so for Blacks. . . . So I feel that the African American students, most of them were left behind because of No Child Left Behind.

Naomi also mentioned that she did not feel affected by this policy—"I didn't feel the effects of No Child Left Behind because I was taking the higher-level classes"—so this was not a personal issue. Instead, Naomi, like others, felt that education and education policies were important because of the special effects that they have on the lives of Blacks in the U.S. In addition to the issues of education, health care, and social welfare, African Americans also responded that issues around race relations and integration, as well as prisoners' rights, were important to them. Again, each of these issues has a disparate effect on Blacks in comparison to white Americans.

Among Black immigrant respondents, health care and education were also at the top of their agenda. About 54 percent (seven out of thirteen) of these respondents mentioned that health care was an important issue to them. This issue was followed by education and immigration, both being named by 38.5 percent of the respondents as important issues.

Even though my group of respondents is not statistically representative of the national Black population, they do respond much like larger, nationally representative survey respondents. When examining the American National Election Study conducted between 1960 and 2000, Laird discovered that of the twenty times the survey was distributed, African Americans reported "social welfare" as "the most important problem facing this country" ten times. Moreover, Laird also analyzed the National Black Election Studies, and she found that discrimination, education, and unemployment were the top three most important issues identified by African Americans. The African Americans' and Black immigrants' responses in my study mirror the sentiments of Blacks nationally.[35]

African American and Black immigrant respondents felt that issues such as abortion and lesbian and gay rights (LGBT issues) were important to them. What is interesting about these issues is that even though they are not obviously racialized—that is, associated with any particular racial group—the respondents at times noted how these issues are related to Blacks. African American respondents in my sample were more likely to expound on this point. For example, Candace had very strong, liberal attitudes toward abortion and women's reproductive rights. She also felt that these issues were racialized, which was why they were so important to her:

> But like abortion, like, it is racialized, and people are like, "Oh, Planned Parenthood is racist." Well, no. Like there are a lot of Planned Parenthoods in Black neighborhoods because they provide reduced health services to pregnant women who are trying to keep their children, that like Black people who don't have health insurance can't afford. That, you know, you need to have healthy babies and to have, you know, healthy toddlers, so I think that's also part of the health disparity problem.

Similarly, LGBT issues were often seen to be connected to issues that Blacks face. Amir, for example, explained why gay and lesbian issues are on his radar: "Giving equality to people who are gay or lesbian is important to me just because I feel a connection with that community based on the struggle that Black folks have gone through." Most of the policy matters that both African Americans and Black immigrants reported as important were those they felt affected Black people in general. The first hypothesis—which asserts that the issues that are most important to African Americans and Black immigrants are issues that clearly affect Blacks in a disparate way, such as poverty, education, and health care—is supported. The respondents communicated that these issues were most important to them, and they also explained that their racial identity influenced the way they structured their political attitudes. Here, we can also get a better understanding of the results from chapter 5, which showed that African Americans' sense of linked fate led them to be more supportive of LGBT rights and women's rights too.

The data also reveal some differences between African Americans and Black immigrants. Only African Americans considered criminal justice and race relations as issues important to them. Conversely, while only 6 percent of African Americans in the sample said that immigration was important, 38.5 percent of Black immigrants indicated that immigration was important to them. Laura, the one African American who explicitly named immigrant rights as an important issue, explained, "I really think we need social justice for everyone, you know. I believe in gay rights, immigrant rights, everything. So anything that will promote the full and equal and equitable participation of all people in society." Although Laura felt that immigrant rights were important, her answer was qualitatively different from those of the Black immigrants who felt this issue was important. Laura described immigration rights as an issue grouped with many other issues, while Black immigrant respondents tended to name issues surrounding immigration as a distinct set of issues. For example, Nym, a Nigerian man, named only one pressing issue when I asked him what policy matters were important to him. He answered, "Immigration reform is a big one. That's, yeah—that's my . . . why I kind of want to get into immigrant policy reform. That's like *the* political issue." I asked him what kind of reforms he would like to see. Nym detailed the kinds of reforms he is passionate about and named issues of family reunification, making the federal government solely responsible for immigrant deportation—rather than allowing states and cities to assist—and inhumane deportation policies.

Similarly, Vanessa, a Dominican woman, identified immigration as her only issue of concern. She said that she did not read or watch the news and did not know much about politics, but she changed her major from premed to prelaw because she felt that it was a personal obligation to push for reform in American immigration laws and to help immigrants learn their rights and learn about the opportunities available to them upon arrival in the United States. Black immigrant respondents were overwhelmingly more likely than African Americans to identify issues of immigration, citizenship, and bilingual education as important issues, providing evidence to support the second hypothesis. African Americans generally did not mention immigration policies as personally important. What do these findings mean for the prospects of intraracial political coalitions?

Prospects for Coalition

The two statements that opened this chapter provide a glimpse into a debate that exists among Blacks in the U.S., a debate that is only further complicated by the increasing ethnic diversity of Blacks in this country. Tunde Adeleke, theorizing on the implications of the color line, explains that the logic of the color line leads one to the idea that because of the racial hierarchy that exists in the U.S., all Blacks—despite their country of origin—should work together. Toni Morrison, conversely, argues that there have been so many cleavages among Blacks in the U.S. that racial unity is unlikely and, perhaps, undesired. I asked respondents their thoughts about racial unity as well as about their desire to see intraracial coalitions formed by African Americans and Black immigrants. Their responses mirror the epigraphs. Some expressed the belief that since Black people in the United States, despite their ethnicity, will be treated similarly, they should focus on building a unified Black agenda. Others stood closer to the other end of the spectrum, suggesting that while Black people should work together on some issues, the prospects for a permanent intraracial coalition is futile and, potentially, detrimental to some groups of Blacks. The following sections elucidate the respondents' attitudes toward Black political unity.

Mandating Racial Unity

Respondents from both groups were on both sides of the debate, but among those who had an opinion about the prospects for coalition, 57 percent of African Americans respondents felt that racial unity was desirable, and 50 percent of Black immigrants expressed similar opinions. Two major themes arose among those who felt that a pan-ethnic coalition among Blacks was the best means by which to improve the status of the group. The first theme centered on the idea that there is power in numbers. For example, when I asked Carmen, an African American woman from Texas, if it is important for African Americans and Black immigrants to work together, she answered, "I think yes, because there's power in numbers. And that's really basically the only reason. The more people you have toward a cause, the more voices will be heard, and the more people will hear your voice." Daise, a Panamanian immigrant, made a similar point and referenced a well-known movement which was successful in undermining a system of racial discrimination: "I think if they [Blacks] could, they should [work together]. There's more strength in numbers. If you . . . if you come—that's why, I guess, civil rights worked so well. It was just huge numbers, and it was constant perseverance." Daise went on to say that Blacks of various ethnicities should continue to work together through more prolonged movements, as we have seen in Black American history. Both Carmen and Daise felt that if Blacks work together, they can accomplish more. For them and for people like them, politics is primarily a game of numbers, in which more is more, and more is better.

Perhaps the more prominent and also more militant theme that arose from those who supported a pan-ethnic coalition is the notion that Blacks need to work together because the color line mandates racial unity. Seven of the respondents suggested that African Americans and Black immigrants need to work together in politics because, despite their differences, a racialized social system distributes advantages and disadvantages on the basis of race rather than ethnicity. I asked Kimberly, an African American woman from Chicago, if she thought Black immigrants and African Americans should work together in politics. She responded,

Definitely. The more cohesion they have, the more represented Blacks would be. Because I feel like rather than being Black immigrant versus being Black American, whatever you want to call it, when whites look at you, you're Black. They could look at you without you even opening your mouth, and the first association they're going to give you: you're Black, regardless. And then you can, you know, argue or articulate in any way or manner—"No, I'm a Black immigrant"; "I'm from Nigeria"; "I'm from X, Y, and Z"—but at the end of the day, you're Black. We were all Black immigrants at one time or another from our ancestry, but at the end of the day, you're Black.

Evelyn, a second-generation Dominican woman, articulated the same idea. When I asked her if she thought it was important for African American and Black immigrants to share a political agenda, she answered,

Yes. I mean, my immediate answer would be yes. I do think there's a lot of diversity within all those communities and ethnicities, and that needs to be highlighted as well. And there are different needs and wants, but I do think in general, because of the history of the United States—having all these immigrant communities coming in, having a continual African American community—like it's important to make sure that . . . Because they're not going to be the dominant structural power or whatever, they're not going to hold the power, I think it's important. There's power in numbers.

Evelyn notes that there are differences among various Black communities, and while she suggests that it is important to be cognizant of those differences, she emphasizes that these ethnic differences do not matter in a society that is organized by race. She notes that Black people, of all ethnicities, are "not going to be the dominant structural power," so it is imperative that Blacks form a coalition. Joshua, an African American from Dallas, provides another example:

Yes, I think that is important [to work together] because to a certain extent we are all treated the same. Until some qualifier that makes a Black immigrant more known as a Black immigrant is exposed, you're going to be looked at as a Black person. And I think that if that's the case, we should work together to . . . *I mean, if we're going to be treated as a group, we might as well act as one.*

Similarly, Ahmad, a second-generation Eritrean immigrant, said,

We can see throughout history, you know, when people ban together, people are able to promote a certain agenda, or it's easier for them to promote an agenda, their agenda, their interests. And whether you want to accept it or not, from the outside looking in, we might have these issues of "I'm Black," "I'm African American, and you're an African immigrant to the United States." From the outside looking in, you guys are the same. And in that way, people are going to treat you the same. And in that sense, your experiences are going to be similar. So you might as well promote that agenda.

Joshua's and Ahmad's statements encapsulate the notion of linked fate. For these two men, as well as for other African Americans and Black immigrants, the idea that Blacks should work as a group since they are treated as a group is the bedrock of Black political behavior.[36] Even in the Obama era, these young Black respondents feel that their race is inextricably linked to their life chances and, further, that their individual life chances are related to the racial group. From their perspective, the color line is still a major division in society, whereby all Blacks are similarly categorized despite the increasing ethnic diversity among them, and consequently, they feel that it is necessary for racial group members to work together despite their ethnic differences.

Moving Beyond Racial Unity

A minority of African Americans (43 percent) and half of Black immigrant respondents suggested that racial unity in the political realm is undesirable. This group of respondents seems especially aware of the notion of intersectionality. Intersectionality "helps us to understand both the differences between and within groups."[37] What is particularly interesting about these responses is that they demonstrate that Black people are simultaneously aware of the ethnic diversity that exists and the potentially negative consequences diversity has for any particular subgroup; more specifically, they recognize how being Black and also being immigrant will have special implications on the lives of foreign-born Blacks. Intersectionality, after all, describes the process by which "multiple identities collide to create new oppressions and new perspectives on inequality."[38]

Kimberlé Crenshaw outlines three forms of intersectionality as they relate to violence against women of color, but we can see how two of these forms become apparent in the responses in my interviews, namely, structural intersectionality and political intersectionality.[39] Structural intersectionality "refers to the complex ways in which deeply embedded inequalities not only amplify, but also uniquely define" individuals who are in multiple minority groups.[40] We might consider, for example, the idea that "immigrants from the Caribbean, Asia, Latin America and Africa who cannot pass as white encounter more difficulty gaining citizenship than immigrants from European nations," but once they have gained citizenship, "they encounter the challenges of being treated as second-class citizens."[41] Or similarly, one might recall the fact that immigrants from Haiti have been turned away in their efforts for political asylum in the U.S., but (white) Cubans have been accepted for the same reason.

Political intersectionality, in this case, highlights the fact that immigrants of color are "situated within at least two subordinated groups that frequently pursue conflicting political agendas."[42] Each of the subordinated groups wants to pursue single-axis political approaches, thereby not addressing the needs of those who are simultaneously in both groups. This idea becomes apparent in the concerns of these respondents. Unlike the previous group of respondents, who want to see racial unity at any cost, this group of respondents reflects the idea that racial unity is disadvantageous and impractical, and from their perspective, we should expect intraracial coalitions to be temporary, at best, due to the tensions that arise from the fact that African Americans and Blacks immigrants have different policy priorities.

Respondents such as Naomi, an African American woman from Stone Mountain, Georgia, equivocated on their response to my question concerning the prospects of an Black intraracial political coalition. Naomi responded,

I would say yes, but at the same time even during different Civil Rights eras, I feel like there was separation between Black people, African Americans, based on what they wanted. Like W. E. B. Du Bois, he wanted there to be integration, he wanted people to have—Black people to have—social and educational mobility because they [whites] had economic mobility. Whereas Booker T. Washington thought that Black people should have economic mobility first and do more technical, or vocational, rather, I should say—but I mean, in a way Booker T.'s method seemed more effective just because white people in charge seemed to approve of that. He had more funding, but I feel like both were against each other and excluding each other from their organizations and causes. I feel like both were important for the Black struggle.

Naomi feels two ways about the notion of Black solidarity. On the one hand, she feels that there should be a political coalition, but the majority of her response is dedicated to the fact that there have historically been chasms in Black political thought and political behavior. She points to the idea that various groups of Black people excluded one another but suggests that the difference in political thought was important for "the Black struggle." It seems as if Naomi values diversity in thought and suggests diversity should be valued over undiscriminating racial unity. Candace, an African American woman, responded similarly:

I think it's hard for me to say if they [African Americans and Black immigrants] should or should not [work together in politics]. I think we should because I think if we were all united behind the same issues, it would really just get things done. But, I mean, I'm not going to say to someone that their belief isn't important and isn't like another voice. Because I think it would be dangerous to say, to force the Black community to only have one voice. I think there's an importance to diversity in belief, and I don't think that those differences should divide us because I think that there are issues that everyone can agree on. At the same time, I would say like everyone has to have the same opinions. So I think there are issues that we can unite on, and there are issues that we can be divided on.

Candace has a very nuanced response to my question. She suggests that it would ideal for Blacks of various ethnicities to work together, but she also identifies one criterion that must be met for real political solidarity to come to fruition: "everyone has to have the same opinion," and Candace finds this "dangerous."

Some respondents had more abstract answers about the potential pitfalls of undiscriminating racial unity, but others were more realistic about the prospective points of conflict between the groups. Respondents in this antisolidarity (or cautious coalition) camp suggested that there is a danger that African Americans might marginalize Black immigrants' issues, particularly those issues surrounding immigration. This response was elicited from African Americans and Black immigrants alike. For example, I asked Laura, an African American woman from Maryland, if she thought African Americans and Black immigrants should work together in politics and share a political agenda. She answered,

Yes, definitely, but at the same time, I think that it could come into conflict because I feel like immigrants' voices might not be heard. That's the only thing. Just because, even right now, I don't know a lot about black immigrants, and I'm a student studying political science, you know. And I don't know a lot about Black immigrants' voice in the U.S. So I mean, I think yes, it's important, but at the same time, they have to balance the issues, and I don't really see groups like the NAACP, for example, I don't really see them reaching out to a lot of immigrant issues, except for recently; they stepped up on with the Arizona situation, which was great. But besides that, I haven't seen anything else really from them.

Laura suggests that immigrant issues may be marginalized on a shared, pan-ethnic political agenda. While she sees value in an intraracial political coalition, she also incorporates what she has seen empirically in her consideration of what a pan-ethnic agenda would mean for various subgroups. Her responses also center political elites in the equation of a pan-ethnic coalition. Actually, her analysis is accurate. Reuel Rogers finds that Black immigrant political elites are unlikely to favor working with African American elites because they feel that African Americans neither prioritize issues that are of importance to Black immigrants nor recognize the importance of descriptive representation as it relates to ethnic identity or immigrant status.[43]

Vanessa, a second-generation Dominican immigrant, also predicted that the process of secondary marginalization will come to fruition if African Americans and Black immigrants work together. She was careful with her response to my question of whether Black immigrants and African Americans should work together in politics:

> I think they have . . . I think they have like . . . I think they have different— they have different desires. Whereas Black immigrants who are closer to the consequences of immigration, like me, might be more . . . more . . . might be closer to the . . . to the like . . . to immigration and how it influences their lives. You know what I mean? They might be concerned with different issues. Where Black Americans, because they're so far removed from immigration, because they immigrated way back when, you know, they have different issues that they want to like, you know, bring into the political sphere or eye, whatever. I don't think . . . You ask me if I think they should work together, and I think that they should work together in any areas where they might have the same—they might be fighting for the same thing, but I think that might be hard if they are not fighting for the same thing.

Like Daise, who suggests, "African Americans don't need to care about that [immigration]," Vanessa is a bit less hopeful of the prospects of an intraracial coalition because her most important issue—immigration— may be crowded out. As individuals who see that immigration is a key issue for a small minority of Blacks and, more importantly, that immigration is virtually invisible for the vast majority of Blacks in the U.S., they find that there might be more problems than solutions for Black immigrants if the groups worked together in the political realm.

* * *

We have seen throughout American history times when Black immigrants and African Americans formed and maintained separate communities and political agendas, but we have also seen times when African Americans and Black immigrants have joined together to form intraracial political coalitions. These coalitions have been driven by shared experiences of discrimination, racism, and the constraints of the "one-drop" rule. Issues of immigration were important to Black immigrants in the past, but since their racial group status dictated their well-being, racial issues were prioritized by Black immigrants. This chapter shows that issues of immigration and immigrant rights are still important to Black immigrants, but in this contemporary racial landscape, we see that for Black immigrants, these issues are now prioritized over, or at least alongside, racial issues. This chapter has attempted to discern what this might mean for Black politics and for the prospects of intraracial coalitions in the future.

Black immigrants and African Americans see themselves as equal group members, and they see each other as compatriots in a struggle against institutional racism. But we see here that the contours of the Black political agenda have not expanded beyond those issues that disproportionately affect most Blacks to also include those that disproportionately affect Black immigrants, more specifically. There is considerable overlap in the issues that African Americans and Black immigrants deem important, but there is still a set of pressing issues that influence a small minority of Blacks that is not on African Americans' radars.

I was curious to know what, if anything, this contradiction means for the prospects of intraracial coalition. What I found is that on one hand, there are some African Americans and Black immigrants alike who feel that racial unity is incredibly important in the face of ongoing structural racism. For these individuals, the color line is still important to consider, and they believe it commands racial unity even in the face of increasing diversity among group members. On the other hand, there are members of both groups who are hesitant about the prospects for an intraracial Black coalition. This group primarily focuses on the idea that racial unity would require the stanching of the diversity in opinions that comes from the intersection of race, ethnicity, and immigration status. Furthermore, they suggest that undiscriminating racial unity, in the face of political intersectionality, would do a disservice to some members of the group. Both African Americans and Black immigrants in this group point to the prospect that Black immigrants' issues of concern would be relegated to the bottom of a shared Black political agenda.

Conclusion

My President Is Black?

Barack Obama's racial identity is debated among Americans not only because he is biracial but also because his father was a Black immigrant from Kenya. Most Americans subscribe to the "one-drop" rule, and Obama himself identifies as a Black—not mixed-race—man.[1] But his father's ancestry along with the fact that President Obama has not lived the "average" African American's life has led some to question the extent to which Obama is "really" Black.[2] Soon after Barack Obama was elected as America's forty-fourth president in 2008, rapper Jay-Z wrote an ode to the first Black president of the United States:

> My president is Black
> In fact, he's half white
> So even in a racist mind
> He's half right
> If you have a racist mind
> You be aight
> The president is black
> But his house is all white
> Rosa Parks sat
> So Martin Luther could walk
> Martin Luther walked
> So Barack Obama could run
> Barack Obama ran
> So all the children could fly
> So I'ma spread my wings
> You can meet me in the sky

Jay-Z and a number of other rappers who wrote versions of "My President Is Black" clearly saw Obama as an individual who descended from the legacy of civil rights leaders, such as Martin Luther King Jr., and Rosa Parks. Further, Obama is seen not only as a person who benefited from the actions of civil rights leaders and the Civil Rights Movement but also as a person who is passing down this legacy to young Blacks in the United States. The fact that Obama is biracial is mentioned, but for the most part, Obama is seen as a Black president for most people of African descent in the United States.

But there are others who suggest that Americans should not be so quick to congratulate themselves on electing their first Black president. Ann Coulter has argued that some Blacks are more "Black" than others and that Obama has made claims about his identity that have resulted in undeserved benefits:

> The president who we have now who has benefited from this [the Civil Rights Acts]—"Oh isn't this great? We have our first Black president." Well, he's half Black, and he's not the descendant of Blacks who suffered these Jim Crow laws, who suffered through slavery. I'm not contesting that he was born in America or anything, but he is the son of a Kenyan. He is not the son, the grandson, the great-grandson of American Blacks who went through the American experience. That is Herman Cain![3]

Coulter acts as the identity police, setting up a series of criteria that defines Blackness in America. For Coulter, Black identity is defined by one's heritage. More specifically, she configures Blackness to describe only those who have had experience with slavery within the borders of the U.S. or Jim Crow laws or someone who is the descendant of a person who lived through those darkest parts of American history. She presumes that since Barack Obama's father was Kenyan, neither the son nor father could have experienced Jim Crow racism—even though Obama's father lived in the United States in the late 1950s and 1960s—or any of the more subtle forms of racism that people who are ascribed a Black identity are likely to encounter in contemporary America. (Coulter is not likely to agree that modern racism actually exists, but that is beside the point.)

One might argue that Coulter, a white, right-wing conservative, is the last person I should reference in a debate about Black identity, but there are African Americans who have made a similar argument. Just before Obama announced his candidacy for president of the United States, Steven Colbert on *The Colbert Report* asked author Debra Dickerson, who is Black, if Barack Obama is Black. She responded,

> No, he's not. In the American political context, Black means the son of West African . . . the descendants of West African slaves brought here to labor in the United States. It's not a put-down. It's not to say that he hasn't suffered. It's not to say that he doesn't have a glorious lineage of his own. It's just to say that he and I, who am descended from West African slaves brought to America, we are not the same.[4]

Colbert then asked her, if Obama is not Black, how he should be identified. He suggested "nouveau-Black" and "late-to-the-scene-Blackness" as possible alternatives to "Black." In turn, Dickerson recommended, "Well, we could go with Black-as-the-circumstances-allow." Finally, when Colbert pointed out that he was excited about the prospect of voting for a Black presidential candidate, Dickerson went on to explain, "You can say, 'I voted for an American of African–African American' or 'an American of African immigrant stock.' And he's also a person who has adopted the role of being Black, so he's not my . . . He's a brother, but he's an adopted brother." Even Cornell West has made digs at the authenticity of Obama's Blackness, due, in part, to his father's African ancestry. He asserted,

> I think my dear brother Barack Obama has a certain fear of free black men. It's understandable. As a young brother who grows up in a white context, brilliant African father, he's always had to fear being a white man with black skin. . . . Obama, coming out of Kansas influence, white, loving grandparents, coming out of Hawaii and Indonesia, when he meets these independent black folk who have a history of slavery, Jim Crow, Jane Crow and so on, he is very apprehensive. He has a certain rootlessness, a deracination.[5]

Here we see that members of various groups of American society are participating in a dialogue about what Blackness means today—even in incredibly preposterous ways. This debate is largely inspired by the incredible increase in ethnic diversity among Blacks due to the immigration of Afro-Caribbeans, Afro-Latinos, and Africans to the United States. This upsurge in diversity among Blacks provoked the questions presented in this book about the (potential) changes in Black identity in the United States as well as how this diversity might influence Black politics. The ultimate purpose of the book has been to illuminate the ways in which native- and foreign-born Blacks in the United States take part in shaping and reshaping the boundaries of Black identity and, consequently, the contours of Black politics.

Traditionally, scholars who have been concerned with African American and Black immigrant relations have primarily focused on the ways in which Black immigrants and African Americans differ from one another and have emphasized the idea that native- and foreign-born Blacks tend to distance themselves from one another.[6] Much of the sociology literature tends to suggest that Black immigrants who are most likely to relate to and identify with African Americans are poor, are male, live in racially segregated neighborhoods, and have oppositional identities.[7] On the other side of the same coin, Black politics research has tended to focus on the unity that has historically characterized Black political behavior. Thus far, the two bodies literature have only depicted parts of a very multifaceted story and history of Black intraracial relations. As this project developed, it became clearer to me that a theory that captured the complex, intraracial relationship between African Americans and Black immigrants did not exist. Thus, an additional goal for this project was to develop a theory that helped to better understand the circumstances under which a unified Black identity and Black political agenda might arise and when Blacks might not unite under the duress of interethnic tension.

History shows that while ethnic competition has existed among various groups of Blacks, there have also been instances when a sense of shared identity has arisen in communities of Black immigrants and African Americans. As shown in chapter 1, African Americans' interactions with Afro-Cuban, Haitian, and West Indian immigrants have been influenced by a number of factors: group members' initial stereotypes about one another, America's racialized laws, day-to-day racial discrimination, U.S. foreign policy, immigration policies, and political "ethnic entrepreneurs"—both Black and white. At times, these forces have exacerbated ethnic differences, while at other times, these factors have served to expand the boundaries of Black identity, allowing Blackness to be marked by ethnic diversity. What has followed, thereafter, can best be described as a sinuous, up-and-down, waxing-and-waning relationship between native-born Blacks and Black newcomers. We are likely to see a politics of inclusion and coalition as well as of tension and intraracial competition among Black ethnic groups in the United States.

A theory of diasporic consciousness, which focuses on the individual level—on individuals' attitudes and behaviors—provides a flexible framework that helps us to explain what we see empirically: complexity. A theory of diasporic consciousness asserts that Black immigrants and African Americans mutually recognize each other as compatriots in a struggle against inequalities due to the constrained nature of racial groupings. However, just as class, ideology, and gender have, at times, served to split Black opinion about what is best for the group, ethnicity serves to do so as well. That is to say, African Americans and Black immigrants see each other as group members and want to work toward improving the group, but they might also have some differences in opinion about what issues should be prioritized on the Black agenda. It is this set of countervailing forces that shapes diasporic consciousness—the tightrope that individuals of African descent walk as they try to balance what is good for their racial group with what is good for their ethnic group. When their identities and political priorities overlap, we are likely to see racial unity; conversely, when they do not overlap, we see ethnic distancing, at best, and competition, in the most tense situations.

This book provides a comparative analysis of each step that connects identity to politics so that we can gain a better understanding of diasporic consciousness. The first step was group membership and then group identity, which was followed by group consciousness, and finally, political attitudes, behaviors, and Black political agendas were examined with data from in-depth interviews and survey data. Chapter 3 illuminated the fluidity of racial labels and racial boundaries. The labels that one adopts or is ascribed have incredible importance for identity politics. Chapter 3 showed that racial labels are contextual and constantly redefined over time by political institutions and by members of the dominant racial group in American society but also, and more importantly, by Blacks. Both native- and foreign-born Blacks have agency in shaping the denotation and connotation of the racial and ethnic labels that have been ascribed to them; furthermore, they can reject, embrace, or transform the meaning of these labels. It appears that "African American" is currently being contested by native-born Blacks as well as by African immigrants; both groups feel that the label best describes their ethnic group but for very different reasons. African Americans and Black immigrants alike appear to embrace "Black" as a pan-ethnic term, very much in the way that "Latino" or "Asian" functions among members of those pan-ethnic groups.

Even as African Americans and Black immigrants show that group members have a role in shaping the definition of Blackness as we know it, they also recognize that dominant, white society and U.S. institutions group them together. This shared group membership is transformed into a sense of racial identity, or psychological attachment to the group, among African Americans as well as Black immigrants, most of the time. What is important to note, however, is that respondents still communicated that they view their ethnic identities as important to their self-image. Racial and ethnic identities are not mutually exclusive, but rather, one identity may become more or less salient than another depending on the context.

Chapter 4 provided evidence that Blacks' racial identity is largely influenced by the way others view them as well as by experiences with racism and discrimination. This chapter explored the determinants of racial centrality, private regard, and public regard. Again, we saw that there are real differences between the groups and among a group's members: levels of various dimensions of racial identity differed *between* African Americans and Black immigrants as well as *among* Black immigrant groups. But the results also reveal that experiences seem to have a homogenizing or unifying effect on African Americans' and Black immigrants' racial identity. Overall, the results indicate that experiences with discrimination serve as a significant influence in the development of both African Americans' and Black immigrants' racial identities. Along with the similarities between African Americans and Black immigrants, there also exist important differences.

Chapter 5 moved us to the next step in the identity-to-politics link: group consciousness. The results show that while both native- and foreign-born Blacks have similar levels of linked fate, there is divergence in the role that group consciousness plays in African Americans' and Black immigrants' political attitudes and behaviors. The chapter revealed that linked fate influences a smaller domain of policy attitudes for Black immigrants than for African Americans. Nonetheless, the results also illustrated that Black immigrants' racial identity tends to be mobilized around policies that directly influence Black people. African Americans' sense of linked fate influences policies that affect Blacks directly as well as policy areas that have no clear racial content.

Each of the previous substantive chapters showed that Black immigrants and African Americans have a shared sense of identity and further that this identity can be mobilized around issues that affect Blacks in the United States. Chapter 6 further elucidated that African Americans' and Black immigrants' political concerns center on issues that influence Blacks, but the results also indicate that African Americans are not necessarily concerned with the issues that Black immigrants prioritize. The minority group model and other coalition theories generally assume that minorities will develop respectful relationships with one another and work together because they face similar challenges.[8] Such a theory would certainly presume that an intraracial alliance could be easily developed among African Americans and Black immigrants. The results here indicate that there is potential for an intraracial coalition to develop, but they also intimate that such a coalition may not be permanent.

Some African Americans and Black immigrants are very supportive of intraracial political coalitions and focus on the notion that Blacks need to unite against a discrimination that attacks them on the basis of their shared racial identity rather than their various ethnic identities. Others argue that race is not an ideal site for a pan-ethnic political coalition because unrelenting unity is bound to drive issues to the least common denominators—race and racism—which they find problematic, particularly in the face of increasing ethnic diversity among Blacks. Although there is quite a bit of overlap in the political concerns of African Americans and Black immigrants, the results suggest that Black immigrant issues may be marginalized on a shared Black political agenda. This marginalization, especially at the local or state levels, where the proportion of Black immigrants may be large, could lead to intraracial competition for resources and descriptive representation. The prospects for an intraracial coalition may be bolstered by shared racialized experiences in the U.S., but they may also be hindered by interethnic differences.

Taken together, these findings suggest that ongoing racialized experiences have a major influence on the identities, attitudes, and behaviors of African Americans and Black immigrants. But these results also show that there are just as many similarities in the development processes of identity, group consciousness, and political behaviors and attitudes as there are differences, as a theory of diasporic consciousness suggests. These similarities and differences have major implications on Blacks politics as well as in the way we understand the role of race in American politics, more generally. The study of Blacks in the U.S. has primarily focused on those who have been affected by the legacies of slavery, Jim Crow, and racial segregation (directly or indirectly), but as Black immigrants continue to come to the U.S. and significantly contribute to the growth of the population, it will also be important to understand how country of origin, ethnicity, acculturation, and generational status along with "traditional" factors—such as discriminatory experiences within the borders of the U.S.—interact to influence the identities and political behaviors of Black newcomers and their children. At the very least, social scientists will have to be more specific about which Black people they are discussing (e.g., Americans, foreign-born, second-generation immigrant) when making claims about Black identity and Black politics.

This book has focused on a national sample of Blacks, but in the future, it will be necessary to garner more information on the local level, since, as it is said, all politics is local. I have shown that historical relations in Miami between Haitians and African Americans look very different from Afro-Cuban and African American relations in Tampa, and further, there is yet another set of differences in the relationship between African Americans and West Indians in New York. All of these relationships changed and continue to evolve over time, and a multicity study would be an excellent way to examine the dynamics of intraracial relations and agenda setting at the local level. A multicity study would also allow us to more closely examine the role that institutions and state actors (e.g., local representatives and politicians, the police, state-level legislation on immigration) serve to help or hinder Black intraracial relationships. This will be an important endeavor especially in places where new intraracial interactions are taking place. The introduction of Afro-Mexicans in North Carolina and Somalis in Tennessee are two cases that will require further exploration, and there are still less traditionally studied places where Black immigrants are likely to interact with African Americans: Washington State, Minnesota, and New England, for example.

Taking seriously the ways in which Black people, especially Black immigrants, are influenced by America's racialized social system raises an additional issue of importance that has implications for American politics and American society. I mentioned in the introductory chapter that immigrants of color serve as a canary in the coal mine, helping us to gauge the levels of racial toxicity in our society; they serve as an excellent test of the notion of a colorblind society. Some scholars argue that foreign-born Blacks' upward mobility is evidence that race does not play a key role in the lives of African Americans.[9] But the contents of this book show that by and large Afro-Caribbean, Afro-Latino, and African immigrants' identity, political attitudes, and political behavior are influenced by negative racialized interactions, thereby providing evidence to the contrary. Meanwhile others suggest that we live in a "post-Black era," or a time when "the definitions and boundaries of Blackness are expanding in forty million directions—or really, into infinity."[10] While there is more room to make claim to less traditional identities, racism still constrains the "choices" that Blacks—native- and foreign-born—can make around their identities; Blacks' life chances are still inextricably linked to their racial identity.

Overall, this book has illustrated that racial disparities are clear and prevalent enough that even newcomers to this country and their children experience differential treatment due to race and, consequently, reevaluate their personal identities. Often, this reevaluation leads to a politically mobilized identity aimed to ameliorate racial disparities—a story not unlike the first Black president's. In all, this book's contents have revealed that first- and second-generation immigrants are still quickly racialized into traditional racial categories and treated in relation to their place in America's ethnoracial hierarchy, thereby elucidating the prevalence and the power of race in the United States.

Presentation of Survey Items and Variable Measures

The survey used throughout this book is the National Survey of American Life, which was conducted between 2001 and 2003. This appendix includes survey questions for the measures used in this book.

Socioeconomic Status and Demographics

- *Household income.* What is your total household income? (The values of the income measure are a ten-point income scale from $0–$20,000 to $180,000–$200,000+, in twenty-thousand-dollar increments.)
- *Education.* What is your highest level of education? (This variable was coded in four categories: (1) zero to eleven years of school; (2) earned a high school diploma; (3) some college; (4) college degree or more.)
- *Gender.* What is your gender? (The values of this variable are coded 0 for female, 1 for male.)
- *Age.* What is your age?

Racial Identity Dimensions

For the following questions, please indicate how much you agree with each statement about being Black. (Respondents may choose "Strongly agree," "Somewhat agree," "Somewhat disagree," or "Strongly disagree.")

Racial Centrality (Scale reliability coefficient: .34)

- Being a Black person is a large part of how I think of myself.
- What happens in my life is largely the result of what happens to other Black people in this country.

- I *do not* feel strongly tied to other Black people.
- Being Black is *not* an important part of who I am as a person.

Racial Private Regard (*Scale reliability coefficient: .42*)

- I feel good about other Black people.
- I am *not* happy that I am Black.
- I am proud to be Black.
- Black people have made important contributions to the development of this country.

Racial Public Regard (*Scale reliability coefficient: .64*)

- White people in this country *do not* respect Black people.
- White people in this country *do not* think of Black people as important contributors to this country.
- Other racial and ethnic groups in this country *do not* think of Blacks as intelligent and competent.
- Other racial and ethnic groups in this country are positive about Black people.

Discrimination Indices

Major Discrimination

In the following questions, we are interested in the way people have treated you or your beliefs about how other people treated you. Can you tell me if any of the following has ever happened to you? (The respondents may choose "Yes" or "No.")

- At any time in your life, have you ever been unfairly fired?
- For unfair reasons, have you ever not been hired for a job?
- Have you ever been unfairly denied a promotion?
- Have you ever been unfairly stopped, search, questioned, physically threatened or abused by the police?
- Have you ever been unfairly discouraged by a teacher or advisor from continuing your education?

- Have you ever been unfairly prevented from moving into a neighborhood because the landlord or realtor refused to sell or rent you a house or apartment?
- Have you ever moved into a neighborhood where neighbors made life difficult for your or your family?
- Have you ever been unfairly denied a bank loan?
- Have you ever received service from someone such as a plumber or car mechanic that was worse than what other people get?

Everyday Discrimination

In your day-to-day life how often have any of the following things happened to you? Would you say almost everyday, at least once a week, a few times a month, a few times a year or less than once a year?

- You are treated with less courtesy than other people.
- You are treated with less respect than other people.
- You receive poorer service than other people at restaurants or stores.
- People act as if they are afraid of you.
- People act as if they think you are dishonest.
- People act as if they are better than you are.
- You are called names or insulted.
- You are threatened or harassed.
- You are followed in stores.

Racial Socialization

Parents

When you were growing up, how often did your parents, or the people who raised you, talk about race or racism? (Respondents may choose "Very often," "Fairly often," "Sometimes," "Rarely," or "Never.")

Proximity

When you think about the places where you have lived, gone to school, worked or received services—was it mostly Blacks or Whites there?

(Respondents may choose among seven options ranging between "All Blacks" to "Almost all Whites.")

- The grammar school you went to?
- The junior high school you went to?
- The high school you went to?
- The neighborhood(s) where you grew up?
- Your present neighborhood?

Black Organization

Do you belong to a national group or organization that aims to improve the well-being of Black people in the United States? (This variable is coded 1 for "Yes" and 0 for "No.")

Political Orientation

- *Partisanship.* Which one of the following political groups best describes your political orientation? 1) Strong Democrat; 2) Moderate Democrat; 3) Strong Republican; 4) Moderate Republican; 5) No preference; 6) Independent, please describe; 7) Other. (The partisanship variable combined strong and moderate Democrats, coded as 1. Republicans, no preference, Independents, and other were combined, coded as 0.)
- *Ideology.* We hear a lot of talk these days about liberals and conservatives. Here is a 7-point scale on which the political views that people might hold are from extremely liberal to extremely positive. Where would you place yourself on this scale? (The ideology variable maintains this direction, from "Extremely liberal" (1) to "Extremely conservative" (7).)

Religiosity

- How much guidance does your religion provide in your day-to-day living? None (1), Some (2), Quite a bit (3), A great deal (4).

APPENDIX B

Interview Respondent Characteristics

Name	Age	Self-identity	Country of origin / generational status	Place of residence
African American females				
Naomi	21	Black; mixed race	USA	Stone Mountain, GA
Candace	22	Black or African American	USA	Baltimore, MA
Carmen	19	Black or African American	USA	Dallas, TX
Elle	21	Black	USA	Glen Cove, IL
Kimberly*	21	Black	USA	Chicago, IL
Alexis	20	Black	USA	Trenton, NJ
Joy*	20	African American	USA	Metro Atlanta, GA
Laura*	21	African American	USA	Columbia, MA
Nicole	21	Black	USA	Boston, MA
Lynette	21	African American	USA	Hackensack, NJ
African American males				
Bruce	20	Black	USA	Erwin, NC
Jason	21	Black	USA	Clinton, MA
Amir*	21	Black or African American	USA	Dearborn, SC

Description of current neighborhood	Mother's racial/ethnic identity	Father's racial/ethnic identity	Mother's occupation	Father's occupation
Predominantly Black	African American	White	Social worker	High school teacher
Predominantly white; upper class	African American	African American	Administrator at a private school	Consultant
Changing from white to Black American	African American	African American	Teacher	Pharmacist
Predominantly white; upper class	African American	African American	Realtor	Doctor
Black/Latino; working class	African American	—	Unemployed	—
Black/Latino	African American	African American	Child care	(Stepfather) Truck driver
Predominantly Black; middle class	African American	—	Social worker	—
Racially mixed; mixed income	African American	African American	Information technology	Information technology
Racially mixed; low income	African American	African American	Administrative assistant	Factory worker
African American/Haitian; middle class	African American	African American	Social worker	Retired lithographer
Mixed Black, white, Latino; rural; mixed income	African American	African American	Principal	USPS sales associate
Predominantly white; military base	African American	African American	Stay-at-home mom	(Stepfather) Military
Predominantly Black; mixed income	African American	African American	Federal government civil servant (education)	(Stepfather) Retired federal government civil servant (education)

(*continued*)

Name	Age	Self-identity	Country of origin / generational status	Place of residence
Joshua*	21	African American	USA	Dallas, TX
Noah	21	Black	USA	Atlanta, GA
Peter	20	Black	USA	Rochester, NY
Michael*	21	Black or African American	USA	Spokane, WA
Black immigrant females				
Rosa	21	Ethiopian American	USA / second generation	Durham, NC
Claire	22	African American	USA / second generation	Rock Hill, SC
Daise	22	Panamanian/ Hispanic/Black	Panama / first generation	Key West, FL
Vanessa	22	Hispanic	Dominican Republic / 1.5 generation	Miami, FL
Ann	21	Black	USA / second generation	Baltimore, MD
Evelyn	21	Black/ Dominican	USA / second generation	Brooklyn, NY
Chinwe	20	African American	USA / second generation	Atlanta, GA
Stacy	20	Haitian American / Black	USA / 1.5 generation	Brooklyn, NY
Ashley	21	Black/Ethiopian	USA / second generation	Dallas, TX
Black immigrant males				
Antwon	20	Nigerian/Black	Nigeria / 1.5 generation	Marietta, GA
Nym	21	Nigerian/Black/ American	Nigeria / first generation	Katy, TX
Ahmad*	19	African/American/ Eritrean/Black	USA / second generation	Seattle, WA
John	20	Black	South Africa / first generation	Powell, OH

* Students who did not attend PSU

Description of current neighborhood	Mother's racial/ethnic identity	Father's racial/ethnic identity	Mother's occupation	Father's occupation
Predominantly Black; upper/middle class	African American	African American	FEMA administrator	Pastor
Predominantly white; middle class	African American	African American	Insurance auditor	Software engineer
Predominantly Black; low income	White	African American	Secretary	—
Predominantly white; low income	White	African American	Unemployed	—
Racially mixed; middle class	Ethiopian	Ethiopian	Food services	Custodian, taxi driver
Racially mixed; middle class	African American	Nigerian	Homeschool teacher	Mail carrier
Moved around from year to year	Panamanian	Panamanian	Civil servant— environment	Civil servant— environmental specialist
African American; low income	Dominican	Dominican	Unknown	Unknown
Racially mixed; middle and upper class	Ghanaian	Ghanaian	Administrative assistant	Information analysis
Predominantly Black/ Afro-Caribbean; low income	Dominican	Dominican	Factory worker	Unskilled laborer
—	Sierra Leonian	Nigerian	Registered nurse	Sales manager
West Indian; working class	Haitian	Haitian	Practical nurse	Self-employed; real-estate/ insurance broker
Predominantly white; middle class	Ethiopian	Ethiopian	Weight/balance planner for airline	Aircraft mechanic
Predominantly Black; low income	St. Vincent	Nigerian	Accountant	Unemployed
Predominantly white; middle class	Nigerian	Nigerian	Nurse (U.S.) / microbiologist (Nigeria)	Attorney (Nigeria)
Predominantly Black; mixed income	Eritrean	Eritrean	Stay-at-home mom	Software engineer
Predominantly white; upper class	South African	South African	Stay-at-home mom	Self-employed (information technology)

Semistructured Interview Guide

The interviews lasted between forty-five and ninety minutes. The respondents signed an informed-consent form before we began and provided a pseudonym to use in place of their real name. The following questions guided our conversations. The questions in brackets were only presented to first- and second-generation Black immigrant respondents.

Introduction and Identity

- Tell me about yourself and your family. Where are you all from? Where do you all live? What's the ethnic/racial composition of your neighborhood? What do your parents do for a living? [Do they maintain ties with their home country? How?] [Does your family ever think about going back to their home country? What do you think about that? Would you want to live in your parents' home country?]
- Do you belong to any students groups? Which ones?
- How would you describe your ancestry?
- There are multiple ways that Black people in the U.S. describe their identity. How do you identify? Does this change depending on situation?
- Who is Black? Who is African American? Is there a difference?
- Is being Black an important part of your self-image? Ethnic group?
- What does it mean to be Black?

Group Feelings, Values, and Beliefs

- Do you feel that African Americans and Black immigrants share the same values and outlook on life?

- Some people say that African Americans and Black immigrants do not get along. What is your opinion on this issue? Do you think there is competition and tension between groups of Blacks in the United States? Have you experienced this tension? If so, what is the source of this conflict?
- What stereotypes did you grow up hearing or learning about African Americans? Afro-Caribbeans? Africans? Afro-Latinos?
- Do you think racism and discrimination are important issues in the United States?
- Have you personally been affected by racism or discrimination?
- What, if anything, should be done about it?
- Most African Americans think pretty similarly about the effects of race in the United States. Do you think that it's important for all people of African descent to see eye-to-eye on racial matters and problems?
- How can the increasing achievement gap between Blacks and whites be explained? Why, given all the progress that Blacks as a racial group have made, do they continue to lag behind whites and other groups along various social and economic indicators?
- Do you think that Black immigrants and their children get treated any differently than African Americans, generally? Police? Employers?

Race-Conscious Admissions Policies and Affirmative Action

- What is your interpretation of the goal of race-conscious admissions policies and affirmative action?
- Are these policies necessary?
- Should all students of African descent benefit from these policies?
- Should African Americans and Black immigrants benefit from race-conscious admissions policies and affirmative action, or should they be treated differently?
- First- and second-generation Black immigrants have a large presence at prestigious schools like Harvard. How would you explain that?

Political Attitudes and Behaviors

- What political issues are important to you?
- How, if at all, does your racial identity influence your political attitudes and behavior?

- Is there one party that you tend to support? Does one party represent your views better than others? Which one?
- Is it important to support Black politicians and Black political leaders?
- Thought experiment: There are two candidates who have similar platforms and qualifications. The only difference between the candidates is that one is Black and one is white. Whom do you think you would be more likely to support?
- Do Black political leaders have a responsibility to communicate issues of Black communities?
- What political issues or policy matters do you think are important to African Americans? What about for Black immigrants, like Afro-Caribbean, Afro-Latino, or African immigrants?
- Is anyone capable of representing Black political interests or are Black representatives more suited for this task?
- Are there any political issues that you think all people of African descent should be concerned about in the U.S.?
- Do you think that it's important for people of African decent to share a political agenda? Should they work together in politics? What issues might they differ on?
- Is the political system an efficient way to solve Blacks' social, economic, and political issues?

Barack Obama

- A lot of people thought it was important for Barack Obama to be elected, as the first Black president. What did you think about his election?
- How do you think he is doing as president?
- Do you think it's important for—or even a responsibility for—Obama to talk about racial disparities? Do you think Obama has a responsibility to Black people?

Additional Questions

- What is the American Dream? Who can accomplish it? Is it easier for some than others?
- Does your racial identity affect your life chances?

- Who are you friends? What is the racial makeup of your friends? (If you could think of a proportion or percentage?)
- What does "Black Community" mean to you? To what extent do you think about people of African descent constituting a broader national (or even global) community?
- Has your racial or ethnic identity changed over time, either in the way you describe yourself or in the strength of your identity?

NOTES

NOTES TO THE INTRODUCTION

1. Mary C. Waters, *Ethnic Options: Choosing Identities in America* (Berkeley: University of California Press, 1990).
2. Mary Mederios Kent, "Immigration and America's Black Population" (Washington, DC: Population Reference Bureau, 2007).
3. Douglass S. Massey et al., *The Source of the River: The Social Origins of Freshmen at America's Selective Colleges and Universities* (Princeton: Princeton University Press, 2008); Douglass S. Massey et al., "Black Immigrants and Black Natives Attending Selective Colleges and Universities in the United States," *American Journal of Education* 113, no. 2 (2007).
4. Michael C. Dawson, *Behind the Mule: Race and Class in African-American Politics* (Princeton: Princeton University Press, 1994).
5. Kerry L. Haynie and Candis S. Watts, "Blacks and the Democratic Party: A Resilient Coalition," in *New Directions in American Political Parties*, ed. Jeffrey M. Stonecash (New York: Routledge, 2010).
6. Dawson, *Behind the Mule.*
7. Cathy J. Cohen, *The Boundaries of Blackness: AIDS and the Breakdown of Black Politics* (Chicago: University of Chicago Press, 1999), x.
8. Michael C. Dawson, *Black Visions: The Root of Contemporary African-American Political Ideologies* (Chicago: University of Chicago Press, 2001); Melissa Harris-Lacewell, *Barbershops, Bibles, and BET: Everyday Talk and Black Political Thought* (Princeton: Princeton University Press, 2004); Melanye T. Price, *Dreaming Blackness: Black Nationalism and African American Public Opinion* (New York: NYU Press, 2009).
9. Cohen, *Boundaries of Blackness*; Dawson, *Behind the Mule*; William Julius Wilson, *Declining Significance of Race: Blacks and Changing American Institutions* (Chicago: University of Chicago Press, 1980).
10. Evelyn M. Simien, "Race, Gender, and Linked Fate," *Journal of Black Studies* 35, no. 5 (2005); Evelyn M. Simien and Rosalee A. Clawson, "The Intersection of Race and Gender: An Examination of Feminist Consciousness, Race Consciousness, and Policy Attitudes," *Social Science Quarterly* 85, no. 3 (2004); Wendy Smooth, "Intersectionality in Electoral Politics: A Mess Worth Making," *Politics & Gender* 2, no. 3 (2006).

11. See the following for exceptions: Sharon D. Wright Austin, Richard T. Middleton, and Rachel Yon, "The Effect of Racial Group Consciousness on the Political Participation of African Americans and Black Ethnics in Miami-Dade County, Florida," *Political Research Quarterly* 65, no. 3 (2012); Shayla C. Nunnally, "Linking Blackness or Ethnic Othering? African Americans' Diasporic Linked Fate with West Indian and African Peoples in the United States," *Du Bois Review* 7, no. 2 (2010); Reuel R. Rogers, "Race-Based Coalitions Among Minority Groups: Afro-Caribbean Immigrants and African-Americans in New York City," *Urban Affairs Review* 39, no. 3 (2004); Rogers, *Afro-Caribbean Immigrants and the Politics of Incorporation: Ethnicity, Exception, or Exit* (New York: Cambridge University Press, 2006).

12. Nancy Foner, "West Indian Identity in the Diaspora: Comparative and Historical Perspectives," *Latin American Perspectives* 25, no. 3 (1998); Tatishe Mavovosi Nteta, *"Plus Ça Change, Plus C'est la Même Chose*? An Examination of the Racial Attitudes of New Immigrants in the United States," in *Transforming Politics, Transforming America: The Political and Civic Incorporation of Immigrants in the United States*, ed. Taeku Lee, Karthick Ramakrishnan, and Ricardo Ramirez (Charlottesville: University of Virginia Press, 2006); Mary C. Waters, "The Role of Lineage in Identity Formation among Black Americans," *Qualitiative Sociology* 14, no. 1 (1991); Waters, *Black Identities: West Indian Immigrant Dreams and American Realities* (Cambridge: Harvard University Press, 1999).

13. Susan D. Greenbaum, *More than Black: Afro-Cubans in Tampa* (Gainesville: University Press of Florida, 2002); Philip Kasinitz, *Caribbean New York: Black Immigrants and the Politics of Race* (Ithaca: Cornell University Press, 1992); Claire Jean Kim, *Bitter Fruit: The Politics of Black-Korean Conflict in New York City* (New Haven: Yale University Press, 2000).

14. Orlando Patterson, "Toward a Future That Has No Past—Reflections on the Fate of Blacks in the Americas," *Public Interest* 27 (1972): 25; see also Lisa Brock, "Questioning the Diaspora: Hegemony, Black Intellectual, and Doing International History from Below," *Issue: A Journal of Opinion* 24, no. 2 (1996); Tiffany Ruby Paterson and Robin D. G. Kelley, "Unfinished Migrations: Reflection on the African Diaspora and the Making of the Modern World," *African Studies Review* 43, no. 1 (2000).

15. Brock, "Questioning the Diaspora"; Robin D. G. Kelley, " 'But a Local Phase of a World Problem': Black History's Global Vision, 1883–1950," *Journal of American History* 86, no. 3 (1999); Patterson, "Toward a Future That Has No Past."

16. Paterson and Kelley, "Unfinished Migrations."

17. Jane Junn and Natalie Masuoka, "Asian American Identity: Shared Racial Status and Political Context," *Perspectives on Politics* 6, no. 4 (2008); Taeku Lee, "Pan-ethnic Identity, Linked Fate, and the Political Significance of 'Asian American' " (unpublished paper, University of California, 2005); Alejandro Portes and Ruben G. Rumbaut, *Immigrant American: A Portrait*, 2nd ed. (Berkeley: University of California Press, 1996); Alejandro Portes and Min Zhou, "The New

Second Generation: Segmented Assimilation and Its Variants," *Annals of the American Academy of Political and Social Science* 530 (1993).

18. Ira Berlin, "The Changing Definition of African-American," *Smithsonian Magazine*, February 2010; David J. Hellwig, "Black Meets Black: Afro-American Reactions to West Indian Immigrants in the 1920s," *South Atlantic Quarterly* 77, no. 1 (1978).

19. Berlin, "Changing Definition of African American."

20. Kent, "Immigration and America's Black Population."

21. U.S. Census Bureau, "The American Community—Blacks: 2004" (Washington, DC: U.S. Census Bureau, Department of Commerce, 2007).

22. Kent, "Immigration and America's Black Population."

23. Berlin, "Changing Definition of African-American"; Rachel L. Swarns, "'African-American' Becomes a Term of Debate," *New York Times*, August 29, 2004.

24. Vilna F. Bashi Bobb, "Neither Ignorance nor Bliss: Race, Racism, and the West Indian Immigrant Experience," in *Migration, Transnationalization, and Race in a Changing New York*, ed. Hector Cordero-Guzman, Robert C. Smith, and Ramon Grosfoguel (Philidelphia: Temple University Press, 2001).

25. Greenbaum, *More than Black*; Hellwig, "Black Meets Black."

26. Mary C. Waters, "West Indians and African Americans at Work: Structural Differences and Cultural Stereotypes," in *Immigration and Opportunity: Race, Ethnicity, and Employment in the United States*, ed. Frank D. Bean and Stephanie Bell-Rose (New York: Russell Sage Foundation, 1999b).

27. Pew Research Center, "Optimism about Black Progress Declines: Blacks See Growing Values Gap between Poor and Middle Class" (Washington, DC: Pew Research Center, 2007).

28. Noel Ignatiev, *How the Irish Became White* (New York: Routledge, 1995); David R. Roediger, *Working toward Whiteness: How America's Immigrants Became White: The Strange Journey from Ellis Island to the Suburbs* (New York: Basic Books, 2005); Roediger, *The Wages of Whiteness: Race and the Making of the American Working Class* (London: Verso, 2007).

29. Berlin, "Changing Definition of African-American"; Swarns, "'African-American' Becomes a Term of Debate."

30. Carolle Charles, "Being Black Twice," in *Problematizing Blackness: Self-Ethnographics by Black Immigrants to the United States*, ed. Percy Claude Hintzen and Jean Muteba Rahier (New York: Routledge, 2003); Alex Stepick III, "The Refugees Nobody Wants: Haitians in Miami," in *Miami Now! Immigration, Ethnicity, and Social Change*, ed. Guillermo J. Grenier and Alex Stepick III (Gainesville: University Press of Florida, 1992).

31. Louis E. V. Nevaer, "In Black-Hispanic Debate, West Indians Side with Hispanics," Pacific News Service, *New America Media*, December 4, 2003.

32. Quoted in Marcella Bombardieri, "Harvard's Black Community Reunites," *Boston Globe*, October 5, 2003.

33. Dawson, *Behind the Mule*.

34. Melvin Oliver and Thomas Shapiro, *Black Wealth / White Wealth: A New Perspective on Racial Inequality* (New York: Routledge, 1995).
35. Claire Jean Kim, "The Racial Triangulation of Asian Americans," in *Asian Americans and Politics: Perspectives, Experiences, Prospects*, ed. Gordon H. Chang (Washington, DC: Woodrow Wilson Center Press, 2001), 39.
36. Edna A. Viruell-Fuentes, " 'It's a Lot of Work'": Racialization Processes, Ethnic Identity Formation, and Their Health Implications," *Du Bois Review* 8, no. 1 (2011).
37. Sara Rimer and Karen W. Arenson, "Top Colleges Take More Blacks, but Which Ones?," *New York Times*, June 24, 2004.
38. Portes and Zhou, "New Second Generation"; Waters, *Black Identities*.

NOTES TO CHAPTER 1

1. Ira De Augustine Reid, *The Negro Immigrant: His Background, Characteristics and Social Adjustment, 1899–1937* (New York: Columbia University Press, 1939), 24.
2. Greenbaum, *More than Black*; Hellwig, "Black Meets Black."
3. Kasinitz, *Caribbean New York*; Mary C. Waters, "Immigration, Intermarriage, and the Challenges of Measuring Racial/Ethnic Identities," *American Journal of Public Health* 90, no. 11 (2000).
4. Context also influences U.S.-born Blacks' understanding of racial identity. The context of the Mississippi Delta is different from the context in, say, Chicago or Los Angeles. See David Harris, "Exploring the Determinants of Adult Black Identity: Context and Process," *Social Forces* 74, no. 1 (1995); Isabel Wilkerson, *The Warmth of Other Suns: The Epic Story of America's Great Migration* (New York: Random House, 2010).
5. Shayla C. Nunnally, "Learning Race, Socializing Blackness," *Du Bois Review* 7, no. 1 (2010).
6. The racial histories of the United States, Latin America, and Africa are complex. My aim is to present the dominant features of these societies' construction of racial identity in an effort to illuminate the differences and similarities among them.
7. Jessica L. Davis and Oscar H. Gandy Jr., "Racial Identity and Media Orientation: Exploring the Nature of Constraint," *Journal of Black Studies* 29, no. 3 (1999).
8. Joe R. Feagin, *Racist America: Roots, Current Realities, and Future Reparations* (New York: Routledge, 2000); Gerald M. Oppenheimer, "Paradigm Lost: Race, Ethnicity, and the Search of a New Population Taxonomy," *American Journal of Public Health* 91, no. 7 (2001); Audrey Smedley, "Social Origins of the Idea of Race," in *Race in 21st Century America*, ed. Curtis Stokes, Theresa Melendez, and Genice Rhodes-Reed (East Lansing: Michigan State University Press, 2001).
9. Paula D. McClain and Joseph Stewart Jr., *Can We All Get Along? Racial and Ethnic Minorities in American Politics*, 5th ed. (Boulder, CO: Westview, 2010).
10. Patricia Hill Collins, "Like One of the Family: Race, Ethnicity, and the Paradox of US National Identity," *Ethnic and Racial Studies* 24, no. 1 (2001).

11. Benjamin Bailey, "Dominican-American Ethnic/Racial Identities and United States Social Categories," *International Migration Review* 35, no. 3 (2001): 686.
12. Gilberto Freye, *The Masters and the Slaves* (New York: Kopf, 1947); Jay Kinsbruner, *Not of Pure Blood: The Free People of Color and Prejudice in Nineteenth-Century Puerto Rico* (Durham: Duke University Press, 1996).
13. Freye, *Masters and the Slaves*; Kinsbruner, *Not of Pure Blood*.
14. Jose Itzigsohn and Carlos Dore-Cabral, "Competing Identities? Race, Ethnicity and Panethnicity among Dominicans in the United States," *Sociological Forum* 15, no. 2 (2000); Foner, "West Indian Identity in the Diaspora."
15. Foner, "West Indian Identity in the Diaspora"; Milton Vickerman, "Tweaking a Monolith: The West Indian Immigrant Encounter with 'Blackness,'" in *Islands in the City: West Indian Migration to New York*, ed. Nancy Foner (Berkeley: University of California Press, 2001).
16. Itzigsohn and Dore-Cabral, "Competing Identities?"; Melissa Nobles, *Shades of Citizenship: Race and the Census in Modern Politics* (Stanford: Standford University Press, 2000); Anthony W. Marx, *Making Race and Nation: A Comparison of the United States, South Africa and Brazil* (Cambridge: Cambridge University Press, 1998); Peter Wade, *Race and Ethnicity in Latin America* (London: Pluto, 1997).
17. Foner, "West Indian Identity in the Diaspora."
18. Ibid., 175.
19. Vickerman, "Tweaking a Monolith."
20. George Reid Andrews, *Afro-Latin America, 1800–2000* (Oxford: Oxford University Press, 2004); Mark Q. Sawyer, *Racial Politics in Post-Revolutionary Cuba* (New York: Cambridge University Press, 2006).
21. Freye, *Masters and the Slaves*; Antonio Sérgio Guimarães, "The Misadventures of Nonracialism in Brazil," in *Beyond Racism: Race and Inequality in Brazil, South Africa, and the United States*, ed. Charles V. Hamilton et al. (Boulder, CO: Lynne Rienner, 2001); Wade, *Race and Ethnicity in Latin America*.
22. Ariel E. Dulitzy, "A Region in Denial: Racial Discrimination and Racism in Latin America," in *Neither Enemies nor Friends: Latinos, Blacks, Afro-Latinos*, ed. Anani Dzidzienyo and Suzanne Oboler (New York: Palgrave Macmillian, 2005); Anani Dzidzienyo and Suzanne Oboler, "Flows and Counterflows: Latinas/os, Blackness, and Racialization in Hemispheric Perspective," in ibid.
23. William A. Darity Jr., Jason Dietrich, and Darrick Hamilton, "Bleach in the Rainbow: Latin Ethnicity and Preference for Whiteness," *Transforming Anthropology* 13, no. 2 (2005).
24. Margaret L. Hunter, "'If You're Light You're Alright': Light Skin Color as Social Capital for Women of Color," *Gender and Society* 16, no. 2 (2002).
25. Elisa Larkin Nascimento, "Aspects of Afro-Brazilian Experience," *Journal of Black Studies* 11, no. 2 (1980).
26. Dulitzy, "Region in Denial."
27. Sawyer, *Racial Politics in Post-Revolutionary Cuba*.

28. Eduardo Bonilla-Silva and David R. Dietrich, "The Latin Americanization of Racial Stratification in the U.S.," in *Racism in the 21st Century: An Empirical Analysis of Skin Color*, ed. Robert E. Hall (New York: Springer, 2008).

29. Philip Gourevitch, *We Wish to Inform You That Tomorrow We Will Be Killed with Our Families: Stories from Rwanda* (New York: Farrar, Straus and Giroux, 1998); Andrew C. Okolie, "The Appropriation of Difference: State and the Construction of Ethnic Identities in Nigeria," *Identity* 3, no. 1 (2003).

30. Francis Kornegay, "Pan-African Citizenship and Identity Formation in Southern Africa: An Overview of Problems, Prospects and Possibilities" (Johannesburg: Center for Policy Studies, 2006); Wyatt MacGaffey, "Concepts of Race in the Historiography of Northeast Africa," *Journal of African History* 7, no. 1 (1966); Marx, *Making Race and Nation*; Deborah Posel, "Race as Common Sense: Racial Classification in Twentieth-Century South Africa," *African Studies Review* 44, no. 2 (2001).

31. MacGaffey, "Concepts of Race in the Historiography of Northeast Africa"; Marx, *Making Race and Nation*; Posel, "Race as Common Sense."

32. James R. Brennan, "Realizing Civilization through Patrilineal Descent: The Intellectual Making of an African Racial Nationalism in Tanzania, 1920–1950," *Social Identities* 12, no. 4 (2006): 408.

33. Ibid.

34. Ibid.

35. Gourevitch, *We Wish to Inform You.*

36. Greenbaum, *More than Black*; Kasinitz, *Caribbean New York.*

37. Roy Simon Bryce-Laporte, "Black Immigrants: The Experience of Invisibility and Inequality," *Journal of Black Studies* 3, no. 1 (1972): 31; emphasis in original.

38. These individuals have not necessarily made an effort to make salient their immigrant background to the public. Even though Obama has mentioned and written about his Kenyan father, he generally identifies as a Black person; when provided the opportunity to "mark one or more" racial categories on the 2010 U.S. Census, Obama selected "Black/African American/Negro." There have been a number of notable and recent rising politicians who have put their immigrant identities at the center of their political campaigns and rhetoric. Yvette D. Clarke (D-NY, Ninth District) and Ludmya "Mia" Bourdeau Love, Republican mayor of Saratoga Springs, Utah are two examples.

39. Lisa Brock and Bijan Bayne, "Not Just Black: African-Americans, Cubans, and Baseball," in *Between Race and Empire: African-Americans and Cubans before the Cuban Revolution*, ed. Lisa Brock and Digna Castañeda Fuertes (Philidelphia: Temple University Press, 1998); Nancy Raquel Mirabal, "Telling Silences and Making Community: Afro-Cubans and African-Americans in Ybor City and Tampa, 1899–1915," in ibid.

40. Mirabal, "Telling Silences and Making Community," 51.

41. Ibid.

42. This is not to say that this was the first time African Americans and Afro-

Cubans interacted. The U.S.'s intervention into the Cuban War for Independence in 1898 was a major impetus for interactions between these two groups in Cuba. See the following sources for additional examples: Brock and Bayne, "Not Just Black"; and Frank Andre Guridy, *Forging Diaspora: Afro-Cubans and African Americans in a World of Empire and Jim Crow* (Chapel Hill: University of North Carolina Press, 2010). This chapter focuses on interactions in the United States.

43. Greenbaum, *More than Black*, 12.
44. Ibid.; Mirabal, "Telling Silences and Making Community."
45. Greenbaum, *More than Black*. It should also be noted that during this time, African Americans primarily identified as Republicans; the shift that African Americans made to the Democratic Party did not occur until the mid-twentieth century. See the following sources for more details: Tasha S. Philpot, *Race, Republicans, and the Return of the Party of Lincoln* (Ann Arbor: University of Michigan Press, 2007); Haynie and Watts, "Blacks and the Democratic Party."
46. Quoted in Greenbaum, *More than Black*, 105.
47. Ibid.
48. Mirabal, "Telling Silences and Making Community," 57.
49. Afro-Cubans' identity as "Cuban" rather than Black and Afro-Cubans' attitudes toward African Americans have striking similarities with Marilyn Halter's portrait of Cape Verdean American immigrants in New England between 1860 and 1965. Halter's dark-skinned Cape Verdean immigrant informants consistently note that they saw themselves as "Portuguese" rather than African or Black, but they were also separated from white Portuguese immigrants themselves; over time, like many Afro-Cubans, Black Cape Verdeans began to develop a sense of racial group consciousness and, consequently, began to relate to African Americans' political attitudes around racial inequality. Marilyn Halter, *Between Race and Ethnicity: Cape Verdean American Immigrants, 1860–1965* (Urbana: University of Illinois Press, 1993).
50. Mirabal, "Telling Silences and Making Community."
51. Brock and Bayne, "Not Just Black," 181.
52. Mirabal, "Telling Silences and Making Community," 60.
53. Ibid.
54. Ira Katznelson, *When Affirmative Action was White: An Untold History of Racial Inequality in Twentieth-Century America* (New York: Norton, 2005).
55. Greenbaum, *More than Black*.
56. Marvin Dunn and Alex Stepick III, "Blacks in Miami," in *Miami Now! Immigration, Ethnicity, and Social Change*, ed. Guillermo J. Grenier and Alex Stepick III (Gainesville: University Press of Florida, 1992).
57. Marvin Dunn, *Black Miami in the Twentieth Century* (Gainesville: Univeristy Press of Florida, 1997), 322.
58. Ibid.
59. Stepick, "Refugees Nobody Wants," 60.
60. Shirley Anita St. Hill Chisholm was also the child of immigrants.

61. Stepick, "Refugees Nobody Wants."

62. Leon D. Pamphile, *Haitians and African Americans* (Gainesville: University Press of Florida, 2001).

63. Dunn, *Black Miami in the Twentieth Century*, 330.

64. Stepick, "Refugees Nobody Wants," 63.

65. David Levering Lewis, *W. E. B. Du Bois, 1919–1963: The Fight for Equality and the American Century* (New York: Holt, 2001), 40.

66. Ibid., 46.

67. Kasinitz, *Caribbean New York*; Lewis, *W. E. B. Du Bois*.

68. Lewis, *W. E. B. Du Bois*, 78–79; Harold Cruse, *The Crisis of the Negro Intellectual* (New York: Morrow, 1967).

69. W. A. Domingo and Chandler Owen, "The Policy of the *Messenger* on West Indian and American Negroes," *Messenger*, March 1923.

70. Lewis, *W. E. B. Du Bois*, 79.

71. Cruse, *Crisis of the Negro Intellectual*; Hellwig, "Black Meets Black."

72. Hellwig, "Black Meets Black"; Irma Watkins-Owens, *Blood Relations: Caribbean Immigrants and the Harlem Community, 1900–1930* (Bloomington: Indiana University Press, 1996).

73. Alvin Bernard Tillery and Michell Chresfield, "Model Blacks or "Ras the Exhorter" A Quantitative Content Analysis of Black Newspapers' Coverage of the First Wave of Afro-Caribbean Immigration to the United States," *Journal of Black Studies* 43, no. 5 (2012). This was not an uncommon way to think about Black immigrants, and in many ways, this stereotype continues to linger in contemporary media and in the academy. Also see George Edmund Haynes, *The Negro at Work in New York City: A Study in Economic Progress* (New York: Longman, 1912); Reid, *Negro Immigrant*; Thomas Sowell, "Ethnicity in a Changing America," *Daedalus* 107, no. 1 (1978); and Portes and Zhou, "New Second Generation." For critiques, see Jemima Pierre, "Black Immigrants in the United States and the 'Cultural Narratives' of Ethnicity," *Identities: Global Studies in Culture and Power* 11 (2004).

74. Hellwig, "Black Meets Black."

75. Cruse, *Crisis of the Negro Intellectual*, 424; Violet Showers Johnson, "Relentless Ex-Colonials and Militant Immigrants: Protest Strategies of Boston's West Indian Immigrants, 1910–1950," in *The Civil Rights Movement Revisted: Critical Perspectives on the Struggle for Racial Equality in the United States*, ed. Patrick B. Miller, Therese Frey Steffen, and Elisabeth Schäfer-Wünsche (New Brunswick, NJ: Transaction, 2001).

76. Cruse, *Crisis of the Negro Intellectual*, 428.

77. Kasinitz, *Caribbean New York*; John C. Walter, "Black Immigrants and Political Radicalism in the Harlem Renaissance," *Western Journal of Black Studies* 1, no. 2 (1977).

78. Walter, "Black Immigrants and Political Radicalism," 131.

79. Lewis, *W. E. B. Du Bois*; Walter, "Black Immigrants and Political Radicalism."

80. Dawson, *Black Visions.*

81. Walter, "Black Immigrants and Political Radicalism," 315.

82. Lewis, *W. E. B. Du Bois*; Walter, "Black Immigrants and Political Radicalism"; Watkins-Owens, *Blood Relations.*

83. Reid, *Negro Immigrant*, 231.

84. Hellwig, "Black Meets Black."

85. Kasinitz, *Caribbean New York*, 219.

86. Domingo and Owen, "Policy of the *Messenger* on West Indian and American Negroes."

87. Hellwig, "Black Meets Black."

88. Berlin, "Changing Definition of African-American."

89. Kasinitz, *Caribbean New York.*

90. Ibid., 9.

91. Foner, "West Indian Identity in the Diaspora"; Kasinitz, *Caribbean New York.* Harold Cruse has also noted that "perceptive whites" in the 1950s played on the division between African Americans and Black immigrants and used it to their advantage (*Crisis of the Negro Intellectual*).

92. Kasinitz, *Caribbean New York.*

93. Ibid.

94. Kim, "Racial Triangulation."

95. Rogers, "Race-Based Coalitions among Minority Groups"; Rogers, *Afro-Caribbean Immigrants and the Politics of Incorporation.*

96. Rogers, *Afro-Caribbean Immigrants and the Politics of Incorporation.*

97. Jorge Durand, Douglass S. Massey, and Fernando Charvet, "The Changing Geography of Mexican Immigration to the United States: 1910–1996," *Social Science Quarterly* 81, no. 1 (2000); Paula D. McClain et al., "Racial Distancing in a Southern City: Latino Immigrants' Views of Black Americans," *Journal of Politics* 68, no. 3 (2006).

98. Durand, Massey, and Charvet, "Changing Geography of Mexican Immigration to the United States"; McClain et al., "Racial Distancing in a Southern City"; Paula D. McClain et al., "Intergroup Relations in Three Southern Cities," in *Just Neighbors? Research on African American and Latinos Relations in the United States*, ed. Edward Telles, Mark Q. Sawyer, and Gaspar Rivera-Salgado (New York: Russell Sage Foundation, 2011); Monica McDermott, "Black Attitudes and Hispanic Immigrants in South Carolina," in ibid.; Helen Marrow, "Hispanic Immigration, Black Population Size, and Intergroup Relations in the Rural and Small-Town South," in *New Faces in New Places: The Changing Geography of American Immigration*, ed. Douglas S. Massey (New York: Russell Sage Foundation, 2008).

99. Lisa Hoppenjas and Ted Richardson, "Mexican Ways, African Roots," *Winston-Salem Journal*, June 19, 2005.

100. Marrow, "Hispanic Immigration, Black Population Size"; McClain et al., "Racial Distancing in a Southern City"; Bobby Vaughn and Ben Vinson III, "Unfinished

Migrations: From the Mexican South to the American South," in *Beyond Slavery: The Multilayered Legacy of Africans in Latin America and the Caribbean*, ed. Darién J. Davis (Lanham, MD: Rowman and Littlefield, 2007).

101. Vaughn and Vinson, "Unfinished Migrations," 231.

102. Hoppenjas and Richardson, "Mexican Ways, African Roots"; Jennifer A. Jones, "Blacks May Be Second Class, but They Can't Make Them Leave: Mexican Racial Formation and Immigrant Status in Winston-Salem," *Latino Studies* 10, no. 1 (2012).

103. Elizabeth Barnett, "'Somos Costeños': Afro-Mexican Transnational Migration and Community Formation in Mexico and Winston-Salem, NC" (unpublished paper, Connecticut College, 2011).

104. Vaughn and Vinson, "Unfinished Migrations."

105. Jones, "Blacks May Be Second Class, but They Can't Make Them Leave," 68.

106. Ibid., 72–73.

107. Ibid., 75.

108. Galen Spencer Hull, "Immigrant Entrepreneurs: The Face of the New Nashville," *iBusiness* 2 (2009).

109. *Welcome to Shelbyville*, directed by Kim A. Snyder, *Independent Lens*, PBS, 2011.

110. Ginetta E. B. Candelario, *Black behind the Ears: Dominican Racial Identity from Museums to Beauty Shops* (Durham: Duke University Press, 2007), 164.

111. Ibid.

112. Kasinitz, *Caribbean New York*.

113. Rogers, *Afro-Caribbean Immigrants and the Politics of Incorporation*.

114. Darryl Fears, "In Diversity Push, Top Universities Enrolling More Black Immigrants," *Washington Post*, March 6, 2007; Sawyer, *Racial Politics in Post-Revolutionary Cuba*; Swarns, "'African-American' Becomes a Term of Debate."

NOTES TO CHAPTER 2

1. Foner, "West Indian Identity in the Diaspora"; Waters, *Black Identities*; Mary C. Waters, "Ethnic and Racial Identities of Second-Generation Black Immigrants in New York City," *International Migration Review* 29, no. 4 (1994).

2. Dawson, *Behind the Mule*.

3. Dawson, *Black Visions*, 44.

4. Dawson, *Behind the Mule*; Haynie and Watts, "Blacks and the Democratic Party"; Paula McClain et al., "Group Membership, Group Identity, and Group Consciousness: Measures of Racial Identity in American Politics?," *Annual Review of Political Science* 12 (2009); McClain and Stewart, *Can We All Get Along?*; Richard D. Shingles, "Black Consciousness and Political Participation: The Missing Link," *American Political Science Review* 75, no. 1 (1981); Sidney Verba and Norman Nie, *Participation in America: Political Democracy and Social Equality* (New York: Harper and Row, 1972).

5. Yvette M. Alex-Assensoh, "African Immigrants and African-Americans: An

Analysis of Voluntary African Immigration and the Evolution of Black Ethnic Politics in America," *African and Asian Studies* 8, nos. 1–2 (2009).

6. Candelario, *Black behind the Ears*; Greenbaum, *More than Black*; Kasinitz, *Caribbean New York*; Kim, *Bitter Fruit*.

7. Robert M. Sellers et al., "Multidimensional Model of Racial Identity: A Reconceptualization of African American Racial Identity," *Personality and Social Psychology Review* 2, no. 1 (1998); Robert M. Sellers and J. Nicole Shelton, "The Role of Racial Identity in Perceived Racial Discrimination," *Journal of Personality and Social Psychology* 84, no. 5 (2003); J. Nicole Shelton and Robert M. Sellers, "Situational Stability in African American Racial Identity," *Journal of Black Psychology* 26, no. 1 (2000).

8. Rawi Abdelal et al., "Identity as a Variable," *Perspectives on Politics* 4, no. 4 (2006): 695.

9. Zoltan L. Hajnal and Taeku Lee, *Why Americans Don't Join the Party: Race, Immigration, and the Failure (of Political Parties) to Engage the Electorate* (Princeton: Princeton University Press, 2011).

10. Ibid.; Taeku Lee, "Race, Immigration, and the Identity-to-Politics Link," *Annual Review of Political Science* 11, no. 1 (2008).

11. Pamela Johnston Conover, "The Role of Social Groups in Political Thinking," *British Journal of Political Science* 18, no. 1 (1988): 52.

12. Ibid.

13. Vilna F. Bashi, "Racial Categories Matter Because Racial Hierarchies Matter: A Commentary," *Ethnic and Racial Studies* 21, no. 5 (1998); James F. Davis, *Who Is Black? One Nation's Definition* (University Park: Pennsylvania State University Press, 1991); Ian F. Haney-López, *White by Law: The Legal Construction of Race* (New York: NYU Press, 2006); Nobles, *Shades of Citizenship*; Kim M. Williams, *Mark One or More: Civil Rights in Multiracial America* (Ann Arbor: University of Michigan Press, 2006).

14. Bashi, "Racial Categories Matter"; Eduardo Bonilla-Silva, "Rethinking Racism: Toward a Structural Interpretation," *American Sociological Review* 62, no. 3 (1997); Christine E. Guarneri and Christopher Dick, "Methods of Assigning Race and Hispanic Origin to Births from Vital Statistics Data" (paper presented at the annual meeting of the Federal Committee on Statistical Methodology, Washington, DC, 2012).

15. Conover, "Role of Social Groups in Political Thinking."

16. Hajnal and Lee, *Why Americans Don't Join the Party*, 115.

17. Dennis Chong and Reuel Rogers, "Reviving Group Consciousness," in *The Politics of Democratic Inclusion*, ed. Christina Wolbrecht and Rodney E. Hero (Philidelphia: Temple University Press, 2005); Lee, "Race, Immigration, and the Identity-to-Politics Link."

18. McClain et al., "Group Membership, Group Identity, and Group Consciousness," 476.

19. Chong and Rogers, "Reviving Group Consciousness."
20. Patricia Gurin, Shirley Hatchett, and James Sidney Jackson, *Hope and Independence: Blacks' Response to Electoral and Party Politics* (New York: Russell Sage Foundation, 1989), vii. There were also important works prior to this era that discussed racial group consciousness. See W. O. Brown, "The Nature of Race Consciousness," *Social Forces* 10, no. 1 (1931); Brown, "Race Consciousness among South African Natives," *American Journal of Sociology* 40, no. 5 (1935); and Elizabeth A. Ferguson, "Race Consciousness among American Negroes," *Journal of Negro Education* 7, no. 1 (1938). Works that came after the Civil Rights Movement include Mary R. Jackman and Robert W. Jackman, "An Interpretation of the Relation between Objective and Subjective Social Status," *American Sociological Review* 38, no. 5 (1973); Patricia Gurin, Arthur H. Miller, and Gerald Gurin, "Stratum Identification and Consciousness," *Social Psychology Quarterly* 43, no. 1 (1980); Shingles, "Black Consciousness and Political Participation"; and Verba and Nie, *Participation in America*.
21. Gurin, Hatchett, and Jackson, *Hope and Independence*, vii.
22. Ibid.; Haynie and Watts, "Blacks and the Democratic Party"; Katherine Tate, *From Protest to Politics: The New Black Politics in American Elections* (New York: Russell Sage Foundation, 1994).
23. Verba and Nie, *Participation in America*.
24. Shingles, "Black Consciousness and Political Participation," 77; Verba and Nie, *Participation in America*.
25. Haynie and Watts, "Blacks and the Democratic Party."
26. Jan E. Leighley and Arnold Vedlitz, "Race, Ethnicity, and Political Participation: Competing Models and Contrasting Explanations," *Journal of Politics* 61, no. 4 (1999); Clyde Wilcox and Leopoldo Gomez, "Religion, Group Identification, and Politics among African Americans," *Sociological Analysis* 51, no. 3 (1990).
27. Chong and Rogers, "Reviving Group Consciousness"; Dawson, *Behind the Mule*; Junn and Masuoka, "Asian American Identity"; Tate, *From Protest to Politics*.
28. Tate, *From Protest to Politics*.
29. Chong and Rogers, "Reviving Group Consciousness."
30. Waters, "Immigration, Intermarriage, and the Challenges."
31. Reuel R. Rogers, "'Black Like Who?' Afro-Caribbean Immigrants, African Americans, and the Politics of Group Identity," in *Islands in the City: West Indian Migration to New York*, ed. Nancy Foner (Berkeley: University of California Press, 2001).
32. Nteta, "*Plus Ça Change, Plus C'est la Même Chose*?"; Alejandro Portes, "For the Second Generation, One Step at a Time," in *Reinventing the Melting Pot: The New Immigrants and What it Means to Be American*, ed. Tamar Jacoby (New York: Basic Books, 2004); Waters, *Black Identities*.
33. Nteta, "*Plus Ça Change, Plus C'est la Même Chose*?"; Waters, "Role of Lineage"; Waters, *Black Identities*.
34. Teceta Thomas Tormala and Kay Deaux, "Black Immigrants to the United

States: Confronting and Constructing Ethnicity and Race," in *Cultural Psychology of Immigrants*, ed. Ramaswami Mahalingam (Mahway, NJ: Erlbaum, 2006); Milton Vickerman, *Crosscurrents: West Indian Immigrants and Race* (Oxford: Oxford University Press, 1999); Vickerman, "Jamaicans: Balancing Race and Ethnicity," in *New Immigrants in New York*, ed. Nancy Foner (New York: Columbia University Press, 2001); Waters, "Role of Lineage"; Waters, *Black Identities*.

35. Kasinitz, *Caribbean New York*; Nteta, *"Plus Ça Change, Plus C'est la Même Chose?"*

36. Waters, *Black Identities*; Mary C. Waters, "Growing Up West Indian and African American: Gender and Class Differences in the Second Generation," in *Islands in the City: West Indian Migration to New York*, ed. Nancy Foner (Berkeley: University of California Press, 2001).

37. Portes, "For the Second Generation, One Step at a Time"; Portes and Rumbaut, *Immigrant American*; Portes and Zhou, "The New Second Generation."

38. Sherri-Ann P. Butterfield, "Challenging American Conceptions of Race and Ethnicity: Second-Generation West Indian Immigrants," *International Journal of Sociology and Social Policy* 24, nos. 7–8 (2004); Butterfield, " 'We're Just Black': The Racial and Ethnic Identities of Second-Generation West Indians in New York," in *Becoming New Yorkers: Ethnographies of the New Second Generation*, ed. Philip Kasinitz, John H. Mollenkopf, and Mary C. Waters (New York: Russell Sage Foundation, 2004); Schekeva P. Hall and Robert T. Carter, "The Relationship between Racial Identity, Ethnic Identity, and Perceptions of Racial Discrimination in an Afro-Caribbean Descent Sample," *Journal of Black Psychology* 32, no. 2 (2006); Waters, *Black Identities*.

39. Sunil Bhatia and Anjali Ram, "Rethinking 'Aculturation' in Relation to Diasporic Cultures and Postcolonial Identities," *Human Development* 44 (2001): 13.

40. Michael Omi and Howard Winant, *Racial Formation in the United States: From the 1960s to the 1990s*, 2nd ed. (New York: Routledge, 1994).

41. Amadou Diallo was a twenty-three-year-old immigrant from Guinea. In reaction to Diallo's attempt to show identification, four New York City police officers, who assumed he was reaching for a weapon, fired forty-one shots at him; nineteen of them struck Diallo. Diallo was unarmed. The officers were acquitted, but the situation illuminated issues of racial profiling and police brutality. For a more in-depth analysis of the case, see Leslie V. Dery, "Amadou Diallo and the 'Foreigner' Meme: Interpreting the Application of Federal Court Interpreter Laws," *Florida Law Review* 53 (2001).

42. Nancy Foner, "The Jamaicans: Race and Ethnicity among Migrants in New York," in *New Immigrants in New York*, ed. Nancy Foner (New York: Columbia University Press, 1987).

43. Richard D. Alba, *Ethnic Idenitty: The Transformation of White America* (New Haven: Yale University Press, 1990); Ignatiev, *How the Irish Became White*; Robert Orsi, "The Religious Boundaries of an Inbetween People: Street *Feste* and the Problem of the Dark-Skinned Other in Italian Harlem, 1920–1990," *American Quarterly* 44, no. 3 (1992); Joseph Pugliese, "Race as Category Crisis: Whiteness

and the Topical Assignation of Race," *Social Semiotics* 12, no. 2 (2002); Roediger, *Wages of Whiteness*; Rogers, "Black Like Who?"

44. Rowland T. Berthoff, "Southern Attitudes toward Immigration, 1895–1914," *Journal of Southern History* 17, no. 3 (1951); Ignatiev, *How the Irish Became White*; Orsi, "Religious Boundaries of an Inbetween People"; Frederick B. Parker, "The Status of the Foreign Stock in the South-East: A Region-Nation Comparison," *Social Forces* 27, no. 2 (1948); Pugliese, "Race as Category Crisis"; Roediger, *Wages of Whiteness*; Rogers, "Black Like Who?"

45. Ignatiev, *How the Irish Became White*.

46. Berthoff, "Southern Attitudes toward Immigration"; Orsi, "Religious Boundaries of an Inbetween People"; Pugliese, "Race as Category Crisis."

47. Pugliese, "Race as Category Crisis."

48. Victoria Hattam, *In the Shadow of Race: Jews, Latinos, and Immigrant Politics in the United States* (Chicago: University of Chicago Press, 2007); Ignatiev, *How the Irish Became White*; Orsi, "Religious Boundaries of an Inbetween People"; Roediger, *Working toward Whiteness*; Roediger, *Wages of Whiteness*.

49. Berthoff, "Southern Attitudes toward Immigration," 344.

50. Stephen Steinberg, *The Ethnic Myth: Race, Ethnicity, and Class in America* (Boston: Beacon, 2001).

51. Ibid., 42.

52. Bob Blaumer, *Racial Oppression in America* (New York: Harper and Row, 1972); Steinberg, *Ethnic Myth*.

53. James W. Loewen, *The Mississippi Chinese: Between Black and White* (Cambridge: Harvard University Press, 1971).

54. Kim, "Racial Triangulation."

55. Nancy A. Denton and Douglas S. Massey, "Racial Identity among Caribbean Hispanics: The Effect of Double Minority Status on Residential Segregation," *American Sociological Review* 54, no. 5 (1989); Arthur H. Kim and Michael J. White, "Pathethnicity, Ethnic Diversity, and Residential Segregation," *American Journal of Sociology* 115, no. 5 (2010).

56. Bailey, "Dominican-American Ethnic/Racial Identities and United States Social Categories."

57. Bonilla-Silva, "Rethinking Racism."

58. Omi and Winant, *Racial Formation in the United States*.

59. Joane Nagel, "Constructing Ethnicity: Creating and Recreating Ethnic Identity and Culture," *Social Problems* 41, no. 1 (1994): 156.

60. Michael Jones-Correa and David L. Leal, "Becoming 'Hispanic': Secondary Panethnic Identification among Latin American–Origin Populations in the United States," *Hispanic Journal of Behavioral Sciences* 18, no. 2 (1996).

61. Lee, "Pan-Ethnic Identity, Linked Fate," 6.

62. David Lopez and Yan Espiritu, "Panethnicity in the United States: A Theoretical Framework," *Ethnic and Racial Studies* 13, no. 2 (1990); Nagel, "Constructing Ethnicity."

63. Alejandro Portes and Ruben G. Rumbaut, *Legacies: The Story of the Immigrant Second Generation* (Berkeley: University of California Press, 2001), 150.
64. Kim and White, "Pathethnicity, Ethnic Diversity, and Residential Segregation"; Nobles, *Shades of Citizenship*; Williams, *Mark One or More*.
65. Kim and White, "Pathethnicity, Ethnic Diversity, and Residential Segregation."
66. Dina G. Okamoto, "Institutional Panethnicity: Boundary Formation in Asian American Organizing," *Social Forces* 85, no. 1 (2006): 2; Nagel, "Constructing Ethnicity."
67. Felix M. Padilla, *Latino Ethnic Consciousness: The Case of Mexian Americans and Puerto Ricans in Chicago* (Notre Dame, IN: University of Notre Dame Press, 1985).
68. Portes and Rumbaut, *Immigrant American*.
69. Joane Nagel, "American Indian Ethnic Renewal: Politics and the Resurgence of Identity," *American Sociological Review* 60, no. 6 (1995).
70. Yan Espiritu, *Asian American Panethnicity: Bridging Institutions and Identities* (Philadelphia: Temple University Press, 1992).
71. Kim, *Bitter Fruit*.
72. Dina G. Okamoto, "Toward a Theory of Panethnicity: Explaining Asian American Collective Action," *American Sociological Review* 68, no. 6 (2003).
73. Phillip Kasinitz and Milton Vickerman, "Ethnic Niches and Racial Traps: Jamaicans in the New York Regional Economy," in *Migration, Transnationalization, and Race in a Changing New York*, ed. Héctor Cordero-Guzmán, Robert C. Smith, and Ramón Grosfoguel (Philidelphia: Temple University Press, 2001).
74. Milagros Ricourt and Ruby Danta, *Hispanas de Queens: Latino Panethnicty in a New York City Neighborhood* (Ithaca: Cornell University Press, 2003).
75. Louis DeSipio, "More than the Sum of Its Parts: The Building Blocks of a Pan-Ethnic Latino Identity," in *The Politics of Minority Coalitions: Race, Ethnicity, and Shared Uncertainties*, ed. Wilbur C. Rich (Westport, CT: Praeger 1996).
76. Lopez and Espiritu, "Panethnicity in the United States."
77. Kyle D. Crowder, "Residential Segregation of West Indians in the New York / New Jersey Metropolital Area: The Roles of Race and Ethnicity," *International Migration Review* 33, no. 1 (1999); Denton and Massey, "Racial Identity among Caribbean Hispanics"; Kim and White, "Pathethnicity, Ethnic Diversity, and Residential Segregation"; Douglas S. Massey and Nancy A. Denton, *American Apartheid: Segregation and the Making of the Underclass* (Cambridge: Harvard University Press, 1993).
78. Okamoto, "Institutional Panethnicity."
79. Ricourt and Danta, *Hispanas de Queens*.
80. Espiritu, *Asian American Panethnicity*; Okamoto, "Institutional Panethnicity."
81. Pei-te Lien, M. Margaret Conway, and Janelle Wong, "The Contours and Sources of Ethnic Identity Choices among Asian Americans," *Social Science Quarterly* 84, no. 2 (2003); McClain et al., "Group Membership, Group Identity, and Group Consciousness"; McClain and Stewart, *Can We All Get*

Along?; Okamoto, "Toward a Theory of Panethnicity"; Okamoto, "Institutional Panethnicity."

82. Lien, Conway, and Wong, "Contours and Sources of Ethnic Identity," 463.
83. Patrick L. Mason, "Culture and Intraracial Wage Inequality," *American Economic Review* 100 (2010); Waters, "West Indians and African Americans at Work."
84. Foner, "West Indian Identity in the Diaspora"; Nteta, *"Plus Ça Change, Plus C'est la Même Chose?"*; Olúfẹ́mi Táíwò, "The Prison Called My Skin: On Being Black in America," in *Problematizing Blackness: Self-Ethnographics by Black Immigrants to the United States*, ed. Percy C. Hintzen and Jean Muteba Rahier (New York: Routledge, 2003); Waters, *Black Identities*.
85. See for example Jane Junn and Kerry L. Haynie, *New Race Politics in America: Understanding Minority and Immigrant Politics* (New York: Cambridge University Press, 2008); McClain and Stewart, *Can We All Get Along?*
86. Stokely Carmichael and Charles Hamilton, *Black Power: The Politics of Liberation in America* (New York: Random House, 1967).
87. McClain and Stewart, *Can We All Get Along?*; Nicolas C. Vaca, *The Presumed Alliance: The Unspoken Conflict between Latinos and Blacks and What It Means for America* (New York: HarperCollins, 2004).
88. Kim, *Bitter Fruit*; McClain and Stewart, *Can We All Get Along?*; Raphael J. Sonenshein, *Politics in Black and White* (Princeton: Princeton University Press, 1993).
89. Haynie and Watts, "Blacks and the Democratic Party"; Mark Hugo Lopez, *The Hispanic Vote in the 2008 Election* (Washington, DC: Pew Hispanic Center, 2008); Mark Hugo Lopez and Paul Taylor, *Dissecting the 2008 Electorate: Most Diverse in U.S. History* (Washington, DC: Pew Research Center, 2009).
90. Bonilla-Silva, "Rethinking Racism"; Feagin, *Racist America*; Kim, *Bitter Fruit*.
91. Kim, *Bitter Fruit*, 10.
92. Waters, *Black Identities*.
93. Foner, "West Indian Identity in the Diaspora"; Nteta, *"Plus Ça Change, Plus C'est la Même Chose?"*; Waters, "Role of Lineage"; Waters, *Black Identities*.
94. Joe R. Feagin and José A. Cobas, "Latinos/as and White Racial Frame: The Procrustean Bed of Assimilation," *Sociological Inquiry* 78, no. 1 (2008).
95. Paula D. McClain et al., "Racial Distancing in a Southern City: Latino Immigrants' Views of Black Americans," *Journal of Politics* 68, no. 3 (2006).
96. Kim, "Racial Triangulation."
97. Cohen, *Boundaries of Blackness*; Mark Q. Sawyer, "Race Politics in Multiethnic America: Black and Latina/o Identities," in *Neither Enemies nor Friends: Latinos, Blacks, Afro-Latinos*, ed. Anani Dzidzienyo and Suzanne Oboler (New York: Palgrave Macmillian, 2005).
98. Cohen, *Boundaries of Blackness*; Cathy J. Cohen, *Democracy Remixed: Black Youth and the Future of American Politics* (Oxford: Oxford University Press, 2010).
99. Nunnally, "Linking Blackness or Ethnic Othering?"
100. Foner, "West Indian Identity in the Diaspora"; Waters, *Black Identities*. African

Americans also espouse negative stereotypes about Black immigrants. Ira Reid lists several stereotypes about Black immigrants (*Negro Immigrant*), and Mary Waters similarly notes that some African Americans harbor negative feelings toward Black immigrants.

101. William A. Darity Jr., Darrick Hamilton, and Jason Dietrich, "Passing on Blackness: Latinos, Race, and Earnings in the USA," *Applied Economics Letters* 9 (2002); Sawyer, *Racial Politics in Post-Revolutionary Cuba*.

102. Táíwò, "The Prison Called My Skin."

103. Eduardo Bonilla-Silva, *Racism without Racists: Color-Blind Racism and Racial Inequality in Contemporary America*, 3rd ed. (Lanham, MD: Rowman and Littlefield, 2010); Kim, "Racial Triangulation"; Pierre, "Black Immigrants in the United States and the 'Cultural Narratives' of Ethnicity."

104. Darity, Hamilton, and Dietrich, "Passing on Blackness"; Ignatiev, *How the Irish Became White*; Roediger, *Working toward Whiteness*; Roediger, *Wages of Whiteness*.

105. Vilna F. Bashi, "Globalized Anti-Blackness: Transnationalizing Western Immigration Law, Policy, and Practice," *Ethnic and Racial Studies* 27, no. 4 (2004); Brock, "Questioning the Diaspora"; Kelley, "But a Local Phase of a World Problem"; Paterson and Kelley, "Unfinished Migrations"; Sawyer, "Race Politics in Multiethnic America."

106. Vickerman, *Crosscurrents*; Vickerman, "Jamaicans."

107. Butterfield, "Challenging American Conceptions of Race and Ethnicity"; Butterfield, "We're Just Black."

108. We might also consider the possibility of allegiances and coalitions along class lines. Middle-class African Americans and Black immigrants alike often make distinctions by class and make an effort to distance themselves from low-income Blacks. Butterfield, "Challenging American Conceptions of Race and Ethnicity"; Cohen, *Democracy Remixed*; E. Franklin Frazier, *The Black Bourgeoisie: The Rise of the New Middle Class in the United States* (New York: Free Press, 1957); Pew Research Center, *Optimism about Black Progress Declines: Blacks See Growing Values Gap between Poor and Middle Class* (Washington, DC: Pew Research Center, 2007).

109. Dawson, *Black Visions*; Harris-Lacewell, *Barbershops, Bibles, and BET*; Price, *Dreaming Blackness*.

110. Kimberlé W. Crenshaw, "Demarginalizing the Intersection of Race and Sex," *University of Chicago Legal Forum* 43 (1989); Simien, "Race, Gender, and Linked Fate"; Simien and Clawson, "Intersection of Race and Gender."

111. Cohen, *Boundaries of Blackness*; Dawson, *Behind the Mule*.

112. Alex-Assensoh, "African Immigrants and African-Americans"; Dawson, *Behind the Mule*; Dawson, *Black Visions*.

113. Lee, "Race, Immigration, and the Identity-to-Politics Link."

114. To be clear, when I talk about "generational status," I do not mean "generation" in the Mannheimian sense of the word. "Generational status" throughout this

work refers to one's lineage in the U.S.; more specifically, I mean to talk about whether Blacks are new to the United States (first-generation immigrants), whether they were born elsewhere but moved to the U.S. around the time of adolescence (1.5 generation), or whether they are they were born in the U.S. but are the children of immigrants (second-generation immigrants). There has been important foundational work in the Black politics literature that analyzes Mannheimian generational differences among African Americans, particularly in an effort to gain a sense of the extent to which those African Americans who came of age before, during, or after the Civil Rights Movement see the world differently. See, for example, Cathy J. Cohen, "Millennials and the Myth of the Post-racial Society: Black Youth, Intra-generational Divisions and the Continuing Racial Divide in American Politics," *Daedalus* 140, no. 2 (2011); Ellis Cose, *The End of Anger: A New Generation's Take on Race and Rage* (New York: Harper-Collins, 2011); and Andrea Simpson, *The Tie That Binds: Identity and Political Attitudes in the Post–Civil Rights Generation* (New York: NYU Press, 1998). See also Karl Mannheim, "The Problem of Generations," in *Essays on the Sociology of Knowledge*, ed. Karl Mannheim and Paul Kecskemeti (New York: Oxford University Press, 1952).

NOTES TO CHAPTER 3

1. Omi and Winant, *Racial Formation in the United States*; Viruell-Fuentes, "It's a Lot of Work."
2. Nagel, "Constructing Ethnicity"; Omi and Winant, *Racial Formation in the United States*.
3. Kasinitz, *Caribbean New York*; Waters, "Growing Up West Indian and African American."
4. Michael C. Thornton, Robert Joseph Taylor, and Tony N. Brown, "Correlates of Racial Label Use among Americans of African Descent: Colored, Negro, Black, and African American," *Race and Society* 2, no. 2 (2000).
5. William E. Cross Jr., *Shades of Black: Diversity in African-American Identity* (Philadelphia: Temple University Press, 1991), 190.
6. William E. Cross Jr., "Negro-to-Black Conversion Experience: Toward a Psychology of Black LIberation," *Black World* 20, no. 9 (1971); William E. Cross Jr., "The Thomas and Cross Models of Psychological Nigrescence: A Review," *Journal of Black Psychology* 5, no. 1 (1978); William E. Cross Jr., Thomas A. Parham, and Janet E. Helms, "Nigrescence Revisited: Theory and Research," in *African American Identity Development: Theory, Research, and Intervention*, ed. Reginald L. Jones (Hampton, VA: Cobb and Henry, 1998); Cross, *Shades of Black*.
7. Cross, *Shades of Black*, 199.
8. Ibid., 214.
9. Tom W. Smith, "Changing Racial Labels: From 'Colored' to 'Negro' to 'Black' to 'African American,'" *Public Opinion Quarterly* 56, no. 4 (1992).
10. Brown, "Nature of Race Consciousness."

11. Davis, *Who Is Black?*; Haney-López, *White by Law*; Nobles, *Shades of Citizenship*.
12. Bashi, "Racial Categories Matter."
13. Halford H. Fairchild, "Black, Negro, or Afro-American? The Differences Are Crucial!," *Journal of Black Studies* 16, no. 1 (1985).
14. Bashi, "Racial Categories Matter."
15. Swarns, "'African-American' Becomes a Term of Debate."
16. Jose Itzigsohn, Silvia Giorguli, and Obed Vazquez, "Immigrant Incorporation and Racial Identity: Racial Self-Identification among Dominican Immigrants," *Ethnic and Racial Studies* 28, no. 1 (2005): 51.
17. Kasinitz, *Caribbean New York*.
18. Jeffery M. Jones, "Racial or Ethnic Labels Make Little Difference to Blacks, Hispanics" (Gallup News Service, September 11, 2001); Lee Sigelman, Steven A. Tuch, and Jack K. Martin, "What's in a Name? Preference for 'Black' versus 'African-American' among Americans of African Descent," *Public Opinion Quarterly* 69, no. 3 (2005).
19. Carol K. Sigelman et al., "Black Candidates, White Voters: Understanding Racial Bias in Political Perceptions," *American Journal of Political Science* 39, no. 1 (1995).
20. U.S. Census Bureau, "American Community—Blacks: 2004."
21. Williams, *Mark One or More*.
22. Greenbaum, *More than Black*; Hellwig, "Black Meets Black."
23. Kasinitz, *Caribbean New York*; Waters, "Immigration, Intermarriage, and the Challenges."
24. Mary Herring, Thomas B. Jankowski, and Ronald E. Brown, "Pro-Black Doesn't Mean Anti-White: The Structure of African-American Group Identity," *Journal of Politics* 61, no. 3 (1999).
25. Crowder, "Residential Segregation of West Indians"; Denton and Massey, "Racial Identity among Caribbean Hispanics"; Kim and White, "Pathethnicity, Ethnic Diversity, and Residential Segregation"; Massey and Denton, *American Apartheid*; Suzzane Model, "Caribbean Immigrants: A Black Success Story?," *International Migration Review* 25, no. 2 (1991); Jen'nan Ghazal Read and Michael O. Emerson, "Racial Context, Black Immigration and the U.S. Black/White Health Disparity," *Social Forces* 84, no. 1 (2005). Wilson, *Declining Significance of Race*.
26. Butterfield, "Challenging American Conceptions of Race and Ethnicity"; Butterfield, "We're Just Black."
27. Haitians are separated from the sample because there was a large enough sample size to look at this group in isolation (n = 236). Respondents from English-speaking Caribbean countries were grouped together. There was only a small contingent of respondents from African countries (in total forty-nine), so separating them out by country of origin would not have been analytically fruitful.
28. Foner, "West Indian Identity in the Diaspora"; Waters, *Black Identities*.
29. Butterfield, "Challenging American Conceptions of Race and Ethnicity"; Butterfield, "We're Just Black."

30. Clifford L. Broman, Harold W. Neighbors, and James S. Jackson, "Racial Group Identification among Black Adults," *Social Forces* 67, no. 1 (1988); David H. Demo and Michael Hughes, "Socialization and Racial Identity among Black Americans," *Social Psychology Quarterly* 53, no. 4 (1990); Sigelman, Tuch, and Martin, "What's in a Name?"; Smith, "Changing Racial Labels."
31. Sigelman, Tuch, and Martin, "What's in a Name?," 437.
32. Vickerman, *Crosscurrents*; Waters, "Growing Up West Indian and African American."
33. Not all the respondents were asked the questions on the portion of the survey that included questions of "proximity" and "closeness"; thus, the number of respondents decreases significantly from the initially asked question about preference for racial or ethnic labels.
34. Portes, "For the Second Generation, One Step at a Time"; Portes and Rumbaut, *Immigrant American*; Portes and Rumbaut, *Legacies*; Portes and Zhou, "New Second Generation"; Waters, *Black Identities*.
35. Vilna F. Bashi Bobb and Averil Y. Clarke, "Experiencing Success: Structuring the Perception of Opportunities for West Indians," in *Islands in the City: West Indian Migration to New York*, ed. Nancy Foner (Berkeley: University of California Press, 2001).
36. Butterfield, ""We're Just Black.""
37. Quoted in Swarns, "'African-American' Becomes a Term of Debate."
38. Jones, "Racial or Ethnic Labels Make Little Difference to Blacks, Hispanics."
39. I am aware that there are multiple Black communities. The question wording was, "When you say or hear the phrase 'Black community,' who are you thinking of? Who is included?"
40. Cross, Parham, and Helms, "Nigrescence Revisited," 11.
41. Bashi, "Globalized Anti-Blackness"; Brock, "Questioning the Diaspora"; Paterson and Kelley, "Unfinished Migrations."
42. Quoted in Kelley, "But a Local Phase of a World Problem," 1054.
43. Dawson, *Behind the Mule*.
44. Feagin and Cobas, "Latinos/as and White Racial Frame."

NOTES TO CHAPTER 4

1. Bryce-Laporte, "Black Immigrants"; Vickerman, "Jamaicans"; Vickerman, "Tweaking a Monolith."
2. Stephen Cornell and Douglas Hartmann, *Ethnicity and Race: Making Identities in a Changing World*, 2nd ed. (Thousand Oaks, CA: Pine Forge, 2007), 26.
3. Vilna F. Bashi and Antonio McDaniel, "A Theory of Immigration and Racial Stratification," *Journal of Black Studies* 27, no. 5 (1997); Bashi, "Racial Categories Matter."
4. A racialized social system is a society where political, economic, and social advantages are distributed based on racial group membership, where some

groups are disproportionately rewarded while others are penalized. For a full explanation of the theory, see Bonilla-Silva, "Rethinking Racism."

5. Sellers et al., "Multidimensional Model of Racial Identity."

6. Ibid., 23.

7. Ibid., 25.

8. Ibid., 26.

9. Ibid., 27.

10. Sellers et al., "Multidimensional Model of Racial Identity," 24.

11. Broman, Neighbors, and Jackson, "Racial Group Identification among Black Adults."

12. Ibid.

13. Richard L. Allen, Michael C. Dawson, and Ronald E. Brown, "A Schema-Based Approach to Modeling an African-American Racial Belief System," *American Political Science Review* 83, no. 2 (1989).

14. Demo and Hughes, "Socialization and Racial Identity among Black Americans"; Harris, "Exploring the Determinants of Adult Black Identity."

15. Jennifer Lee and Frank D. Bean, "America's Changing Color Lines: Immigration, Race/Ethnicity, and Multiracial Identification," *Annual Review of Sociology* 30 (2004): 225.

16. Bhatia and Ram, "Rethinking 'Aculturation' "; Margaret A. Gibson, "Immigrant Adaptation and Patterns of Acculturation," *Human Development* 44, no. 1 (January–February 2001).

17. Bhatia and Ram, "Rethinking 'Aculturation,' " 13.

18. Ibid.; Gibson, "Immigrant Adaptation and Patterns of Acculturation."

19. Nteta, "*Plus Ça Change, Plus C'est la Même Chose?*"; Vickerman, *Crosscurrents*; Waters, "Role of Lineage"; Waters, "Ethnic and Racial Identities"; Waters, *Black Identities*.

20. Foner, "West Indian Identity in the Diaspora."

21. Waters, *Black Identities*.

22. David O. Sears et al., "Race in American Politics: Framing the Debates," in *Racialized Politics: The Debate about Racism in America*, ed. David O. Sears, Jim Sidanius, and Lawrence Bobo (Chicago: University of Chicago Press, 2000).

23. Tormala and Deaux, "Black Immigrants to the United States"; Vickerman, *Crosscurrents*; Vickerman, "Jamaicans"; Waters, "Ethnic and Racial Identities."

24. Tormala and Deaux, "Black Immigrants to the United States."

25. Rogers, *Afro-Caribbean Immigrants and the Politics of Incorporation.*

26. Mason, "Culture and Intraracial Wage Inequality"; Katherine S. Newman, *No Shame in My Game: The Working Poor in the Inner City* (New York: Russell Sage Foundation, 1999); Roger Waldinger, *Still the Promised City?* (Cambridge: Harvard University Press, 1996).

27. Nteta, "*Plus Ça Change, Plus C'est la Même Chose?*"

28. Foner, "West Indian Identity in the Diaspora"; Vickerman, *Crosscurrents*.

29. Rogers, *Afro-Caribbean Immigrants and the Politics of Incorporation.*
30. Bobb and Clarke, "Experiencing Success"; Jean S. Phinney and Mukosolu Onwughalu, "Racial Identity and Perception of American Ideals among African American and African Students in the United States," *International Journal of Intercultural Relations* 20, no. 2 (1996); Vickerman, *Crosscurrents*; Vickerman, "Jamaicans."
31. Steven Song, "Finding One's Place: Shifting Ethnic Identities of Recent Immigrant Children from China, Haiti, and Mexico in the United States," *Ethnic and Racial Studies* 33, no. 6 (2010).
32. Portes and Rumbaut, *Immigrant American*; Portes and Zhou, "New Second Generation."
33. Portes, "For the Second Generation, One Step at a Time"; Portes and Rumbaut, *Immigrant American*; Portes and Rumbaut, *Legacies*; Portes and Zhou, "New Second Generation."
34. Waters, *Black Identities*; Waters, "Growing Up West Indian and African American."
35. Stephen Steinberg, "Immigration, African Americans, and Race Discourse," *New Politics* 38 (2005): 50.
36. Bobb and Clarke, "Experiencing Success."
37. Alford Young Jr., "Black Men, Racefulness, and Getting Ahead in American Society: A Cultural Paradigm Reconstituted" (paper presented at the Race Workshop, Duke University, February 23, 2010).
38. Philip Kasinitz et al., *Inheriting the City: The Children of Immigrants Come of Age* (New York: Russell Sage Foundation, 2008).
39. Cross, *Shades of Black.*
40. Butterfield, "Challenging American Conceptions of Race and Ethnicity"; Butterfield, "We're Just Black"; Hall and Carter, "Relationship between Racial Identity, Ethnic Identity, and Perceptions of Racial Discrimination."
41. Butterfield, "Challenging American Conceptions of Race and Ethnicity"; Butterfield, "We're Just Black"; Waters, *Black Identities*; Waters, "Growing Up West Indian and African American."
42. Butterfield, "We're Just Black."
43. Song, "Finding One's Place."
44. Butterfield, "Challenging American Conceptions of Race and Ethnicity"; Butterfield, "We're Just Black."
45. Broman, Neighbors, and Jackson, "Racial Group Identification among Black Adults"; Demo and Hughes, "Socialization and Racial Identity among Black Americans"; Harris, "Exploring the Determinants of Adult Black Identity"; Earl Lewis, "To Turn as on a Pivot: Writing African Americans into a History of Overlapping Diasporas," *American Historical Review* 100, no. 3 (1995); Nunnally, "Learning Race, Socializing Blackness"; Song, "Finding One's Place."
46. Nunnally, "Learning Race, Socializing Blackness."
47. Demo and Hughes, "Socialization and Racial Identity among Black Americans."

48. Michael C. Dawson, "A Black Counterpublic? Economic Earthquakes, Racial Agenda(s), and Black Politics," *Public Culture* 7, no. 1 (1994); Harris-Lacewell, *Barbershops, Bibles, and BET.*
49. Nagel, "Constructing Ethnicity."
50. Foner, "West Indian Identity in the Diaspora"; Vickerman, "Jamaicans."
51. Butterfield, "We're Just Black"; Denton and Massey, "Racial Identity among Caribbean Hispanics."
52. Butterfield, "Challenging American Conceptions of Race and Ethnicity"; Butterfield, "We're Just Black."
53. Bonilla-Silva, *Racism without Racists*; Feagin and Cobas, "Latinos/as and White Racial Frame."
54. Bonilla-Silva, *Racism without Racists*, 28.
55. Ibid.; Cohen, *Democracy Remixed.*
56. Ellis Cose, *The Rage of a Priviledged Class* (New York: HarperPerennial, 1993); Dawson, *Behind the Mule*; Jennifer L. Hochschild, *Facing Up to the American Dream: Race, Class, and the Soul of the Nation* (Princeton: Princeton University Press, 1995).
57. Portes and Zhou, "New Second Generation."

NOTES TO CHAPTER 5

1. Dennis Chong and Reuel Rogers, "Racial Solidarity and Political Participation," *Political Behavior* 27, no. 4 (2005); Chong and Rogers, "Reviving Group Consciousness"; Dawson, *Behind the Mule*; Tate, *From Protest to Politics.*
2. Gabriel R. Sanchez, "The Role of Group Consciousness in Latino Public Opinion," *Political Research Quarterly* 59, no. 3 (2006): 436.
3. Chong and Rogers, "Racial Solidarity and Political Participation," 350.
4. Dawson, *Behind the Mule*, 10.
5. Ibid.
6. Crowder, "Residential Segregation of West Indians"; Denton and Massey, "Racial Identity among Caribbean Hispanics"; Kim and White, "Pathethnicity, Ethnic Diversity, and Residential Segregation."
7. Brown, "Nature of Race Consciousness"; Marx, *Making Race and Nation*; McClain et al., "Group Membership, Group Identity, and Group Consciousness."
8. Foner, "West Indian Identity in the Diaspora"; Nteta, "*Plus Ça Change, Plus C'est la Même Chose?*"; Portes and Rumbaut, *Immigrant American*; Waters, *Black Identities.*
9. Chong and Rogers, "Racial Solidarity and Political Participation," 350.
10. McClain et al., "Group Membership, Group Identity, and Group Consciousness," 476.
11. Allen, Dawson, and Brown, "Schema-Based Approach"; Dawson, *Behind the Mule.*
12. Chong and Rogers, "Racial Solidarity and Political Participation"; Dawson, *Behind the Mule*; Haynie and Watts, "Blacks and the Democratic Party."

13. McClain and Stewart, *Can We All Get Along?*; Arthur H. Miller et al., "Group Consciousness and Political Participation," *American Journal of Political Science* 25, no. 3 (1981).
14. Milton Lodge and Ruth Hamill, "A Partisan Schema for Political Information Processing," *American Political Science Review* 80, no. 2 (1986): 506; Pamela Johnston Conover and Stanley Feldman, "How People Organize the Political World: A Schematic Model," *American Journal of Political Science* 28, no. 1 (1984).
15. Allen, Dawson, and Brown, "Schema-Based Approach," 422.
16. Robert P. Abelson, "Differences between Belief and Knowledge Systems," *Cognitive Science* 3, no. 4 (1979): 355–60.
17. Katherine Tate, *What's Going On? Political Incorporation and the Transformation of Black Public Opinion* (Washington, DC: Georgetown University Press, 2010).
18. Dawson, *Behind the Mule*; Patricia Gurin, Shirley Hatchett, and James Sidney Jackson, *Hope and Independence: Blacks' Response to Electoral and Party Politics* (New York: Russell Sage Foundation, 1989).
19. Tate, *What's Going On?*, 5.
20. Haynie and Watts, "Blacks and the Democratic Party."
21. Chong and Rogers, "Reviving Group Consciousness."
22. Lawrence Bobo and Franklin D. Gilliam Jr., "Race, Sociopolitical Participation, and Black Empowerment," *American Political Science Review* 84, no. 2 (1990); Leighley and Vedlitz, "Race, Ethnicity, and Political Participation"; Wilcox and Gomez, "Religion, Group Identification, and Politics."
23. Bobo and Gilliam, "Race, Sociopolitical Participation, and Black Empowerment."
24. Chong and Rogers, "Reviving Group Consciousness"; Dawson, *Behind the Mule*; Junn and Masuoka, "Asian American Identity"; McClain et al., "Group Membership, Group Identity, and Group Consciousness."
25. Crowder, "Residential Segregation of West Indians"; Denton and Massey, "Racial Identity among Caribbean Hispanics"; Kim and White, "Pathethnicity, Ethnic Diversity, and Residential Segregation."
26. Read and Emerson, "Racial Context, Black Immigration and the U.S. Black/White Health Disparity"; Andrew M. Ryan, Gilbert C. Gee, and David F. Laflamme, "The Association between Self-Reported Discrimination, Physical Health and Blood Pressure: Findings from African Americans, Black Immigrants, and Latino Immigrants in New Hampshire," *Journal of Health Care for the Poor and Underserved* 17 (2006).
27. McClain et al., "Group Membership, Group Identity, and Group Consciousness."
28. Foner, "West Indian Identity in the Diaspora"; Nteta, "*Plus Ça Change, Plus C'est la Même Chose?*"; Portes, "For the Second Generation, One Step at a Time"; Waters, *Black Identities*.
29. Rogers, *Afro-Caribbean Immigrants and the Politics of Incorporation*.

30. Rogers, "Black Like Who?"; Rogers, *Afro-Caribbean Immigrants and the Politics of Incorporation*.

31. Miller et al., "Group Consciousness and Political Participation."

32. Foner, "West Indian Identity in the Diaspora"; Nteta, "*Plus Ça Change, Plus C'est la Même Chose*?"; Rogers, "Black Like Who?"; Waters, *Black Identities*.

33. Butterfield, "Challenging American Conceptions of Race and Ethnicity"; Butterfield, "We're Just Black"; Tormala and Deaux, "Black Immigrants to the United States."

34. Butterfield, "We're Just Black."

35. Vickerman, "Jamaicans."

36. Greenbaum, *More than Black*.

37. Candelario, *Black behind the Ears*.

38. Kasinitz, *Caribbean New York*; Kim, *Bitter Fruit*.

39. Junn and Masuoka, "Asian American Identity," 729.

40. Cohen, *Boundaries of Blackness*; Price, *Dreaming Blackness*.

41. McClain et al., "Group Membership, Group Identity, and Group Consciousness," 476.

42. Miller et al., "Group Consciousness and Political Participation."

43. Chong and Rogers, "Reviving Group Consciousness"; Lee, "Race, Immigration, and the Identity-to-Politics Link"; McClain et al., "Group Membership, Group Identity, and Group Consciousness."

44. There is no statistical difference between the proportion of African respondents and second-generation respondents who responded that they do not feel a sense of linked fate, but there were significantly more African respondents who responded "not very much" than second-generation respondents who did.

45. Butterfield, "Challenging American Conceptions of Race and Ethnicity"; Butterfield, "We're Just Black."

46. Adriane Danette Lentz-Smith, *Freedom Struggle: African Americans and World War I* (Cambridge: Harvard University Press, 2009).

47. I only asked about half the respondents this question because I was able to develop more pointed, useful questions as I interviewed more respondents; I utilized the methods of grounded theory.

48. Stuart Hall et al., *Policing the Crisis: Mugging, the State and Law and Order* (New York: Palgrave Macmillan, 1978).

49. Miller et al., "Group Consciousness and Political Participation."

50. McClain and Stewart, *Can We All Get Along?*

51. Allen, Dawson, and Brown, "Schema-Based Approach"; Broman, Neighbors, and Jackson, "Racial Group Identification among Black Adults"; Cose, *Rage of a Priviledged Class*; Dawson, *Behind the Mule*; Thomas J. Durrant and Kathleen H. Sparrow, "Race and Class Consciousness among Lower- and Middle-Class Blacks," *Journal of Black Studies* 27, no. 3 (1997); Hochschild, *Facing Up to the American Dream*.

52. Demo and Hughes, "Socialization and Racial Identity among Black Americans";

Claudine Gay, "Putting Race in Context: Identifying the Environmental Determinants of Black Racial Attitudes," *American Political Science Review* 98, no. 4
(2004); Nunnally, "Learning Race, Socializing Blackness."

53. Harris, "Exploring the Determinants of Adult Black Identity," 228.
54. I thank the anonymous reviewer for making this suggestion.
55. Cose, *The Rage of a Priviledged Class*; Dawson, *Behind the Mule*; Durrant and
Sparrow, "Race and Class Consciousness among Lower- and Middle-Class
Blacks"; Hochschild, *Facing Up to the American Dream*.
56. Foner, "West Indian Identity in the Diaspora"; Greenbaum, *More than Black*;
Hellwig, "Black Meets Black"; Kasinitz, *Caribbean New York*; Kim, *Bitter Fruit*.
57. Vincent L. Hutchings and Nicholas A. Valentino, "The Centrality of Race in
American Politics," *Annual Review of Political Science* 7(2004).
58. Rachel Allison, "Race, Gender, and Attitudes toward War in Chicago: An Intersectional Analysis," *Sociological Forum* 26, no. 3 (2011).
59. Alvin B. Tillery, *Between Homeland and Motherland: Africa, U.S. Foreign Policy,
and Black Leadership in America* (Ithaca: Cornell University Press, 2011), 11.
60. Rogers, *Afro-Caribbean Immigrants and the Politics of Incorporation*.
61. Ibid.
62. Unfortunately, the NSAL does not ask its respondents about their attitudes concerning immigration.
63. McClain and Stewart, *Can We All Get Along?*
64. Recent research shows that more Blacks are exiting the Democratic Party, or
at least, there has been an increase in the proportion of Blacks who identify as
Independent. However, there were very few respondents in the NSAL who identified either as Independent or as members of the Republican Party. See Hajnal
and Lee, *Why Americans Don't Join the Party*; Haynie and Watts, "Blacks and the
Democratic Party."
65. Espiritu, *Asian American Panethnicity*; Okamoto, "Institutional Panethnicity."
66. A note on missing data: The NSAL asked less than half its respondents the
policy questions analyzed here. As such, you will see a decrease in the sample
size between the descriptive tables (all respondents queried about linked fate)
and the multivariate analyses. Further, those with missing responses were not
included in the analyses. With such a dramatic drop-off, I was not able to do
additional analyses that included specific ethnic groups for Black immigrants.
67. Rogers, *Afro-Caribbean Immigrants and the Politics of Incorporation*.
68. I also ran analyses on abortion and LBGT attitudes that included religiosity as a
predictor, not shown here. Religion played an important role for African Americans and Black immigrants, leading them to be less supportive of these issues,
but linked fate remained a statistically significant determinant of these attitudes
for African Americans.
69. Dawson, *Behind the Mule*.
70. Tate, *What's Going On?*
71. Cohen, *Boundaries of Blackness*.

72. Cheryl Corley, "After NAACP Marriage Stance, Discord and Discussion," *Morning Edition*, National Public Radio, 2012.
73. John R. Arvizu and F. Chris Garcia, "Latino Voting Participation: Explaining and Differentiating Latino Voting Turnout," *Hispanic Journal of Behavioral Sciences* 18, no. 2 (1996); Atiya Kai Stokes, "Latino Group Consciousness and Political Participation," *American Politics Research* 31 (2003).
74. Chong and Rogers, "Reviving Group Consciousness."
75. Ibid.
76. Bobo and Gilliam, "Race, Sociopolitical Participation, and Black Empowerment."
77. Chong and Rogers, "Reviving Group Consciousness"; Junn and Masuoka, "Asian American Identity"; McClain et al., "Group Membership, Group Identity, and Group Consciousness."
78. Chong and Rogers, "Reviving Group Consciousness."

NOTES TO CHAPTER 6

1. Dawson, *Black Visions*; Harris-Lacewell, *Barbershops, Bibles, and BET*; Price, *Dreaming Blackness*.
2. Dawson, *Black Visions*, 44.
3. Adolph Reed Jr., *Stirrings in the Jug: Black Politics in the Post-Segregation Era* (Minneapollis: University of Minnesota Press, 1999).
4. Harris-Lacewell, *Barbershops, Bibles, and BET*; Tate, *What's Going On?*
5. Dawson, *Black Visions*.
6. Chong and Rogers, "Reviving Group Consciousness"; Junn and Masuoka, "Asian American Identity"; Lee, "Race, Immigration, and the Identity-to-Politics Link."
7. William Raspberry, "There Is No Black Agenda," *Washington Post*, November 18, 1988; Raspberry, "The Incredible Shrinking Black Agenda," *Washington Post*, February 9, 2001.
8. Matthew B. Platt, "A Change Narrative of Black Agenda Setting" (unpublished paper, University of Rochester, 2008), 1.
9. Ibid.
10. Dona C. Hamilton and Charles V. Hamilton, *The Dual Agenda: Race and Social Welfare Policies of Civil Rights Organizations* (New York: Columbia University Press, 1997).
11. Hanes Walton Jr. and Robert C. Smith, *American Politics and the African American Quest for Universal Freedom*, 5th ed. (New York: Pearson, 2010), 115.
12. Chryl Laird, "Defining the Black Agenda: An Analysis of Black Public Opinion and Agenda Setting" (paper presented at the annual meeting of the Midwest Political Science Association, Chicago, April 23, 2010).
13. Price, *Dreaming Blackness*.
14. Cohen, *Boundaries of Blackness*; Dawson, *Black Visions*; Harris-Lacewell, *Barbershops, Bibles, and BET*; Price, *Dreaming Blackness*.

15. Vickerman, "Tweaking a Monolith"; Williams, *Mark One or More*.

16. David J. Hellwig, "Black Leaders and United States Immigration Policy, 1917–1929," *Journal of Negro History* 66, no. 2 (1981).

17. Ibid., 110.

18. Jeff Diamond, "African-American Attitudes towards United States Immigration Policy," *International Migration Review* 32, no. 2 (1998): 458.

19. Ibid.

20. Ibid.

21. Ibid.

22. Niambi M. Carter, "The Black/White Paradigm Revisited: African Americans, Immigration, Race, and Nation in Durham, North Carolina" (Ph.D. diss., Duke Univeristy, 2007); Diamond, "African-American Attitudes."

23. Carter, "Black/White Paradigm Revisited"; Cohen, *Boundaries of Blackness*; Diamond, "African-American Attitudes."

24. Carter, "Black/White Paradigm Revisited," 43.

25. Quoted in Bombardieri, "Harvard's Black Community Reunites."

26. Massey et al., "Black Immigrants and Black Natives," 245.

27. Waters, "West Indians and African Americans at Work."

28. Cohen, *Boundaries of Blackness*, 11.

29. Ibid., 24.

30. Ibid.; Cohen, *Democracy Remixed*.

31. Cohen, *Boundaries of Blackness*; Sawyer, "Race Politics in Multiethnic America."

32. I tallied the responses. I grouped issues of homelessness and policies that concern assisting the poor and economically disadvantaged under the "social welfare/justice" label. The other category labels are recorded verbatim.

33. National Coalition for the Homeless, "How Many People Experience Homelessness?" (Washington, DC: National Coalition for the Homeless, 2009).

34. Jonathan Kozol, *Savage Inequalities: Children in America's Schools* (New York: Crown, 1992); Nicolas Miller Restituto and Gerald Miller, "Education and Racial Inequality" (unpublished paper, Rockhurst University, 2005).

35. Laird, "Defining the Black Agenda."

36. Dawson, *Behind the Mule*; Dawson, *Black Visions*.

37. Julia S. Jordan-Zachery, "Am I a Black Woman or a Woman Who Is Black? A Few Thoughts on the Meaning of Intersectionality," *Politics & Gender* 3, no. 2 (2007): 256.

38. Andra Gillespie and Amber Perez, "Race, Religion, and Post-9/11America: The Election of Keith Ellison," in *Whose Black Politics? Cases in Post-racial Black Leadership*, ed. Andra Gillespie (New York: NYU Press, 2010), 275. See also Nikol G. Alexander-Floyd, "Disappearing Acts: Reclaiming Intersectionality in the Social Sciences in a Post-Black Feminist Era," *Feminist Formations* 24, no. 1 (2012); Kimberlé Crenshaw, "Mapping the Margins: Intersectionality, Identity Politics, and Violence against Women of Color," *Stanford Law Review* 43, no. 6 (1991); Ange-Marie Hancock, "When Multiplication Doesn't Equal Quick

Addition: Examining Intersectionality as a Research Paradigm," *Perspectives on Politics* 5, no. 1 (2007); Jordan-Zachery, "Am I a Black Woman or a Woman Who Is Black?"
39. Crenshaw, "Mapping the Margins."
40. Alexander-Floyd, "Disappearing Acts," 8.
41. Collins, "Like One of the Family," 20.
42. Crenshaw, "Mapping the Margins," 1252.
43. Rogers, "Race-Based Coalitions among Minority Groups."

NOTES TO THE CONCLUSION
1. Leslie Rojas, "Black or Mixed Race? Obama's Census Choice Sparks Debate over How People Identify," *Multi-American* (blog), Southern California Public Radio, April 4, 2011, http://www.scpr.org/blogs/multiamerican/2011/04/04/7160/black-or-mixed-race-obamas-census-choice-sparks-de/; Abigail Thernstrom, "Obama's Census Identity," *Wall Street Journal*, April 6, 2010.
2. Melissa Harris-Perry, "Black by Choice," *Nation*, May 3, 2010.
3. *The Sean Hannity Show*, Fox News, November 1, 2011.
4. *The Colbert Report*, Comedy Central, February 8, 2007, http://www.colbertnation.com/the-colbert-report-videos/81955/february-08-2007/debra-dickerson.
5. Quoted in Chris Hedges, "The Obama Deception: Why Cornel West Went Ballistic," Truthdig, May 16, 2011, http://www.truthdig.com/report/print/the_obama_deception_why_cornel_west_went_ballistic_20110516.
6. Nteta, "*Plus Ça Change, Plus C'est la Même Chose*?"; Portes and Zhou, "New Second Generation"; Waters, *Black Identities*.
7. Portes and Rumbaut, *Legacies*; Portes and Zhou, "New Second Generation"; Waters, *Black Identities*.
8. McClain and Stewart, *Can We All Get Along?*
9. Sowell, "Ethnicity in a Changing America."
10. Touré, *Who's Afraid of Post-Blackness? What It Means to Be Black Now* (New York: Free Press, 2011), 12.

BIBLIOGRAPHY

Abdelal, Rawi, Yoshiko M. Herrera, Alastair Iain Johnston, and Rose McDermott. "Identity as a Variable." *Perspectives on Politics* 4, no. 4 (2006): 695–711.

Abelson, Robert P. "Differences between Belief and Knowledge Systems." *Cognitive Science* 3, no. 4 (1979): 355–66.

Alba, Richard D. *Ethnic Idenitty: The Transformation of White America.* New Haven: Yale University Press, 1990.

Alexander-Floyd, Nikol G. "Disappearing Acts: Reclaiming Intersectionality in the Social Sciences in a Post-Black Feminist Era." *Feminist Formations* 24, no. 1 (2012): 1–25.

Alex-Assensoh, Yvette M. "African Immigrants and African-Americans: An Analysis of Voluntary African Immigration and the Evolution of Black Ethnic Politics in America." *African and Asian Studies* 8, nos. 1–2 (2009): 89–124.

Allen, Richard L., Michael C. Dawson, and Ronald E. Brown. "A Schema-Based Approach to Modeling an African-American Racial Belief System." *American Political Science Review* 83, no. 2 (1989): 421–41.

Allison, Rachel. "Race, Gender, and Attitudes toward War in Chicago: An Intersectional Analysis." *Sociological Forum* 26, no. 3 (2011): 668–91.

Andrews, George Reid. *Afro-Latin America, 1800–2000.* Oxford: Oxford University Press, 2004.

Arvizu, John R., and F. Chris Garcia. "Latino Voting Participation: Explaining and Differentiating Latino Voting Turnout." *Hispanic Journal of Behavioral Sciences* 18, no. 2 (1996): 104–28.

Austin, Sharon D. Wright, Richard T. Middleton, and Rachel Yon. "The Effect of Racial Group Consciousness on the Political Participation of African Americans and Black Ethnics in Miami-Dade County, Florida." *Political Research Quarterly* 65, no. 3 (2012): 629–41.

Bailey, Benjamin. "Dominican-American Ethnic/Racial Identities and United States Social Categories." *International Migration Review* 35, no. 3 (2001): 677–708.

Barnett, Elizabeth. "'Somos Costeños': Afro-Mexican Transnational Migration and Community Formation in Mexico and Winston-Salem, NC." Unpublished paper, Connecticut College, 2011.

Bashi, Vilna F. "Globalized Anti-Blackness: Transnationalizing Western Immigration Law, Policy, and Practice." *Ethnic and Racial Studies* 27, no. 4 (2004): 584–606.

Bashi, Vilna F. "Racial Categories Matter Because Racial Hierarchies Matter: A Commentary." *Ethnic and Racial Studies* 21, no. 5 (1998): 959–68.

———. *See also* Bobb, Vilna F. Bashi.

Bashi, Vilna F., and Antonio McDaniel. "A Theory of Immigration and Racial Stratification." *Journal of Black Studies* 27, no. 5 (1997): 668–82.

Berlin, Ira. "The Changing Definition of African-American." *Smithsonian Magazine,* February 2010. http://www.smithsonianmag.com/history/the-changing-definition -of-african-american-4905887/.

Berthoff, Rowland T. "Southern Attitudes toward Immigration, 1895–1914." *Journal of Southern History* 17, no. 3 (1951): 328–60.

Bhatia, Sunil, and Anjali Ram. "Rethinking 'Aculturation' in Relation to Diasporic Cultures and Postcolonial Identities." *Human Development* 44 (2001): 1–18.

Blaumer, Bob. *Racial Oppression in America.* New York: Harper and Row, 1972.

Bobb, Vilna F. Bashi. "Neither Ignorance nor Bliss: Race, Racism, and the West Indian Immigrant Experience." In *Migration, Transnationalization, and Race in a Changing New York,* edited by Héctor Cordero-Guzmán, Robert C. Smith, and Ramón Grosfoguel, 212–38. Philidelphia: Temple University Press, 2001.

———. *See also* Bashi, Vilna F.

Bobb, Vilna F. Bashi, and Averil Y. Clarke. "Experiencing Success: Structuring the Perception of Opportunities for West Indians." In *Islands in the City: West Indian Migration to New York,* edited by Nancy Foner, 216–36. Berkeley: University of California Press, 2001.

Bobo, Lawrence, and Franklin D. Gilliam Jr. "Race, Sociopolitical Participation, and Black Empowerment." *American Political Science Review* 84, no. 2 (1990): 377–93.

Bombardieri, Marcella. "Harvard's Black Community Reunites." *Boston Globe,* October 5, 2003, B1.

Bonilla-Silva, Eduardo. *Racism without Racists: Color-Blind Racism and Racial Inequality in Contemporary America.* 3rd ed. Lanham, MD: Rowman and Littlefield, 2010.

———. "Rethinking Racism: Toward a Structural Interpretation." *American Sociological Review* 62, no. 3 (1997): 465–80.

Bonilla-Silva, Eduardo, and David R. Dietrich. "The Latin Americanization of Racial Stratification in the U.S." In *Racism in the 21st Century: An Empirical Analysis of Skin Color,* edited by Robert E. Hall, 151–70. New York: Springer, 2008.

Brennan, James R. "Realizing Civilization through Patrilineal Descent: The Intellectual Making of an African Racial Nationalism in Tanzania, 1920–1950." *Social Identities* 12, no. 4 (2006): 405–23.

Brock, Lisa. "Questioning the Diaspora: Hegemony, Black Intellectural, and Doing International History from Below." *Issue: A Journal of Opinion* 24, no. 2 (1996): 9–12.

Brock, Lisa, and Bijan Bayne. "Not Just Black: African-Americans, Cubans, and Baseball." In *Between Race and Empire: African-Americans and Cubans before the Cuban Revolution,* edited by Lisa Brock and Digna Castañeda Fuertes, 168–204. Philidelphia: Temple University Press, 1998.

Broman, Clifford L., Harold W. Neighbors, and James S. Jackson. "Racial Group Identification among Black Adults." *Social Forces* 67, no. 1 (1988): 146–58.

Brown, W. O. "The Nature of Race Consciousness." *Social Forces* 10, no. 1 (1931): 90–97.

———. "Race Consciousness among South African Natives." *American Journal of Sociology* 40, no. 5 (1935): 569–81.

Bryce-Laporte, Roy Simon. "Black Immigrants: The Experience of Invisibility and Inequality." *Journal of Black Studies* 3, no. 1 (1972): 29–56.

Butterfield, Sherri-Ann P. "Challenging American Conceptions of Race and Ethnicity: Second-Generation West Indian Immigrants." *International Journal of Sociology and Social Policy* 24, nos. 7–8 (2004): 75–102.

———. " 'We're Just Black': The Racial and Ethnic Identities of Second-Generation West Indians in New York." In *Becoming New Yorkers: Ethnographies of the New Second Generation*, edited by Philip Kasinitz, John H. Mollenkopf, and Mary C. Waters, 288–312. New York: Russell Sage Foundation, 2004.

Candelario, Ginetta E. B. *Black behind the Ears: Dominican Racial Identity from Museums to Beauty Shops.* Durham: Duke University Press, 2007.

Carmichael, Stokely, and Charles Hamilton. *Black Power: The Politics of Liberation in America.* New York: Random House, 1967.

Carter, Niambi M. "The Black/White Paradigm Revisited: African Americans, Immigration, Race, and Nation in Durham, North Carolina." Ph.D. diss., Duke University, 2007.

Charles, Carolle. "Being Black Twice." In *Problematizing Blackness: Self-Ethnographics by Black Immigrants to the United States*, edited by Percy Claude Hintzen and Jean Muteba Rahier, 169–80. New York: Routledge, 2003.

Chong, Dennis, and Reuel Rogers. "Racial Solidarity and Political Participation." *Political Behavior* 27, no. 4 (2005): 347–74.

———. "Reviving Group Consciousness." In *The Politics of Democratic Inclusion*, edited by Christina Wolbrecht and Rodney E. Hero, 45–74. Philidelphia: Temple University Press, 2005.

Cohen, Cathy J. *The Boundaries of Blackness: AIDS and the Breakdown of Black Politics.* Chicago: University of Chicago Press, 1999.

———. *Democracy Remixed: Black Youth and the Future of American Politics.* Oxford: Oxford University Press, 2010.

———. "Millennials and the Myth of the Post-racial Society: Black Youth, Intra-generational Divisions and the Continuing Racial Divide in American Politics." *Daedalus* 140, no. 2 (2011): 197–205.

Colbert Report, The. Comedy Central. February 8, 2007. http://www.colbertnation.com/the-colbert-report-videos/81955/february-08-2007/debra-dickerson.

Collins, Patricia Hill. "Like One of the Family: Race, Ethnicity, and the Paradox of US National Identity." *Ethnic and Racial Studies* 24, no. 1 (2001): 3–28.

Conover, Pamela Johnston. "The Role of Social Groups in Political Thinking." *British Journal of Political Science* 18, no. 1 (1988): 51–76.

Conover, Pamela Johnston, and Stanley Feldman. "How People Organize the Political

World: A Schematic Model." *American Journal of Political Science* 28, no. 1 (1984): 95–126.

Corley, Cheryl. "After NAACP Marriage Stanace, Discord and Discussion." *Morning Edition*, National Public Radio, June 8, 2012.

Cornell, Stephen, and Douglas Hartmann. *Ethnicity and Race: Making Identities in a Changing World*. 2nd ed. Thousand Oaks, CA: Pine Forge, 2007.

Cose, Ellis. *The End of Anger: A New Generation's Take on Race and Rage*. New York: HarperCollins, 2011.

———. *The Rage of a Priviledged Class*. New York: HarperPerennial, 1993.

Crenshaw, Kimberlé W. "Demarginalizing the Intersection of Race and Sex." *University of Chicago Legal Forum* 43 (1989): 1241–99.

———. "Mapping the Margins: Intersectionality, Identity Politics, and Violence against Women of Color." *Stanford Law Review* 43, no. 6 (1991): 1241–99.

Cross, William E., Jr. "Negro-to-Black Conversion Experience: Toward a Psychology of Black Liberation." *Black World* 20, no. 9 (1971): 13–27.

———. *Shades of Black: Diversity in African-American Identity*. Philadelphia: Temple University Press, 1991.

———. "The Thomas and Cross Models of Psychological Nigrescence: A Review." *Journal of Black Psychology* 5, no. 1 (1978): 13–31.

Cross, William E., Jr., Thomas A. Parham, and Janet E. Helms. "Nigrescence Revisited: Theory and Research." In *African American Identity Development: Theory, Research, and Intervention*, edited by Reginald L. Jones, 3–71. Hampton, VA: Cobb and Henry, 1998.

Crowder, Kyle D. "Residential Segregation of West Indians in the New York / New Jersey Metropolital Area: The Roles of Race and Ethnicity." *International Migration Review* 33, no. 1 (1999): 79–113.

Cruse, Harold. *The Crisis of the Negro Intellectual*. New York: Morrow, 1967.

Darity, William A., Jr., Jason Dietrich, and Darrick Hamilton. "Bleach in the Rainbow: Latin Ethnicity and Preference for Whiteness." *Transforming Anthropology* 13, no. 2 (2005): 103–9.

Darity, William A., Jr., Darrick Hamilton, and Jason Dietrich. "Passing on Blackness: Latinos, Race, and Earnings in the USA." *Applied Economics Letters* 9 (2002): 847–53.

Davis, James F. *Who Is Black? One Nation's Definition*. University Park: Pennsylvania State University Press, 1991.

Davis, Jessica L., and Oscar H. Gandy Jr. "Racial Identity and Media Orientation: Exploring the Nature of Constraint." *Journal of Black Studies* 29, no. 3 (1999): 367–97.

Dawson, Michael C. *Behind the Mule: Race and Class in African-American Politics*. Princeton: Princeton University Press, 1994.

———. "A Black Counterpublic? Economic Earthquakes, Racial Agenda(s), and Black Politics." *Public Culture* 7, no. 1 (1994): 195–223.

———. *Black Visions: The Root of Contemporary African-American Political Ideologies.* Chicago: University of Chicago Press, 2001.

Demo, David H., and Michael Hughes. "Socialization and Racial Identity among Black Americans." *Social Psychology Quarterly* 53, no. 4 (1990): 364–74.

Denton, Nancy A., and Douglas S. Massey. "Racial Identity among Caribbean Hispanics: The Effect of Double Minority Status on Residential Segregation." *American Sociological Review* 54, no. 5 (1989): 790–808.

Dery, Leslie V. "Amadou Diallo and the 'Foreigner' Meme: Interpreting the Application of Federal Court Interpreter Laws." *Florida Law Review* 53 (2001): 239–91.

DeSipio, Louis. "More than the Sum of Its Parts: The Building Blocks of a Pan-Ethnic Latino Identity." In *The Politics of Minority Coalitions: Race, Ethnicity, and Shared Uncertainties*, edited by Wilbur C. Rich, 177–89. Westport, CT: Praeger 1996.

Diamond, Jeff. "African-American Attitudes towards United States Immigration Policy." *International Migration Review* 32, no. 2 (1998): 451–70.

Domingo, W. A., and Chandler Owen. "The Policy of the *Messenger* on West Indian and American Negroes." *Messenger*, March 1923, 639–47.

Dulitzy, Ariel E. "A Region in Denial: Racial Discrimination and Racism in Latin America." In *Neither Enemies nor Friends: Latinos, Blacks, Afro-Latinos*, edited by Anani Dzidzienyo and Suzanne Oboler, 39–59. New York: Palgrave Macmillian, 2005.

Dunn, Marvin. *Black Miami in the Twentieth Century.* Gainesville: Univeristy Press of Florida, 1997.

Dunn, Marvin, and Alex Stepick III. "Blacks in Miami." In *Miami Now! Immigration, Ethnicity, and Social Change*, edited by Guillermo J. Grenier and Alex Stepick III, 41–56. Gainesville: University Press of Florida, 1992.

Durand, Jorge, Douglass S. Massey, and Fernando Charvet. "The Changing Geography of Mexican Immigration to the United States: 1910–1996." *Social Science Quarterly* 81, no. 1 (2000): 1–15.

Durrant, Thomas J., and Kathleen H. Sparrow. "Race and Class Consciousness among Lower- and Middle-Class Blacks." *Journal of Black Studies* 27, no. 3 (1997): 334–51.

Dzidzienyo, Anani, and Suzanne Oboler. "Flows and Counterflows: Latinas/os, Blackness, and Racialization in Hemispheric Perspective." In *Neither Enemies nor Friends: Latinos, Blacks, Afro-Latinos*, edited by Anani Dzidzienyo and Suzanne Oboler, 3–36. New York: Palgrave Macmillian, 2005.

Espiritu, Yan. *Asian American Panethnicity: Bridging Institutions and Identities.* Philadelphia: Temple University Press, 1992.

Fairchild, Halford H. "Black, Negro, or Afro-American? The Differences Are Crucial!" *Journal of Black Studies* 16, no. 1 (1985): 47–55.

Feagin, Joe R. *Racist America: Roots, Current Realities, and Future Reparations.* New York: Routledge, 2000.

Feagin, Joe R., and José A. Cobas. "Latinos/as and White Racial Frame: The Procrustean Bed of Assimilation." *Sociological Inquiry* 78, no. 1 (2008): 39–53.

Fears, Darryl. "In Diversity Push, Top Universities Enrolling More Black Immigrants." *Washington Post*, March 6, 2007.

Ferguson, Elizabeth A. "Race Consciousness among American Negroes." *Journal of Negro Education* 7, no. 1 (1938): 32–40.

Foner, Nancy. "The Jamaicans: Race and Ethnicity among Migrants in New York." In *New Immigrants in New York*, edited by Nancy Foner, 195–217. New York: Columbia University Press, 1987.

———. "West Indian Identity in the Diaspora: Comparative and Historical Perspectives." *Latin American Perspectives* 25, no. 3 (1998): 173–88.

Frazier, E. Franklin. *The Black Bourgeoisie: The Rise of the New Middle Class in the United States*. New York: Free Press, 1957.

Freye, Gilberto. *The Masters and the Slaves*. New York: Knopf, 1947.

Gay, Claudine. "Putting Race in Context: Identifying the Environmental Determinants of Black Racial Attitudes." *American Political Science Review* 98, no. 4 (2004): 547–62.

Gibson, Margaret A. "Immigrant Adaptation and Patterns of Acculturation." *Human Development* 44, no. 1 (January–February 2001): 19–23.

Gillespie, Andra, and Amber Perez. "Race, Religion, and Post-9/11 America: The Election of Keith Ellison." In *Whose Black Politics? Cases in Post-racial Black Leadership*, edited by Andra Gillespie, 273–92. New York: NYU Press, 2010.

Gourevitch, Philip. *We Wish to Inform You That Tomorrow We Will Be Killed with Our Families: Stories from Rwanda*. New York: Farrar, Straus and Giroux, 1998.

Greenbaum, Susan D. *More than Black: Afro-Cubans in Tampa*. Gainesville: University Press of Florida, 2002.

Guarneri, Christine E., and Christopher Dick. "Methods of Assigning Race and Hispanic Origin to Births from Vital Statistics Data." Paper presented at the annual meeting of the Federal Committee on Statistical Methodology, Washington, DC, 2012.

Guimarães, Antonio Sérgio. "The Misadventures of Nonracialism in Brazil." In *Beyond Racism: Race and Inequality in Brazil, South Africa, and the United States*, edited by Charles V. Hamilton, Lynn Huntley, Neville Alexander, Antonio Sérgio Guimarães, and Wilmot James. Boulder, CO: Lynne Rienner, 2001.

Guridy, Frank Andre. *Forging Diaspora: Afro-Cubans and African Americans in a World of Empire and Jim Crow*. Chapel Hill: University of North Carolina Press, 2010.

Gurin, Patricia, Shirley Hatchett, and James Sidney Jackson. *Hope and Independence: Blacks' Response to Electoral and Party Politics*. New York: Russell Sage Foundation, 1989.

Gurin, Patricia, Arthur H. Miller, and Gerald Gurin. "Stratum Identification and Consciousness." *Social Psychology Quarterly* 43, no. 1 (1980): 30–47.

Hajnal, Zoltan L., and Taeku Lee. *Why Americans Don't Join the Party: Race, Immigration, and the Failure (of Political Parties) to Engage the Electorate*. Princeton: Princeton University Press, 2011.

Hall, Schekeva P., and Robert T. Carter. "The Relationship between Racial Identity, Ethnic Identity, and Perceptions of Racial Discrimination in an Afro-Caribbean Descent Sample." *Journal of Black Psychology* 32, no. 2 (2006): 155–75.

Hall, Stuart, Chas Critcher, Tony Jefferson, John Clarke, and Brian Roberts. *Policing the Crisis: Mugging, the State and Law and Order*. New York: Palgrave Macmillan, 1978.

Halter, Marilyn. *Between Race and Ethnicity: Cape Verdean American Immigrants, 1860–1965*. Urbana: University of Illinois Press, 1993.

Hamilton, Dona C., and Charles V. Hamilton. *The Dual Agenda: Race and Social Welfare Policies of Civil Rights Organizations*. New York: Columbia University Press, 1997.

Hancock, Ange-Marie. "When Multiplication Doesn't Equal Quick Addition: Examining Intersectionality as a Research Paradigm." *Perspectives on Politics* 5, no. 1 (2007): 63–79.

Haney-López, Ian F. *White by Law: The Legal Construction of Race*. New York: NYU Press, 2006.

Harris, David. "Exploring the Determinants of Adult Black Identity: Context and Process." *Social Forces* 74, no. 1 (1995): 227–41.

Harris-Lacewell, Melissa. *Barbershops, Bibles, and BET: Everyday Talk and Black Political Thought*. Princeton: Princeton University Press, 2004.

Harris-Perry, Melissa. "Black by Choice." *Nation*, May 3, 2010.

Hattam, Victoria. *In the Shadow of Race: Jews, Latinos, and Immigrant Politics in the United States*. Chicago: University of Chicago Press, 2007.

Haynes, George Edmund. *The Negro at Work in New York City: A Study in Economic Progress*. New York: Longman, 1912.

Haynie, Kerry L., and Candis S. Watts. "Blacks and the Democratic Party: A Resilient Coalition." In *New Directions in American Political Parties*, edited by Jeffrey M. Stonecash, 93–109. New York: Routledge, 2010.

Hedges, Chris. "The Obama Deception: Why Cornel West Went Ballistic." Truthdig, May 16, 2011. http://www.truthdig.com/report/print/the_obama_deception_why_ cornel_west_went_ballistic_20110516.

Hellwig, David J. "Black Leaders and United States Immigration Policy, 1917–1929." *Journal of Negro History* 66, no. 2 (1981): 110–27.

———. "Black Meets Black: Afro-American Reactions to West Indian Immigrants in the 1920s." *South Atlantic Quarterly* 77, no. 1 (1978): 206–24.

Herring, Mary, Thomas B. Jankowski, and Ronald E. Brown. "Pro-Black Doesn't Mean Anti-White: The Structure of African-American Group Identity." *Journal of Politics* 61, no. 3 (1999): 363–86.

Hochschild, Jennifer L. *Facing Up to the American Dream: Race, Class, and the Soul of the Nation*. Princeton: Princeton University Press, 1995.

Hoppenjas, Lisa, and Ted Richardson. "Mexican Ways, African Roots." *Winston-Salem Journal*, June 19, 2005, A1, A12, A13.

Hull, Galen Spencer. "Immigrant Entrepreneurs: The Face of the New Nashville."

iBusiness 2 (2009). http://www.scirp.org/journal/PaperInformation.aspx?paperID=
1435#.Ux5KOVzAJLE.

Hunter, Margaret L. " 'If You're Light You're Alright': Light Skin Color as Social Capital
for Women of Color." *Gender and Society* 16, no. 2 (2002): 175–93.

Hutchings, Vincent L., and Nicholas A. Valentino. "The Centrality of Race in American Politics." *Annual Review of Political Science* 7 (2004): 383–408.

Ignatiev, Noel. *How the Irish Became White*. New York: Routledge, 1995.

Itzigsohn, Jose, and Carlos Dore-Cabral. "Competing Identities? Race, Ethnicity and
Panethnicity among Dominicans in the United States." *Sociological Forum* 15, no. 2
(2000): 225–47.

Itzigsohn, Jose, Silvia Giorguli, and Obed Vazquez. "Immigrant Incorporation and
Racial Identity: Racial Self-Identification among Dominican Immigrants." *Ethnic
and Racial Studies* 28, no. 1 (2005): 50–78.

Jackman, Mary R., and Robert W. Jackman. "An Interpretation of the Relation between
Objective and Subjective Social Status." *American Sociological Review* 38, no. 5
(1973): 569–82.

Johnson, Violet Showers. "Relentless Ex-Colonials and Militant Immigrants: Protest
Strategies of Boston's West Indian Immigrants, 1910–1950." In *The Civil Rights
Movement Revisted: Critical Perspectives on the Struggle for Racial Equality in
the United States*, edited by Patrick B. Miller, Therese Frey Steffen, and Elisabeth
Schäfer-Wünsche, 9–20. New Brunswick, NJ: Transaction, 2001.

Jones, Jeffery M. "Racial or Ethnic Labels Make Little Difference to Blacks, Hispanics."
Gallup News Service, September 11, 2001. http://www.gallup.com/poll/4873/Racial
-Ethnic-Labels-Make-Little-Difference-Blacks-Hispanics.aspx.

Jones, Jennifer A. "Blacks May Be Second Class, but They Can't Make Them Leave:
Mexican Racial Formation and Immigrant Status in Winston-Salem." *Latino Studies*
10, no. 1 (2012): 60–80.

Jones-Correa, Michael, and David L. Leal. "Becoming 'Hispanic': Secondary Panethnic
Identification among Latin American–Origin Populations in the United States."
Hispanic Journal of Behavioral Sciences 18, no. 2 (1996): 214–54.

Jordan-Zachery, Julia S. "Am I a Black Woman or a Woman Who Is Black? A Few
Thoughts on the Meaning of Intersectionality." *Politics & Gender* 3, no. 2 (2007):
254–63.

Junn, Jane, and Kerry L. Haynie. *New Race Politics in America: Understanding Minority
and Immigrant Politics*. New York: Cambridge University Press, 2008.

Junn, Jane, and Natalie Masuoka. "Asian American Identity: Shared Racial Status and
Political Context." *Perspectives on Politics* 6, no. 4 (2008): 729–40.

Kasinitz, Philip. *Caribbean New York: Black Immigrants and the Politics of Race*. Ithaca:
Cornell University Press, 1992.

Kasinitz, Philip, John H. Mollenkopf, Mary C. Waters, and Jennifer Holdaway. *Inheriting the City: The Children of Immigrants Come of Age*. New York: Russell Sage Foundation, 2008.

Kasinitz, Philip, and Milton Vickerman. "Ethnic Niches and Racial Traps: Jamaicans in the New York Regional Economy." In *Migration, Transnationalization, and Race in a Changing New York*, edited by Héctor Cordero-Guzmán, Robert C. Smith, and Ramón Grosfoguel, 191–211. Philidelphia: Temple University Press, 2001.

Katznelson, Ira. *When Affirmative Action Was White: An Untold History of Racial Inequality in Twentieth-Century America.* New York: Norton, 2005.

Kelley, Robin D. G. "'But a Local Phase of a World Problem': Black History's Global Vision, 1883–1950." *Journal of American History* 86, no. 3 (1999): 1045–77.

Kent, Mary Mederios. "Immigration and America's Black Population." Washington, DC: Population Reference Bureau, 2007.

Kim, Arthur H., and Michael J. White. "Pathethnicity, Ethnic Diversity, and Residential Segregation." *American Journal of Sociology* 115, no. 5 (2010): 1558–96.

Kim, Claire Jean. *Bitter Fruit: The Politics of Black-Korean Conflict in New York City.* New Haven: Yale University Press, 2000.

———. "The Racial Triangulation of Asian Americans." In *Asian Americans and Politics: Perspectives, Experiences, Prospects*, edited by Gordon H. Chang, 39–78. Washington, DC: Woodrow Wilson Center Press, 2001.

Kinsbruner, Jay. *Not of Pure Blood: The Free People of Color and Prejudice in Nineteenth-Century Puerto Rico.* Durham: Duke University Press, 1996.

Kornegay, Francis. "Pan-African Citizenship and Identity Formation in Southern Africa: An Overview of Problems, Prospects and Possibilities." Johannesburg: Center for Policy Studies, 2006.

Kozol, Jonathan. *Savage Inequalities: Children in America's Schools.* New York: Crown, 1992.

Laird, Chryl. "Defining the Black Agenda: An Analysis of Black Public Opinion and Agenda Setting." Paper presented at the annual meeting of the Midwest Political Science Association, Chicago, April 23, 2010.

Lee, Jennifer, and Frank D. Bean. "America's Changing Color Lines: Immigration, Race/Ethnicity, and Multiracial Identification." *Annual Review of Sociology* 30 (2004): 221–42.

Lee, Taeku. "Pan-Ethnic Identity, Linked Fate, and the Political Significance of 'Asian American.'" Unpublished paper, University of California, 2005.

———. "Race, Immigration, and the Identity-to-Politics Link." *Annual Review of Political Science* 11, no. 1 (2008): 457–78.

Leighley, Jan E., and Arnold Vedlitz. "Race, Ethnicity, and Political Participation: Competing Models and Contrasting Explanations." *Journal of Politics* 61, no. 4 (1999): 1092–114.

Lentz-Smith, Adriane Danette. *Freedom Struggle: African Americans and World War I.* Cambridge: Harvard University Press, 2009.

Lewis, David Levering. *W. E. B. Du Bois, 1919–1963: The Fight for Equality and the American Century.* New York: Holt, 2001.

Lewis, Earl. "To Turn as on a Pivot: Writing African Americans into a History of Overlapping Diasporas." *American Historical Review* 100, no. 3 (1995): 765–87.

Lien, Pei-te, M. Margaret Conway, and Janelle Wong. "The Contours and Sources of

Ethnic Identity Choices among Asian Americans." *Social Science Quarterly* 84, no. 2 (2003): 461–81.

Lodge, Milton, and Ruth Hamill. "A Partisan Schema for Political Information Processing." *American Political Science Review* 80, no. 2 (1986): 505–20.

Loewen, James W. *The Mississippi Chinese: Between Black and White.* Cambridge: Harvard University Press, 1971.

Lopez, David, and Yan Espiritu. "Panethnicity in the United States: A Theoretical Framework." *Ethnic and Racial Studies* 13, no. 2 (1990): 198–224.

Lopez, Mark Hugo. "The Hispanic Vote in the 2008 Election." Washington, DC: Pew Hispanic Center, 2008.

Lopez, Mark Hugo, and Paul Taylor. "Dissecting the 2008 Electorate: Most Diverse in U.S. History." Washington, DC: Pew Research Center, 2009.

MacGaffey, Wyatt. "Concepts of Race in the Historiography of Northeast Africa." *Journal of African History* 7, no. 1 (1966): 1–17.

Mannheim, Karl. "The Problem of Generations." In *Essays on the Sociology of Knowledge*, edited by Karl Mannheim and Paul Kecskemeti, 276–80. New York: Oxford University Press, 1952.

Marrow, Helen. "Hispanic Immigration, Black Population Size, and Intergroup Relations in the Rural and Small-Town South." In *New Faces in New Places: The Changing Geography of American Immigration*, edited by Douglas S. Massey, 211–48. New York: Russell Sage Foundation, 2008.

Marx, Anthony W. *Making Race and Nation: A Comparison of the United States, South Africa and Brazil.* Cambridge: Cambridge University Press, 1998.

Mason, Patrick L. "Culture and Intraracial Wage Inequality." *American Economic Review* 100 (2010): 309–15.

Massey, Douglass S., Camille Z. Charles, Garvey Lundy, and Mary J. Fischer. *The Source of the River: The Social Origins of Freshmen at America's Selective Colleges and Universities.* Princeton: Princeton University Press, 2008.

Massey, Douglas S., and Nancy A. Denton. *American Apartheid: Segregation and the Making of the Underclass.* Cambridge: Harvard University Press, 1993.

Massey, Douglass S., Margarita Mooney, Kimberly C. Torres, and Camille Z. Charles. "Black Immigrants and Black Natives Attending Selective Colleges and Universities in the United States." *American Journal of Education* 113, no. 2 (2007): 243–71.

McClain, Paula, Jessica D. Johnson Carew, Eugene Walton Jr., and Candis S. Watts. "Group Membership, Group Identity, and Group Consciousness: Measures of Racial Identity in American Politics?" *Annual Review of Political Science* 12 (2009): 471–84.

McClain, Paula D., Niambi M. Carter, Victoria M. DeFrancesco Soto, and Monique L. Lyle. "Racial Distancing in a Southern City: Latino Immigrants' Views of Black Americans." *Journal of Politics* 68, no. 3 (2006): 571–84.

McClain, Paula D., Niambi M. Carter, Victoria M. DeFrancesco Soto, Monique L. Lyle, Jeffrey D. Grynaviski, Shayla C. Nunnally, Thomas J. Scotto, et al. "Racial Distancing in a Southern City: Latino Immigrants' Views of Black Americans." *Journal of Politics* 68, no. 3 (2006): 571–84.

McClain, Paula D., Gerald E. Lackey, Efren O. Perez, Niambi M. Carter, Jessica D. Johnson Carew, Candis Watts Smith, Eugene Walton Jr., Monique L. Lyle, and Shayla C. Nunnally. "Intergroup Relations in Three Southern Cities." In *Just Neighbors? Research on African American and Latinos Relations in the United States*, edited by Edward Telles, Mark Q. Sawyer, and Gaspar Rivera-Salgado, 201–41. New York: Russell Sage Foundation, 2011.

McClain, Paula D., and Joseph Stewart Jr. *Can We All Get Along? Racial and Ethnic Minorities in American Politics*. 5th ed. Boulder, CO: Westview, 2010.

McDermott, Monica. "Black Attitudes and Hispanic Immigrants in South Carolina." In *Just Neighbors? Research on African American and Latinos Relations in the United States*, edited by Edward Telles, Mark Q. Sawyer, and Gaspar Rivera-Salgado, 242–63. New York: Russell Sage Foundation, 2011.

Miller, Arthur H., Patricia Gurin, Gerald Gurin, and Oksana Malanchuk. "Group Consciousness and Political Participation." *American Journal of Political Science* 25, no. 3 (1981): 494–511.

Mirabal, Nancy Raquel. "Telling Silences and Making Community: Afro-Cubans and African-Americans in Ybor City and Tampa, 1899–1915." In *Between Race and Empire: African-Americans and Cubans before the Cuban Revolution*, edited by Lisa Brock and Digna Castañeda Fuertes, 49–69. Philidelphia: Temple University Press, 1998.

Model, Suzzane. "Caribbean Immigrants: A Black Success Story?" *International Migration Review* 25, no. 2 (1991): 248–76.

Nagel, Joane. "American Indian Ethnic Renewal: Politics and the Resurgence of Identity." *American Sociological Review* 60, no. 6 (1995): 947–65.

———. "Constructing Ethnicity: Creating and Recreating Ethnic Identity and Culture." *Social Problems* 41, no. 1 (1994): 152–76.

Nascimento, Elisa Larkin. "Aspects of Afro-Brazilian Experience." *Journal of Black Studies* 11, no. 2 (1980): 195–216.

National Coalition for the Homeless. "How Many People Experience Homelessness?" Washington, DC: National Coalition for the Homeless, 2009.

Nevaer, Louis E. V. "In Black-Hispanic Debate, West Indians Side with Hispanics." Pacific News Service. *New America Media*, December 4, 2003. http://news .newamericamedia.org/news/view_article.html?article_id=524a919cf3f2101954 cff10de9f11e96.

Newman, Katherine S. *No Shame in My Game: The Working Poor in the Inner City*. New York: Russell Sage Foundation, 1999.

Nobles, Melissa. *Shades of Citizenship: Race and the Census in Modern Politics*. Stanford: Stanford University Press, 2000.

Nteta, Tatishe Mavovosi. "*Plus Ça Change, Plus C'est La Même Chose*? An Examination of the Racial Attitudes of New Immigrants in the United States." In *Transforming Politics, Transforming America: The Political and Civic Incorporation of Immigrants in the United States*, edited by Taeku Lee, Karthick Ramakrishnan, and Ricardo Ramirez, 194–216. Charlottesville: University of Virginia Press, 2006.

Nunnally, Shayla C. "Learning Race, Socializing Blackness." *Du Bois Review* 7, no. 1 (2010): 185–217.

———. "Linking Blackness or Ethnic Othering? African Americans' Diasporic Linked Fate with West Indian and African Peoples in the United States." *Du Bois Review* 7, no. 2 (2010): 335–55.

Okamoto, Dina G. "Institutional Panethnicity: Boundary Formation in Asian American Organizing." *Social Forces* 85, no. 1 (2006): 1–25.

———. "Toward a Theory of Panethnicity: Explaining Asian American Collective Action." *American Sociological Review* 68, no. 6 (2003): 811–42.

Okolie, Andrew C. "The Appropriation of Difference: State and the Construction of Ethnic Identities in Nigeria." *Identity* 3, no. 1 (2003): 67–92.

Oliver, Melvin, and Thomas Shapiro. *Black Wealth / White Wealth: A New Perspective on Racial Inequality*. New York: Routledge, 1995.

Omi, Michael, and Howard Winant. *Racial Formation in the United States: From the 1960s to the 1990s*. 2nd ed. New York: Routledge, 1994.

Oppenheimer, Gerald M. "Paradigm Lost: Race, Ethnicity, and the Search of a New Population Taxonomy." *American Journal of Public Health* 91, no. 7 (2001): 1049–55.

Orsi, Robert. "The Religious Boundaries of an Inbetween People: Street *Feste* and the Problem of the Dark-Skinned Other in Italian Harlem, 1920–1990." *American Quarterly* 44, no. 3 (1992): 313–47.

Padilla, Felix M. *Latino Ethnic Consciousness: The Case of Mexian Americans and Puerto Ricans in Chicago*. Notre Dame, IN: University of Notre Dame Press, 1985.

Pamphile, Leon D. *Haitians and African Americans*. Gainesville: University Press of Florida, 2001.

Parker, Frederick B. "The Status of the Foreign Stock in the South-East: A Region-Nation Comparison." *Social Forces* 27, no. 2 (1948): 136–43.

Paterson, Tiffany Ruby, and Robin D. G. Kelley. "Unfinished Migrations: Reflection on the African Diaspora and the Making of the Modern World." *African Studies Review* 43, no. 1 (2000): 11–45.

Patterson, Orlando. "Toward a Future That Has No Past—Reflections on the Fate of Blacks in the Americas." *Public Interest* 27 (1972): 25–62.

Pew Research Center. *Optimism about Black Progress Declines: Blacks See Growing Values Gap between Poor and Middle Class*. Washington, DC: Pew Research Center, 2007.

Philpot, Tasha S. *Race, Republicans, and the Return of the Party of Lincoln*. Ann Arbor: University of Michigan Press, 2007.

Phinney, Jean S., and Mukosolu Onwughalu. "Racial Identity and Perception of American Ideals among African American and African Students in the United States." *International Journal of Intercultural Relations* 20, no. 2 (1996): 127–40.

Pierre, Jemima. "Black Immigrants in the United States and the 'Cultural Narratives' of Ethnicity." *Identities: Global Studies in Culture and Power* 11 (2004): 141–70.

Platt, Matthew B. "A Change Narrative of Black Agenda Setting." Unpublished paper, University of Rochester, 2008.

Portes, Alejandro. "For the Second Generation, One Step at a Time." In *Reinventing the Melting Pot: The New Immigrants and What It Means to Be American*, edited by Tamar Jacoby, 155–66. New York: Basic Books, 2004.

Portes, Alejandro, and Ruben G. Rumbaut. *Immigrant American: A Portrait*. 2nd ed. Berkeley: University of California Press, 1996.

———. *Legacies: The Story of the Immigrant Second Generation*. Berkeley: University of California Press, 2001.

Portes, Alejandro, and Min Zhou. "The New Second Generation: Segmented Assimilation and Its Variants." *Annals of the American Academy of Political and Social Science* 530 (1993): 74–96.

Posel, Deborah. "Race as Common Sense: Racial Classification in Twentieth-Century South Africa." *African Studies Review* 44, no. 2 (2001): 87–113.

Price, Melanye T. *Dreaming Blackness: Black Nationalism and African American Public Opinion*. New York: NYU Press, 2009.

Pugliese, Joseph. "Race as Category Crisis: Whiteness and the Topical Assignation of Race." *Social Semiotics* 12, no. 2 (2002): 149–68.

Raspberry, William. "The Incredible Shrinking Black Agenda." *Washington Post*, February 9, 2001.

———. "There Is No Black Agenda." *Washington Post*, November 18, 1988.

Read, Jen'nan Ghazal, and Michael O. Emerson. "Racial Context, Black Immigration and the U.S. Black/White Health Disparity." *Social Forces* 84, no. 1 (2005): 181–99.

Reed, Adolph, Jr. *Stirrings in the Jug: Black Politics in the Post-Segregation Eea*. Minneapollis: University of Minnesota Press, 1999.

Reid, Ira De Augustine. *The Negro Immigrant: His Background, Characteristics and Social Adjustment, 1899–1937*. New York: Columbia University Press, 1939.

Restituto, Nicolas Miller, and Gerald Miller. "Education and Racial Inequality." Unpublished paper, Rockhurst University, 2005.

Ricourt, Milagros, and Ruby Danta. *Hispanas de Queens: Latino Panethnicty in a New York City Neighborhood*. Ithaca: Cornell University Press, 2003.

Rimer, Sara, and Karen W. Arenson. "Top Colleges Take More Blacks, but Which Ones?" *New York Times*, June 24, 2004, A18.

Roediger, David R. *The Wages of Whiteness: Race and the Making of the American Working Class*. London: Verso, 2007.

———. *Working toward Whiteness: How America's Immigrants Became White; The Strange Journey from Ellis Island to the Suburbs*. New York: Basic Books, 2005.

Rogers, Reuel R. *Afro-Caribbean Immigrants and the Politics of Incorporation: Ethnicity, Exception, or Exit*. New York: Cambridge University Press, 2006.

———. "'Black Like Who?': Afro-Caribbean Immigrants, African Americans, and the Politics of Group Identity." In *Islands in the City: West Indian Migration to New York*, edited by Nancy Foner, 163–92. Berkeley: University of California Press, 2001.

———. "Race-Based Coalitions among Minority Groups: Afro-Caribbean Immigrants and African-Americans in New York City." *Urban Affairs Review* 39, no. 3 (2004): 283–317.

Rojas, Leslie. "Black or Mixed Race? Obama's Census Choice Sparks Debate over How People Identify." *Multi-American* (blog), Southern California Public Radio, April 4, 2011. http://www.scpr.org/blogs/multiamerican/2011/04/04/7160/black-or-mixed-race-obamas-census-choice-sparks-de/.

Ryan, Andrew M., Gilbert C. Gee, and David F. Laflamme. "The Association between Self-Reported Discrimination, Physical Health, and Blood Pressure: Findings from African Americans, Black Immigrants, and Latino Immigrants in New Hampshire." *Journal of Health Care for the Poor and Underserved* 17 (2006): 116–32.

Sanchez, Gabriel R. "The Role of Group Consciousness in Latino Public Opinion." *Political Research Quarterly* 59, no. 3 (2006): 435–46.

Sawyer, Mark Q. "Race Politics in Multiethnic America: Black and Latina/o Identities." In *Neither Enemies nor Friends: Latinos, Blacks, Afro-Latinos*, edited by Anani Dzidzienyo and Suzanne Oboler, 265–79. New York: Palgrave Macmillian, 2005.

———. *Racial Politics in Post-Revolutionary Cuba*. New York: Cambridge University Press, 2006.

Sean Hannity Show, The. Fox News. November 1, 2011.

Sears, David O., John J. Hetts, Jim Sidanius, and Lawrence Bobo. "Race in American Politics: Framing the Debates." In *Racialized Politics: The Debate about Racism in America*, edited by David O. Sears, Jim Sidanius, and Lawrence Bobo, 1–43. Chicago: University of Chicago Press, 2000.

Sellers, Robert M., and J. Nicole Shelton. "The Role of Racial Identity in Perceived Racial Discrimination." *Journal of Personality and Social Psychology* 84, no. 5 (2003): 1079–92.

Sellers, Robert M., Mia A. Smith, J. Nicole Shelton, Stephanie A. J. Rowley, and Tabbye M. Chavous. "Multidimensional Model of Racial Identity: A Reconceptualization of African American Racial Identity." *Personality and Social Psychology Review* 2, no. 1 (1998): 18–39.

Shelton, J. Nicole, and Robert M. Sellers. "Situational Stability in African American Racial Identity." *Journal of Black Psychology* 26, no. 1 (2000): 27–50.

Shingles, Richard D. "Black Consciousness and Political Participation: The Missing Link." *American Political Science Review* 75, no. 1 (1981): 76–91.

Sigelman, Carol K., Lee Sigelman, Barbara J. Walkosz, and Michael Nitz. "Black Candidates, White Voters: Understanding Racial Bias in Political Perceptions." *American Journal of Political Science* 39, no. 1 (1995): 243–65.

Sigelman, Lee, Steven A. Tuch, and Jack K. Martin. "What's in a Name? Preference for 'Black' versus 'African-American' among Americans of African Descent." *Public Opinion Quarterly* 69, no. 3 (2005): 429–38.

Simien, Evelyn M. "Race, Gender, and Linked Fate." *Journal of Black Studies* 35, no. 5 (2005): 529–50.

Simien, Evelyn M., and Rosalee A. Clawson. "The Intersection of Race and Gender: An Examination of Feminist Consciousness, Race Consciousness, and Policy Attitudes." *Social Science Quarterly* 85, no. 3 (2004): 793–810.

Simpson, Andrea. *The Tie That Binds: Identity and Political Attitudes in the Post-Civil Rights Generation.* New York: NYU Press, 1998.

Smedley, Audrey. "Social Origins of the Idea of Race." In *Race in 21st Century America,* edited by Curtis Stokes, Theresa Melendez, and Genice Rhodes-Reed, 3–23. East Lansing: Michigan State University Press, 2001.

Smith, Tom W. "Changing Racial Labels: From 'Colored' to 'Negro' to 'Black' to 'African American.'" *Public Opinion Quarterly* 56, no. 4 (1992): 496–514.

Smooth, Wendy. "Intersectionality in Electoral Politics: A Mess Worth Making." *Politics & Gender* 2, no. 3 (2006): 400–414.

Sonenshein, Raphael J. *Politics in Black and White.* Princeton: Princeton University Press, 1993.

Song, Steven. "Finding One's Place: Shifting Ethnic Identities of Recent Immigrant Children from China, Haiti, and Mexico in the United States." *Ethnic and Racial Studies* 33, no. 6 (2010): 1006–31.

Sowell, Thomas. "Ethnicity in a Changing America." *Daedalus* 107, no. 1 (1978): 213–37.

Steinberg, Stephen. *The Ethnic Myth: Race, Ethnicity, and Class in America.* Boston: Beacon, 2001.

———. "Immigration, African Americans, and Race Discourse." *New Politics* 38 (2005): 42–54.

Stepick, Alex, III. "The Refugees Nobody Wants: Haitians in Miami." In *Miami Now! Immigration, Ethnicity, and Social Change,* edited by Guillermo J. Grenier, and Alex Stepick III, 57–82. Gainesville: University Press of Florida, 1992.

Stokes, Atiya Kai. "Latino Group Consciousness and Political Participation." *American Politics Research* 31 (2003): 361–78.

Swarns, Rachel L. "'African-American' Becomes a Term of Debate." *New York Times,* August 29, 2004.

Táíwò, Olúfẹ́mi. "The Prison Called My Skin: On Being Black in America." In *Problematizing Blackness: Self-Ethnographics by Black Immigrants to the United States,* edited by Percy C. Hintzen and Jean Muteba Rahier, 35–52. New York: Routledge, 2003.

Tate, Katherine. *From Protest to Politics: The New Black Politics in American Elections.* New York: Russell Sage Foundation, 1994.

———. *What's Going On? Political Incorporation and the Transformation of Black Public Opinion.* Washington, DC: Georgetown University Press, 2010.

Thernstrom, Abigail. "Obama's Census Identity." *Wall Street Journal,* April 6, 2010.

Thornton, Michael C., Robert Joseph Taylor, and Tony N. Brown. "Correlates of Racial Label Use among Americans of African Descent: Colored, Negro, Black, and African American." *Race and Society* 2, no. 2 (2000): 149–64.

Tillery, Alvin Bernard. *Between Homeland and Motherland: Africa, U.S. Foreign Policy, and Black Leadership in America.* Ithaca: Cornell University Press, 2011.

Tillery, Alvin Bernard, and Michell Chresfield. "Model Blacks or 'Ras the Exhorter': A Quantitative Content Analysis of Black Newspapers' Coverage of the First Wave of

Afro-Caribbean Immigration to the United States." *Journal of Black Studies* 43, no. 5 (2012): 545–70.

Tormala, Teceta Thomas, and Kay Deaux. "Black Immigrants to the United States: Confronting and Constructing Ethnicity and Race." In *Cultural Psychology of Immigrants*, edited by Ramaswami Mahalingam, 331–50. Mahway, NJ: Erlbaum, 2006.

Touré. *Who's Afraid of Post-Blackness? What It Means to Be Black Now.* New York: Free Press, 2011.

U.S. Census Bureau. "The American Community—Blacks: 2004." Washington, DC: U.S. Census Bureau, Department of Commerce, 2007.

Vaca, Nicolas C. *The Presumed Alliance: The Unspoken Conflict between Latinos and Blacks and What It Means for America.* New York: HarperCollins, 2004.

Vaughn, Bobby, and Ben Vinson III. "Unfinished Migrations: From the Mexican South to the American South." In *Beyond Slavery: The Multilayered Legacy of Africans in Latin America and the Caribbean*, edited by Darién J. Davis, 223–45. Lanham, MD: Rowman and Littlefield, 2007.

Verba, Sidney, and Norman Nie. *Participation in America: Political Democracy and Social Equality.* New York: Harper and Row, 1972.

Vickerman, Milton. *Crosscurrents: West Indian Immigrants and Race.* Oxford: Oxford University Press, 1999.

———. "Jamaicans: Balancing Race and Ethnicity." In *New Immigrants in New York*, edited by Nancy Foner, 201–28. New York: Columbia University Press, 2001.

———. "Tweaking a Monolith: The West Indian Immigrant Encounter with 'Blackness.'" In *Islands in the City: West Indian Migration to New York*, edited by Nancy Foner, 237–56. Berkeley: University of California Press, 2001.

Viruell-Fuentes, Edna A. "'It's a Lot of Work': Racialization Processes, Ethnic Identity Formation, and Their Health Implications." *Du Bois Review* 8, no. 1 (2011): 37–52.

Wade, Peter. *Race and Ethnicity in Latin America.* London: Pluto, 1997.

Waldinger, Roger. *Still the Promised City?* Cambridge: Harvard University Press, 1996.

Walter, John C. "Black Immigrants and Political Radicalism in the Harlem Renaissance." *Western Journal of Black Studies* 1, no. 2 (1977): 131–41.

Walton, Hanes, Jr., and Robert C. Smith. *American Politics and the African American Quest for Universal Freedom.* 5th ed. New York: Pearson, 2010.

Waters, Mary C. *Black Identities: West Indian Immigrant Dreams and American Realities.* Cambridge: Harvard University Press, 1999.

———. "Ethnic and Racial Identities of Second-Generation Black Immigrants in New York City." *International Migration Review* 29, no. 4 (1994): 795–820.

———. *Ethnic Options: Choosing Identities in America.* Berkeley: Univeristy of California Press, 1990.

———. "Growing Up West Indian and African American: Gender and Class Differences in the Second Generation." In *Islands in the City: West Indian Migration to New York*, edited by Nancy Foner, 193–215. Berkeley: University of California Press, 2001.

———. "Immigration, Intermarriage, and the Challenges of Measuring Racial/Ethnic Identities." *American Journal of Public Health* 90, no. 11 (2000): 1735–37.

———. "The Role of Lineage in Identity Formation among Black Americans." *Qualitiative Sociology* 14, no. 1 (1991): 57–76.

———. "West Indians and African Americans at Work: Structural Differences and Cultural Stereotypes." In *Immigration and Opportunity: Race, Ethnicity, and Employment in the United States*, edited by Frank D. Bean and Stephanie Bell-Rose, 194–227. New York: Russell Sage Foundation, 1999.

Watkins-Owens, Irma. *Blood Relations: Caribbean Immigrants and the Harlem Community, 1900–1930*. Bloomington: Indiana University Press, 1996.

Welcome to Shelbyville. Directed by Kim A. Snyder. *Independent Lens*, PBS, 60 minutes, 2011.

Wilcox, Clyde, and Leopoldo Gomez. "Religion, Group Identification, and Politics among African Americans." *Sociological Analysis* 51, no. 3 (1990): 271–85.

Wilkerson, Isabel. *The Warmth of Other Suns: The Epic Story of America's Great Migration*. New York: Random House, 2010.

Williams, Kim M. *Mark One or More: Civil Rights in Multiracial America*. Ann Arbor: University of Michigan Press, 2006.

Wilson, William Julius. *Declining Significance of Race: Blacks and Changing American Institutions*. Chicago: University of Chicago Press, 1980.

Young, Alford, Jr. "Black Men, Racefulness, and Getting Ahead in American Society: A Cultural Paradigm Reconstituted." Paper presented at the Race Workshop, Department of Sociology, Duke University, February 23, 2010.

U.S. Census: demographics, 9, 10, 60; racial group categories/classification, 47–48, 53, 55, 57, 72, 73, 74, 107, 178, 224n38

United States: Black-white dichotomy, 11, 113–114; construction of race, 20–21, 222n6; demographic shifts, 8–10, 25–26, 37, 39–43; Jim Crow laws, 22, 27, 28–29, 103, 198–199, 204; miscegenation laws and, 21, 22; slavery within, 20–21; southern region population shift, 39–43

Universal Negro Improvement Association (UNIA), 33, 37

Vanessa (interview respondent), 95, 188, 195, 212–213

Vaughn, Bobby, 40

Verba, Sidney, 49

Vickerman, Milton, 22–23, 110, 139

Villaraigosa, Antonio, 61

Vinson, Ben, 40

voting rights, 15, 30, 35, 49, 51, 61, 115, 137, 166–167, 168–169, 172, 177

Voting Rights Act of 1965, 49

Walter, John, 35

Walton, Hanes, 177

Washington, Booker T., 35–36, 193

Waters, Mary, 1, 51, 52, 61–62, 63, 78–79, 114, 117–119

Welcome to Shelbyville (2011), 41–43

West, Cornell, 199

West Indians, 32–39, 52, 114. *See also* Caribbean, the

White, Michael, 57

white racial frames, 62, 104, 128

whiteness: as absence of Blackness, 21; Asian immigrants and, 55; Black Codes, 27; Black-white dichotomy, 11, 113–114; in Caribbean societies, 22–23; immigrants of color and, 55, 57, 113–114; Latinos and, 55–56; non-Black immigrants and, 55; racial triangulation, 55; racial wedges, 28–29; white ethnic immigrants and, 11, 22–23, 54–56

Winant, Howard, 53

Wong, Janelle, 59–60

X, Malcolm, 72

Young, Alford, 117

Zimbabweans, 24, 93

CARY PUBLIC LIBRARY

ABOUT THE AUTHOR

Candis Watts Smith is an Assistant Professor of Political Science at Williams College.

GARY PUBLIC LIBRARY

BI Stud 305.800973 S 2014
Smith, Candis Watts.
Black mosaic

GARY PUBLIC LIBRARY

3 9222 03083 673 3